OCR GCSE

Humanities

Steve Radford

OCR ★
RECOGNISING ACHIEVEMENT

Heinemann

Official Publisher Partnership

OCR AND HEINEMANN ARE WORKING TOGETHER TO PROVIDE BETTER SUPPORT FOR YOU

Heinemann is an imprint of Pearson Education Limited, a company incorporated in England and Wales, having its registered office at Edinburgh Gate, Harlow, Essex, CM20 2JE. Registered company number: 872828

www.heinemann.co.uk

Heinemann is a registered trademark of Pearson Education Limited

Text © Pearson Education Limited 2009

First published 2009

13
10 9 8 7 6 5 4 3

British Library Cataloguing in Publication Data is available from the British Library on request.

ISBN 978 0 435795 21 4

Edited by Caroline McPherson
Designed by Kamae Design
Typeset by Phoenix Photosetting, Chatham, Kent
Original illustrations © Pearson Education Limited 2009
Illustrated by Julian Mosedale
Picture research by Susie Prescott
Printed in UK by CPI

Websites
There are links to relevant websites in this book. In order to ensure that the links are up-to-date, that the links work, and that the sites are not inadvertently linked to sites that could be considered offensive, we have made the links available on the Heinemann website at www.heinemann.co.uk/hotlinks. When you access the site, the express code is 5214.

Contents

Acknowledgements

The author and publisher would like to thank the following individuals and organisations for permission to reproduce copyright material in this product.

Artwork and text

p.9 Extract from *Global Trends 2007*, © UNHCR; p.12 Extract from *Focus on Ethnicity and Identity*, Office for National Statistics, material from the UK Statistics Authority website www.statisticsauthority.gov.uk © Crown Copyright C2008002221; p.17 Figure 1.8 reproduced with kind permission from www.parliament.co.uk; p.22 Extract from www.conservatives.com quoted with kind permission from the Conservative Party; p.22 © The Labour Party http://www.labour.org.uk/what_is_the_labour_party; pp.22–23 Extract from www.libdem.org quoted with kind permission from the Liberal Democrat Party; p.28 Extract from www.cps.gov.uk © Crown Copyright C2008002221; p.46 Extract from *Young People and Financial Matters*, FSA, © The Chartered Insurance Institute; p.53 Figure 2.7 from *Graduate Market Trends Spring 2003*, data analysis by HECSU. Datasource: Labour Force Survey, reproduced with kind permission from www.prospects.ac.uk; p.57 Table 2.6 reproduced with kind permission from the Certification Officer for Trade Unions and Employers' Associations; p.63 © Climate Change 2007: Synthesis Report. Contribution of Working Groups I, II and III to the Fourth Assessment Report of the Intergovernmental Panel on Climate Change, p. 3. IPCC, Geneva, Switzerland; p.66 Figure 3.4 © World Health Organisation http:// www.who.int/heli/risks/risksmaps/en/index5.html; p.67 Figure 3.5 © Directorate General for Agriculture and Rural Development reproduced with kind permission; pp.67–68 *G8 Report* © Crown Copyright C2008002221; p.68 Extract from a statement by the Director of Global Warming Policy at the Competitive Enterprise Institute reproduced with kind permission from the Competitive Enterprise Institute; p.69 Extract from a statement by Peter Calow, Director of the Environmental Assessment Institute, reproduced with kind permission from Peter Calow, Honorary Professor at Roskilde University (Denmark) and Emeritus Professor at the University of Sheffield (UK), OBE; p.69 Extract from *Global Warming Economics: Facts vs. Myths* reproduced with kind permission from the Competitive Research Institute; p.70 Text adapted from UKCIP02, © Tyndall Centre and Hadley Centre 2002, reproduced with kind permission; pp.71–2 Text adapted from UKCIP02, © Tyndall Centre and Hadley Centre 2002, reproduced with kind permission; p.74 Extract from the United Nations Conference on the Human Environment © United Nations 1972. Reproduced with permission; p.74 Mission statement of the United Nations Environment Programme reproduced with kind permission from the United Nations Environment Programme; p.75 Extract from the Brundtland Commission reproduced with kind permission from the United Nations Department of Economic and Social Affairs; p.76 Extract from the United Nations Convention on Climate Change reproduced with kind permission from the United Nations Climate Change Conference Secretariat; p.80 Figure 3.9 Reproduced from www.carbontrust.co.uk with kind permission from the Carbon Trust; p.120 'The Wellness Quiz' excerpt from *Wellness From Within: The First Step*, American Holistic Health Association (http://ahha.org); p.121 Figure 5.1 reproduced with permission from the NHS website; p.123 Figure 5.3 Material from the UK Statistics Authority website www.statisticsauthority.gov.uk, © Crown Copyright C2008002221; p.128 Table 5.3 © Crown Copyright C2008002221; p.131 Office for National Statistics, © Crown Copyright C2008002221; p.141 Extract from the Health and Safety Executive © Crown Copyright C2008002221; p.142 Table 5.5 reproduced with kind permission from www. revisionworld.co.uk; p.143 Table 5.6, p.144 Table 5.7, p.145 Table 5.8, p.147 Table 5.9 © World Health Organisation http://www.who.int/whr/2002/media_centre/en/whr02_ maps_en.pdf; p.144 Figure 5.11 © World Health Organisation http://gamapserver.who.int/mapLibrary/Files/Maps/ HIVPrevalenceGlobal_200; p.171 Office for National Statistics, © Crown Copyright C2008002221; p.182 © http:// www.icmresearch.co.uk/; pp.184, 186 Extract from Natural Environment Research Council/Centre for Ecology and Hydrology, reproduced with kind permission; p.186 Extracts from the Royal Commission on Environmental Pollution © Crown Copyright C2008002221.

Photos

p.4 The Granger Collection/Topfoto; p.6 Topham Picturepoint; p.8 Mohammed Saber/EPA/Corbis; p.10 Steven Clevenger/Corbis; p.12 Brigitte Bott/Rex Features; p.21 Hulton Archive/Getty Images; p.24 Odd Anderson/AFP/ Getty Images; p.27 Christopher Furlong/Getty Images; p.29 ITV/ Rex Features; p.35 Ricardo Azoury/istockphoto.com; p.37 Claudio Edinger/Corbis; p.42 UPP/Topfoto; p.59 Johnny Green/PA Archive/PA Photos; p.62 Museum of London/ HIP/Topfoto; p.63 Thomas Pickard/istockphoto.com; p.69 Ronaldo Schmidt/AFP/Getty Images; p.71 c.Paramount/ Everett/Rex Features; p.77 Michael SpooneyBarger/AP/ PA Photos; p.79 R Martens/Shutterstock, Churchmouse NZ/istockphoto.com, Jennifer Photography/istockphoto. com, Science Photo Library, Science Photo Library; p.84 Photodisc/Pearson Education; p. 86 Mikhail Levit/ Shutterstock; p.88 Anthony Green/Shutterstock; p.94 Topham Picturepoint; p.95 Christopher Boisvieux/Corbis; p.99 Maziar Nikkholgh/Document Iran/Corbis; p.100 William Campbell/Sygma/Corbis; p.104 Kevin Carter/Megan Patricia Carter Trust/Sygma/Corbis; p.107 Hieronymous Bosch/The Bridgeman Art Library/Getty Images; p.113 David Joel/Photographers Choice/Getty Images; p.116 Pascal Guyot/AFP/Getty Images; p.124 Gerd Ludwig/Terra/Corbis; p.125 Matt Candy/Getty Images; p.126 Advertising Archives, Advertising Archives; p.131 Mary Evans Photo Library; p.134 Jonathan Player/Rex Features; p.139 Department of Transport; p.148 Sipa Press/Rex Features; p.150 The National Archives/HIP/Topfoto; p.152 National Library of Wales/Solo Syndication; p.154 Fotomas/Topfoto.

Every effort has been made to contact copyright holders of material reproduced in this product. Any omissions will be rectified in subsequent printings if notice is given to the publisher.

Welcome to OCR GCSE Humanities

This book has been written specifically to support you during your OCR GCSE Humanities course. Studying GCSE Humanities will help give you an understanding of important topical issues relevant to your life – you will not only develop critical analytical skills, but also learn to apply them to what you see in the world around you.

How to use this book

The OCR GCSE Humanities student book is divided into two units, B031 and B032. Unit B031 has five chapters. Each of these chapters deals with one of the five topics examined on the Cross-Curricular Themes assessment. This unit provides an introduction to the knowledge that you will need to acquire for the end of unit assessment. Unit B032 is much shorter and provides an introduction to the research methods and presentational skills that you will need in the Application of Knowledge assessment and Unit B033 the Humanities Independent Enquiry assessment.

Websites

Throughout the book there are references to websites that will provide additional information on the topics covered in the text. See page ii for access details.

In B031 each unit has a list of the key concepts to be covered in that unit. In both B031 and B032 there is also a list of learning objectives for each unit so that you know what you will learn and which skills you will be developing.

Words which might be new to you will be highlighted in the text. All highlighted words can be found in the Glossary.

Throughout the text there are activities to broaden your understanding of the topics covered.

Below is a reproduction of a sample book spread (pages 4–5):

1: Issues of Citizenship

Unit 1.1 Rights and responsibilities

IN THIS UNIT YOU WILL LEARN:

- what human rights are and how they developed
- UK and international law on human rights
- how individuals, organisations and governments have responsibilities as well as rights
- how individuals, organisations and governments are responsible for upholding human rights in the UK and the world

KEY CONCEPTS

Human rights and responsibilities
Legal, social and political rights
Human rights legislation
Human rights abuses
Human rights protection
Multiculturalism

'It's not fair.' When was the last time that was said to you, or you said it to someone else, and what do you really mean when you say it? We all expect to be treated fairly by a variety of people – parents, friends and the general public – and by a variety of organisations, such as schools, the police and society itself – whatever that is.

How do we judge whether something is fair? Perhaps the next most frequently heard comment on this subject is: 'You can't do that, I know my rights!'

WHAT ARE HUMAN RIGHTS AND WHERE DO THEY COME FROM?

Throughout history, most people had very few 'rights'. The country was run in a 'top down' way. The wealthy people at the top were very powerful and had all the rights; the poor people at the bottom had rights that very much depended on those at the top. They might be lucky if their 'top man' – the local Lord of the Manor – treated them well, but he still had the power of life and death over them. They were not equals.

That they did not have equal rights did not stop many from wanting them. Equality, as we shall see, is a common theme in the demand for human rights. This is because once equality has been achieved, all other rights flow from this one idea:

'From the beginning all men by nature were created alike, and our bondage and servitude came in by the unjust oppression of naughty men.'

This was written by John Ball, a priest who took part in the Peasants' Revolt in England in 1381. John Ball is saying that all people start equal, and the fact that they become *unequal* is because of the power of 'naughty men'. When you feel that things are unfair, you are probably dealing with relatively minor things most of the time. However, if you were a peasant, your Lord would be able to make you do whatever they wanted. They could beat you or even kill you and you would have no rights at all, and that attacks your human rights at a different level to unfairness.

LEGAL, SOCIAL AND POLITICAL RIGHTS

Human rights come in a variety of packages. One obvious package is the law. Every citizen should obey the law and, as a result,

Figure 1.1: This painting shows King John signing the Magna Carta on 15 June 1215. For the first time, the King of England had laws that he had to obey.

4   OCR GCSE Humanities

---

is given rights under that law. The first laws that granted legal rights to people in England were in the Magna Carta agreed by King John and his barons in 1215. Some of the laws written in the Magna Carta still stand today, such as this one:

'No free man shall be seized or imprisoned except by the lawful judgement of his peers.'

Social rights can be more difficult to define because they are generally not written down in the way that laws are, but are things that are generally accepted as the way to behave in a certain society. As we shall see later, this can cause problems in societies where there is more than one acceptable way to behave.

Political rights are related to how a society chooses to govern itself. The UK, as a democracy, gives the right to its people to select representatives to run the country.

ACTIVITY

1. Imagine living in a country where the leaders could do exactly what they liked. Discuss as a class what this might mean for the people who lived in that country.

2. Many people in the UK have suggested we need a Bill of Rights. This would be a law clearly listing citizens' rights. What do you feel would be the essential rights that should be included?

FREEDOM FROM OR FREEDOM TO?

'So, human rights give me the right to do what I want. I can go out and do exactly what I like and no one can stop me!'

This might appear to be quite an attractive prospect, *but* (there always seems to be a but in the good things in life, doesn't there?) if you have the right to do as you want, then so does everyone else. Which is fine, until someone exercising their rights causes you a problem in exercising your rights. A minor example, though it might not feel like it at the time, could be your neighbour exercising their right to play their music as loud as possible. This could seriously affect your right to watch your favourite TV show if you cannot hear it over your neighbour's loud music. A more serious example might be the motorist who decides that their right to drive after drinking too much alcohol is more important than the general public's right not to be killed or injured by a drunk driver. Obviously, rights must have a flip side. Rights that might be seen to be giving the

individual the freedom to do something also place responsibilities on people – the most important responsibility being to respect other people's rights. Human rights cannot give people the right to behave as they please because of the damaging impact this could have on others. Human rights should be seen as giving individuals freedom from the actions of others that they would wish to avoid, rather than giving them the right to do as they please!

ACTIVITY

Copy the rights and responsibilities table into your books and fill in some more rights and their corresponding responsibilities.

Rights	Responsibilities
To be treated with respect	To treat others with respect

THE STRUGGLE FOR HUMAN RIGHTS

What is the human rights position today, and how have we got to where we are? As already mentioned, both the Magna Carta (1215) and the Peasants' Revolt (1381) commented on the unfairness of inequality and the ability for kings and powerful men to deal unfairly with people who had less power and wealth.

All of the protests against inequality and the rights of man were made at times when civil society was in a state of unrest. In more recent history, the American Declaration of Independence (1776), written as the British colonies in America fought for independence from Britain, said:

'We hold these truths to be self evident that all men are created equal.'

A few years later, during the French Revolution, when the French rather bloodily got rid of their King and aristocracy and became a republic, they drew up the Declaration of the Rights of Man (1789), which said in its first article:

'Men are born and remain free and equal in rights.'

The document that has had most influence on the modern approach to human rights was written by a body set up after the horrors of the Second World War. The United Nations Organisation was set up

OCR GCSE Humanities   5

GradeStudio

Grade Studio

Grade Studio is designed for you to improve your chances of achieving the best possible grades. You will find Grade Studio activities at the end of each unit.

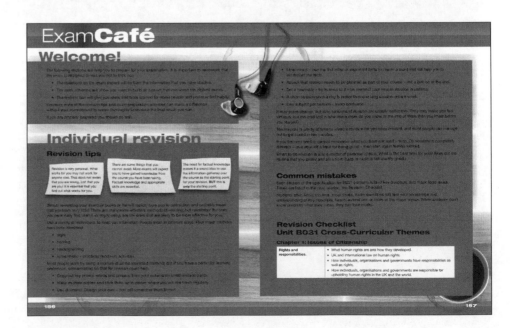

ExamCafé

Exam Café

Exam Café is to be used when revising and preparing for exams. Exam Café could be used in revision classes after school or in revision lessons and can be found at the end of each unit.

The OCR GCSE Humanities course

The table below shows how Unit B031: Cross Curricular Themes, Unit B032: Application of Knowledge and Unit B033: Humanities Independent Enquiry are part of your Humanities course.

Unit B031 Cross-Curricular Themes
Chapter 1 Issues of Citizenship
Chapter 2 Issues of Economic Wellbeing and Financial Capability
Chapter 3 Environmental Issues
Chapter 4 Religious and Moral Issues
Chapter 5 Issues of Health and Welfare
Unit B031 is worth 50 per cent of your final mark.
In Cross-Curricular Themes you will answer questions with different levels of difficulty. There will be straightforward questions which need a short factual answer with no need for further explanation. There will also be structured essay-style questions which need factually detailed and organised answers based on the information which you have learnt during the course. Because the course deals with issues that are in the news, or part of your daily life, you will be able to use knowledge that you have gained from other sources in these questions.

Unit B032 Application of Knowledge
Unit 6.1 Different types and forms of evidence
Unit 6.2 Using and evaluating evidence
Unit 6.3 Managing an enquiry
Unit 6.4 Communicating the results of an enquiry
Unit B032 is worth 25 per cent of your final mark.
In Application of Knowledge you will answer questions with different levels of difficulty. There will be straightforward questions which need a short factual answer with no need for further explanation. There will also be longer questions which test your ability to analyse and evaluate sources of evidence, using your knowledge from the course and information from the sources provided to discuss both sides of a question.

Unit B033 Humanities Independent Enquiry
Unit B033 is worth 25 per cent of your final mark.
In Humanities Independent Enquiry the Examination Board, OCR, will set a choice of ten tasks, two on each of the five chapters of Unit B031. Your school will decide which of these tasks you will undertake. In producing your enquiry you will be expected to select and evaluate evidence. You will be expected to draw reasoned conclusions from this evidence. Finally, you will be expected to present your research findings in a clear way, showing that you understand the limitations of what you have done.

Course objectives

As well as knowing which topics you are going to study, it is important to understand what skills you will be developing and be assessed on.

AO1   Demonstrate Knowledge and Understanding

- Recall, select and communicate your knowledge and understanding of concepts, issues and terminology.

AO2   Analysis, Evaluation and Application

- Apply your knowledge and understanding in familiar and unfamiliar situations.

AO3   Communication and Presentation

- Analyse and evaluate information, sources, arguments and interpretations.

Controlled assessment

Following a coursework review by QCA, controlled assessment is being introduced as part of nearly all GCSEs, to replace coursework. For GCSE Humanities this is the Humanities Independent Enquiry. The aim of this is to make assessments more manageable for both teachers and students. You can find some general guidance and answers to frequently asked questions on OCR's website at

http://www.ocr.org.uk/qualifications/1419changes/gcse/controlled.html

You can find more specific guidance from the OCR Humanities team in section 5 of the specification at:

http://www.ocr.org.uk/Data/publications/key_documents/GCSE_Humanities_Spec.pdf

We hope that you will find the materials provided in this book both useful and interesting and that you will enjoy studying your OCR GCSE Humanities course.

Cross-Curricular Themes B031

1

Chapter 1
Issues of Citizenship

CONTENTS

Unit 1.1 Rights and responsibilities

IN THIS UNIT YOU WILL LEARN ABOUT:

- what human rights are and how they developed
- UK and international law on human rights
- how individuals, organisations and governments have responsibilities as well as rights
- how individuals, organisations and governments are responsible for upholding human rights in the UK and the world.

KEY CONCEPTS

Human rights and responsibilities
Legal, social and political rights
Human rights legislation
Human rights abuses
Human rights protection
Multiculturalism

'It's not fair.' When was the last time that was said to you, or you said it to someone else, and what do you really mean when you say it? We all expect to be treated fairly by a variety of people – parents, friends and the general public – and by a variety of organisations, such as schools, the police and society itself – whatever that is.

How do we judge whether something is fair? Perhaps the next most frequently heard comment on this subject is: 'You can't do that, I know my rights!'

WHAT ARE HUMAN RIGHTS AND WHERE DO THEY COME FROM?

Throughout history, most people had very few 'rights'. The country was run in a 'top-down' way. The wealthy people at the top were very powerful and had all the rights; the poor people at the bottom had rights that very much depended on those at the top. They might be lucky if their 'top man' – the local Lord of the Manor – treated them well, but he still had the power of life and death over them. They were not equals.

That they did not have equal rights did not stop many from wanting them. Equality, as we shall see, is a common theme in the demand for human rights. This is because once equality has been achieved, all other rights flow from this one idea:

'From the beginning all men by nature were created alike, and our bondage and servitude came in by the unjust oppression of naughty men.'

This was written by John Ball, a priest who took part in the Peasants' Revolt in England in 1381. John Ball is saying that all people start equal, and the fact that they become *unequal* is because of the power of 'naughty men'. When you feel that things are unfair, you are probably dealing with relatively minor things most of the time. However, if you were a peasant, your Lord would be able to make you do whatever they wanted. They could beat you or even kill you and you would have no rights at all, and that attacks your human rights at a different level to unfairness.

LEGAL, SOCIAL AND POLITICAL RIGHTS

Human rights come in a variety of packages. One obvious package is the law. Every citizen should obey the law and, as a result,

Figure 1.1: This painting shows King John signing the Magna Carta on 15 June 1215. For the first time, the King of England had laws that he had to obey.

is given rights under that law. The first laws that granted legal rights to people in England were in the Magna Carta agreed by King John and his barons in 1215. Some of the laws written in the Magna Carta still stand today, such as this one:

'No free man shall be seized or imprisoned except by the lawful judgement of his peers.'

Social rights can be more difficult to define because they are generally not written down in the way that laws are, but are things that are generally accepted as the way to behave in a certain society. As we shall see later, this can cause problems in societies where there is more than one acceptable way to behave.

Political rights are related to how a society chooses to govern itself. The UK, as a democracy, gives the right to its people to select representatives to run the country.

ACTIVITY

1. Imagine living in a country where the leaders could do exactly what they liked. Discuss as a class what this might mean for the people who lived in that country.

2. Many people in the UK have suggested we need a Bill of Rights. This would be a law clearly listing citizens' rights. What do you feel would be the essential rights that should be included?

FREEDOM FROM OR FREEDOM TO?

'So, human rights give me the right to do what I want. I can go out and do exactly what I like and no one can stop me!'

This might appear to be quite an attractive prospect, *but* (there always seems to be a *but* in the good things in life, doesn't there?) if you have the right to do as you want, then so does everyone else. Which is fine, until someone exercising their rights causes you a problem in exercising your rights. A minor example, though it might not feel like it at the time, could be your neighbour exercising their right to play their music as loud as possible. This could seriously affect your right to watch your favourite TV show if you cannot hear it over your neighbour's loud music. A more serious example might be the motorist who decides that their right to drive after drinking too much alcohol is more important than the general public's right not to be killed or injured by a drunk driver. Obviously, rights must have a flip side. Rights that might be seen to be giving the individual the freedom to do something also place responsibilities on people – the most important responsibility being to respect other people's rights.

Human rights cannot give people the right to behave as they please because of the damaging impact this could have on others. Human rights should be seen as giving individuals freedom from the actions of others that they would wish to avoid, rather than giving them the right to do as they please!

ACTIVITY

Copy the rights and responsibilities table into your books and fill in some more rights and their corresponding responsibilities.

Rights	Responsibilities
To be treated with respect	To treat others with respect

THE STRUGGLE FOR HUMAN RIGHTS

What is the human rights position today, and how have we got to where we are? As already mentioned, both the Magna Carta (1215) and the Peasants' Revolt (1381) commented on the unfairness of inequality and the ability for kings and powerful men to deal unfairly with people who had less power and wealth.

All of the protests against inequality and the rights of man were made at times when civil society was in a state of unrest. In more recent history, the American Declaration of Independence (1776), written as the British colonies in America fought for independence from Britain, said:

'We hold these truths to be self evident that all men are created equal.'

A few years later, during the French Revolution, when the French rather bloodily got rid of their King and aristocracy and became a republic, they drew up the Declaration of the Rights of Man (1789), which said in its first article:

'Men are born and remain free and equal in rights.'

The document that has had most influence on the modern approach to human rights was written by a body set up after the horrors of the Second World War. The United Nations Organisation was set up to rebuild a shattered world and to attempt to avoid similar catastrophic wars in the future. It published the Universal Declaration of Human Rights in 1948. Article 1 of this document says:

'All human beings are born free and equal in dignity and rights.'

All of these documents have one other thing in common: they are declarations of what some people believe ought to happen. They are not legal documents that can be enforced.

ACTIVITY

1. Find out what happened during the Second World War to prompt the United Nations to draw up the Universal Declaration of Human Rights.

2. What rights do you think people should have? In pairs or small groups come up with a list, then compare them to those in the Universal Declaration of Human Rights; see 'Websites' on page ii.

THE CONVENTION FOR THE PROTECTION OF HUMAN RIGHTS AND FUNDAMENTAL FREEDOMS

Better known as the European Convention on Human Rights, this was agreed by the **Council of Europe** in 1950. It was a European response to the Universal Declaration of Human Rights drawn up by the United Nations. Article 1 says that every country that signs the Convention is to enforce the rights in all the other articles. These are similar to those in the UN Declaration and include the right to life, fair trial and freedom of expression.

The **Council of Europe** was set up in 1949 to work towards European cooperation, and is not the same as the **European Union (EU)** (a political and economic union of 27 states set up in 1993). However, all countries who are members of the EU are also members of the Council. Acceptance of the Convention is therefore effectively a condition of membership of the EU. The UK was a founding member of the Convention and played a large part in setting it up. It was also one of the first countries to agree to implement the treaty.

The European Commission of Human Rights investigates breaches of the Convention either by countries or by individuals. If the Commission believes an individual or a government has broken the Convention, details are then passed onto the European Court of Human Rights.

THE HUMAN RIGHTS ACT

The Human Rights Act, passed in 1998, became law in 2000. When the UK signed the Convention it made it possible for individuals in the UK to take the **government** to the European Court of Human Rights. However, the way of doing this was complicated. Before you could take a case to the Court of Human Rights you had to take it through all the courts in the UK, and this could take years. The Human Rights Act makes the rights protected by the Convention part of UK law. The effect of this Act was to force all government agencies to act in the light of the Convention when making decisions affecting citizens. If they fail to do this, they can be taken to court in the UK.

Figure 1.2: What rights were the suffragettes fighting for? What rights is the suffragette being deprived of in this picture and why?

STRETCH AND CHALLENGE

The European Court of Human Rights is the final court of appeal for European citizens. Research a case that has been taken to this Court.

- What was the case about?

- What rights did the person or people feel were being infringed?

- What was the judgement?

- Prepare a short presentation for the rest of the group.

Who is responsible for making sure rights are balanced, supported and protected?

By the end of the 20th century, basic human rights had been included in national and international law. However, it is one thing to have a right and have it protected by law, and quite another to make sure that these rights are supported and protected in practice. The question now is: who should enforce these human rights and how should they do it?

Who do people blame when things go wrong? Typically they do not blame themselves! They look for someone else, someone in authority, to blame. This leads to a fairly common expectation that someone else should sort out the issue. In the UK the most likely 'someone in authority' is the government.

THE ROLE OF THE GOVERNMENT

To some extent this is a reasonable expectation. The government is elected by the people to run the country. It has the power to pass laws through parliament and the means to enforce them through the police, the courts and the prisons. However, not everybody believes that the government is always reliable in protecting human rights.

NON-GOVERNMENTAL ORGANISATIONS

Various organisations that are independent of government have been established in the UK. These provide challenges to the government on issues of human rights. Liberty, also known as the National Council for Civil Liberties, defines its mission as seeking to protect civil liberties and promote human rights for all. It does this by campaigning through the courts, parliament and the community and uses public campaigning, parliamentary lobbying and the giving of free advice.

INTERNATIONAL PROTECTION

The United Nations, which put forward the Universal Declaration of Human Rights, has representatives from almost all the countries of the world as members. On human rights issues the UN High Commissioner for Human Rights is the person who investigates claims of abuse made by either individuals or countries.

Added to this are international lobbying/campaign groups such as Amnesty International, established in 1961 in the UK.

ACTIVITY

Liberty and Amnesty International are just two examples of organisations that campaign on issues of human rights, but there are many others. Find out more about the work of Liberty or Amnesty International or about another organisation that campaigns for human rights.

WEBLINKS

For weblinks of organisations that campaign on issues of human rights, see 'Websites' on page ii.

THE ROLE OF THE INDIVIDUAL

The individual citizen may seem helpless in the face of human rights abuses, yet they can play a vital role. In a democracy, many of the rights granted relate to the right to vote. This gives the individual the opportunity to influence, and if necessary, change national and local government. Individuals also have the right to lobby their elected MPs and councillors.

Organisations such as Liberty and Amnesty International depend on the support, both moral and financial, of individual citizens. By supporting and making their opinions heard through such organisations, individuals can make a massive difference.

An individual commitment, not only to your own human rights, but to supporting the human rights of everyone else as well, is the mark of an active citizen living in a healthy society.

Is human rights legislation effective in protecting people at risk?

Sadly, despite the best efforts of many individuals, humanitarian organisations, national governments and international organisations, the world is not yet a perfectly peaceful place where human rights are automatically respected and protected.

The scope of this challenge to achieve universal human rights is illustrated by the following two case studies.

ACTIVITY

Is it realistic in the modern world to expect the individual to make a contribution to maintaining human rights?

CASE STUDY 1: Victims of armed conflict

Wherever it happens, armed conflict has a devastating effect on civilian populations. Whenever there is armed conflict or internal disturbance, civilians suffer most.

In many parts of the world – Sri Lanka, Afghanistan, Sudan and the Democratic Republic of the Congo – violence has been long-term. The amount of violence can vary, but when it is intense, the civilian population suffers. This suffering can include executions without trial, internal displacement, disappearances and hostage-taking. The most seriously affected are often the weakest.

Humanitarian organisations attempt to influence the fighters to take account of the needs of civilians to try and guarantee the safety and well-being of the people concerned. A major concern is **refugees** who flee their country as a result of conflict and internally displaced persons who are forced to leave their homes and move somewhere else in their country.

Figure 1.3: Humanitarian organisations work to protect vulnerable people such as refugees fleeing war.

Displacement has serious consequences. Victims have to abandon their homes and their material belongings – they lose everything. They also lose years of hard work and effort, their families and their community ties. They lose their land, their possessions and their dreams.

Humanitarian organisations work to deliver food, healthcare and education. They also support projects for sanitation and water supply.

The United Nations High Commission for Refugees (UNHCR)

According to the UNHCR report *Global Trends 2007*, there were 11.4 million refugees outside their countries and 26 million others displaced internally by conflict or persecution at the end of 2007.

The number of refugees and internally displaced persons (IDPs) being looked after by UNHCR in more than 150 countries rose by 2.5 million during 2007 to 25.1 million. Refugees are defined as people who flee to another country to escape persecution and conflict. IDPs are people forced from their homes by conflict but who stay within their own countries.

Table 1.1: The number of refugees of each nationality in 2007.

Nationality	Number of refugees
Afghans	3,000,000
Iraqis	2,000,000
Colombians	552,000
Sudanese	523,000
Somalis	457,000

(*Source:* Global Trends 2007, *UNHCR*)

The top refugee-hosting countries in 2007 were Pakistan, Syria, Iran, Germany and Jordan.

Table 1.2: The number of IDPs in each of these countries in 2007.

Country	Number of IDPs
Colombia	3,000,000
Iraq	2,400,000
Democratic Republic of Congo	1,300,000
Uganda	1,200,000
Somalia	1,000,000

(*Source:* Global Trends 2007, *UNHCR*)

UNHCR's goal is to find lasting solutions for refugees. Those solutions include voluntary repatriation once conditions allow it.

Table 1.3: The number of repatriations of refugees in each of these countries in 2007.

Country	Number of Repatriations
Afghanistan	374,000
Sudan	130,700
Democratic Republic of Congo	60,000
Iraq	45,400
Liberia	44,000

(*Source:* Global Trends 2007, *UNHCR*)

About 2.1 million IDPs went home during 2007.

ACTIVITY

Are the United Nations and humanitarian aid agencies helping victims of armed conflict? Give reasons for your answer.

The scale of the problem

There are an estimated 300,000 child soldiers around the world. Children are used in wars taking place in Sierra Leone, Liberia, Congo, Sudan, Sri Lanka, Afghanistan and Burma, amongst others. They lose their childhood and often take part in horrific violence. They take part in all aspects of modern warfare: combat, acting as human mine detectors, taking part in suicide missions, carrying supplies and acting as spies, messengers or lookouts.

Every year the number grows as more children are recruited for use in active combat.

Recruitment

After attacks on villages, surviving children are abducted and recruited by force. They are removed to special camps where they are held and 'trained'. They are forced to follow orders under the threat of death.

Some children join armed groups out of fear. When society is breaking down they are given food, shelter and a chance for survival. Others join military forces to avenge family members who have been killed. Often they undergo a brutal initiation, sometimes forced to commit violence against their family or neighbours. This stops children trying to escape, as afterwards, they can never return to their own community.

Sometimes the children are initiated into 'secret societies', which they are told gives them magical powers. They believe the magic will protect them and stop enemy bullets.

Lightweight automatic weapons like the AK47 are simple to operate and can be used by children as easily as by adults. This means that boys as young as eight can become soldiers.

Children do as they are told as soldiers because they are emotionally immature. They are easy to bully because they are physically immature. They can be attracted into violence because they are too young to understand.

The youngest children are often placed in the front line. They do not really understand what is happening and this makes them unpredictable and

Figure 1.4: Think about why this picture is disturbing. What rights does this child have that are not being protected?

apparently fearless. Some are given drugs before being sent into combat.

The Convention on the Rights of the Child

This is a universally agreed set of non-negotiable standards and obligations. It was adopted by the United Nations in 1989 and came into force in 1990.

Article 38 bound countries who adopted it to stop young people under 15 taking part in combat or being compulsorily recruited in to the armed forces.

This Convention was amended in 2000 by the Optional Protocol on the Convention on the Rights of the Child. This came into force in 2002. Articles 1 and 2 raise the age in Article 38 to 18 years. More than 110 countries have accepted this amendment.

STRETCH AND CHALLENGE

The UN Convention on the Rights of the Child is supposed to protect children from becoming involved in armed conflicts. Research a conflict in which child soldiers are being used.

- What is the conflict about?

- How are child soldiers recruited and trained?

- How are child soldiers used in the conflict?

- What is the UN and/or the rest of the world doing about the conflict?

- Prepare a short presentation for the rest of the group.

Ethnicity and identity

WHO DO YOU THINK YOU ARE?

When you were younger did you ever write out your address and add silly lines to it?

Caroline Broughton,
16 Winchester Road,
Alton,
Hampshire,
England,
Europe,
The World,
The Universe

Figure 1.5: Where do you live?

This does illustrate an important issue about who we think we are. If you were asked 'Where are you from?', what would your answer be? Your town, your county or region, your country, or all three? Immediately you have several identities.

Location is not the only type of identity you have. If you meet someone for the first time and discover that you have something in common, does that help you to identify with that person? Many people identify with others who work at the same job, speak the same language or share a belief in the same religion.

That is the positive side of identifying who you are. There are negatives as well. An obvious example of this is football supporters. If you are a football supporter, there will generally be one team that you and your fellow supporters dislike more than any other. That kind of identification can spill over into the violent behaviour which used to be common at football matches.

It is not surprising, therefore, that when people are asked what it means to be British there is not one simple answer. One reason for this is the UK is not one country but three: England, Scotland and Wales. Northern Ireland is a part of the UK and many people there regard themselves as British. Another reason is that throughout the UK's history people from many parts of the world have, for a variety of reasons, come to settle.

ACTIVITY

1. Who do you think you are? Briefly write how you see your identity. Give reasons for your choices.

2. 'It's good to like people like yourself and be suspicious of those who are different.' How far do you agree with this statement? Explain your answer.

THE 2001 CENSUS

The most recent **Census** in 2001 showed that the UK today has more people from different cultures than ever before. Before considering the issues raised by this diversity, it is important to look at the facts that gave rise to the statement.

POPULATION SIZE

The majority of the UK population, 54.2 million in 2001, were white (92 per cent). The remaining 4.6 million (7.9 per cent) people belonged to other ethnic groups.

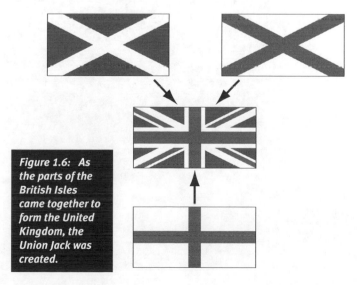

Figure 1.6: As the parts of the British Isles came together to form the United Kingdom, the Union Jack was created.

Table 1.4: The ethnic mix of the UK's population.

Ethnicity	Total population (%)
White	92.1
Mixed	1.2
Indian	1.8
Pakistani	1.2
Bangladeshi	0.5
Other Asian	0.4
Black Caribbean	1.0
Black African	0.8
Black Other	0.2
Chinese	0.4
Other ethnic groups	0.4

(*Source:* Focus on Ethnicity and Identity, *Office for National Statistics, March 2005*)

The number of people from an ethnic group other than white rose by 53 per cent between the 1991 and 2001 Census, from 3.0 million to 4.6 million.

GEOGRAPHIC DISTRIBUTION

Non-white ethnic groups are concentrated in England:

Table 1.5: Where the non-white ethnic groups are most common in the UK.

Country	% of population of country
England	9
Scotland	2
Wales	2
Northern Ireland	1

(*Source:* Focus on Ethnicity and Identity, *Office for National Statistics, March 2005*)

Non-white ethnic groups in England are concentrated in the large urban centres:

Table 1.6: The percentage of non-white ethnic groups found in urban centres throughout the UK.

Urban centre	% of residents
London	29
West Midlands	13
South East	8
North West	8
Yorkshire and the Humber	7

(*Source:* Focus on Ethnicity and Identity, *Office for National Statistics, March 2005*)

Less than 4 per cent of non-white ethnic groups live in the North East or the South West.

Table 1.7: The ethnic mix of non-white groups living in London.

Resident in London	% of ethnic minority group
Black Africans	78
Black Caribbean	61
Bangladeshi	54
Pakistani	19

(*Source:* Focus on Ethnicity and Identity, *Office for National Statistics, March 2005*)

RELIGION

White Christians remain the largest single group. In the UK, 40 million people (70 per cent) said they were white and Christian. Majorities of black people

Figure 1.7: This street reflects the wide range of cultures, and foods, that have become common in UK society.

(71 per cent) and mixed ethnic backgrounds (52 per cent) also identified themselves as Christian. The vast majority of Pakistanis and Bangladeshis were Muslim (90 per cent in each case). Indians were divided between Hindus (50 per cent) and Sikhs (30 per cent).

NATIONAL IDENTITY

In most non-white **ethnic groups** in the UK, the majority of people described their national identity as either British, English, Scottish or Welsh.

The white British group was more likely to describe their national identity as English rather than British.

However, the opposite was true of the non-white groups, who were far more likely to identify themselves as British. For example, 76 per cent of Bangladeshis said they were British and only 5 per cent said they were English, Scottish or Welsh.

ACTIVITY

The data clearly show that the overwhelming majority of the UK population is white. Using the data above, suggest reasons why this fact appears to be wrong in some areas of the country.

MULTICULTURALISM

Multiculturalism is an official acceptance of racial, cultural and ethnic diversity within a country. Society gives equal status to distinct cultural and religious groups, with no one culture predominating.

That the UK is a multicultural society is clearly evident from the data of the 2001 Census. If there was no acceptance of multiculturalism in the UK, then presumably all immigrants would need to adopt the 'British way of life'. But what is the British way of life?

The UK has been a multicultural society since long before recent immigration. The UK is made up of four distinct nations – Wales, Scotland, England and Northern Ireland – with their own diverse cultures and identities.

If multiculturalism did not exist in the UK, it could deprive UK society of diversity in areas that not might immediately spring to mind as multicultural – for example, food!

Recently questions have been asked about multiculturalism. If different groups live completely separate lives, will this split society? Will society fall apart if there is no common identity to hold it together?

The positive view of multiculturalism is that people have their own cultural beliefs and are happy to coexist – but there is a common identity of Britishness to hold society together. There is clear evidence from the Census to indicate the overwhelming majority of non-white ethnic groups share this idea of being British.

MULTICULTURALISM AND RACISM

What is racism?

Multiculturalism can give rise to **racism**. Racism is treating someone differently or unfairly simply because they belong to a different race, culture, religion or nationality. Racism can exist in all races and cultures. Racists feel threatened by anyone who is from a different race or culture.

Racism takes many different forms such as personal attacks of any kind, including violence, written and verbal threats and insults. It can also include damage to property, including graffiti.

It is illegal to treat people differently or unfairly because of their race and it is an offence for which you can be arrested.

ACTIVITY

1. What are the advantages and disadvantages of multiculturalism?

2. If you are coming from another country and want to become a UK citizen you now have to take a test. Make a list of 5–10 questions you think would test a person's 'Britishness'.

SUMMARY

This unit has explored the following points.

- What human rights are and how they have developed.
- The role of individuals and organisations in establishing and maintaining human rights legislation.
- Human rights in practice: their influence and effect.

Unit 1.2 Democratic process in the UK

IN THIS UNIT YOU WILL LEARN ABOUT:

- how parliamentary democracy in the UK works
- alternative systems of democracy
- the rights available in a democracy
- dictatorship
- the importance of active citizenship in elections.

'It's not worth voting, they are all the same – just as bad as each other.' Hands up those who think this is a fair description of UK **democracy** in the 21st century.

ACTIVITY

1. Write down your thoughts for or against this statement (or both if you think there are two sides). Discuss these thoughts as a class and try to come to a conclusion.

2. As a further discussion point: do you feel that you, as a class, have enough knowledge about democracy in the UK to come to a conclusion?

WHAT IS THIS WORD 'DEMOCRACY'?

It is actually an ancient Greek word which means 'rule by the people'. It is from the Greek words *demos*, meaning 'people', and *kratos*, meaning 'authority'. This idea was not at all popular with many wealthy and educated Greeks. They thought rule by the people would be rule by the mob.

However, it was not really rule by the people, but by some of them. Women, slaves and foreigners were not allowed to take part. Democracy was a meeting of men, in a market place, discussing issues and deciding what to do by a majority show of hands.

Representative democracy

It soon became clear that this all-inclusive type of democracy would not work. It was impossible for all the people, or all the men, to take part in democracy all the time. There were too many other things they had to do. If the democratic way of making decisions was to survive, another way to do it had to be found.

The answer the ancient Greeks came up with was **representative democracy**, a clever idea that has lasted a surprisingly long time in one form or another. If all the people (or men) could not take part personally, they could choose, on a regular basis, a small number of representatives who would take decisions on behalf of everyone. These representatives were given very clear guidance as to what their job was. It was:

- to check how the government spent money raised from taxes;
- to represent those who elected them to the government;
- to make decisions and laws.

Fundamental human rights and democracy

Democracies are based on the belief that governments are there to work for the people, not the other way round. While governments continue to protect the people's fundamental rights, people will support the government. An authoritarian government (a **dictatorship**) demands loyalty and service from the people without the need to ask for their agreement to what it is doing.

Democratic governments do not grant the freedoms that individuals have, but they are created to protect those individual's freedoms. Effective guarantees of freedom of speech, press, religion, assembly and equality before the law are essential in a democracy. The making of laws and procedures to protect these rights is the bedrock of a democratic system.

Democracy requires a decision-making system based on majority rule, with minority rights protected.

Freedom of speech is the essential right for any democracy to have. If people are free to exchange ideas and opinions, then truth has the opportunity to triumph over lies.

In contrast, authoritarian governments (dictatorships) control and monitor freedom of speech in all its forms.

Closely linked to freedom of speech is the right to protest and demand that government listens to grievances. Without the right to gather, protest and demand change, freedom of speech would be seriously undermined.

Parliamentary democracy
Modern systems of democracy are sometimes referred to as '**parliamentary democracies**'. Having got an idea of what democracy means, it is perhaps important to get a similar knowledge of the word 'parliament'.

'Parliament' comes from a Norman French word *purler*, meaning 'to speak'. There has been a parliament at Westminster in London since the 1200s, when the language that educated Englishmen spoke was still the French that had been brought to England by the Norman Conquest – therefore, Norman French.

Kings called parliaments to advise them – literally, *to speak* to them. Parliament was a talking shop.

A definition of parliamentary democracy is shown in the boxed text.

Does this definition remind you of anything?

A parliamentary democracy is one in which the people choose representatives at regular elections. These representatives are responsible for a number of functions:
- to form a government;
- to pass laws;
- to check how the government spends public (taxpayers') money;
- to discuss current issues.

ACTIVITY

1. State the differences between ancient Greek democracy and representative democracy.
2. What is the relationship between democracy and fundamental human rights?
3. 'Parliamentary democracy is just another name for representative democracy.' How far do you agree or disagree?

GOVERNMENT AND PARLIAMENT IN THE UK
When people talk about how the country is run, they often use the words 'government' and 'parliament' as if they mean the same thing. In fact they are quite different. So what are the differences? Simply put, the government runs the country, and parliament is there to check how well it does it.

What is government?
Government is the body with the power to make and enforce laws for a country.

Devolved government in the UK
The UK has historically had a centralised system of government. This changed following referendums in 1997 in Scotland and Wales and 1998 in Northern Ireland. These referendums led to a **devolution** of power to these three parts of the UK.

In 1999 the Scottish Parliament, the Welsh National Assembly and the Northern Ireland Assembly were established. The UK parliament in Westminster retains control of all non-devolved aspects of government, which includes foreign policy, defence, social security and trade. Scotland and Northern Ireland have powers to pass law on areas not reserved to the UK parliament, Wales has the right to suggest laws which are then 'fast tracked' at Westminster.

What is parliament?

It sounds as though it should be one thing, but in fact it is made up of three:

- the Queen, because she is Head of State;
- the **House of Commons**, because they are elected Members of Parliament (MPs);
- the **House of Lords**, which is now made up of people who are appointed.

Because MPs are elected, they make the Commons the most important House. These three parts of parliament only meet on rare occasions. The most regular of these is the state opening of parliament.

What does parliament do?

Parliament is an essential part of the workings of UK democracy. Its main jobs are:

- scrutiny – examining and questioning what the government is doing;
- legislation – discussing and passing laws;
- taxation – discussing and agreeing on the taxation that funds government.

How does it check on government?

The government may run the country, but parliament has some powerful weapons it uses to check how well the government is doing. The three main weapons are questions, debates and investigative committees.

Government ministers have to answer questions in parliament. Their answers can be written or verbal. MPs can ask questions on issues that the government might prefer they had not asked, and the government is obliged to answer.

All important national and international issues are debated in parliament. Votes are taken to decide whether MPs are in favour of, or against, what the government is doing.

MPs also meet in small groups called 'select committees'. These committees specialise in questioning the government on particular issues. They can make recommendations to the government.

Making law

Another vital job that parliament does is to make new laws and update old ones. These laws apply to all of us. It used to be the case that there were no legal limits on what laws parliament could make.

That is not quite true any more because, as the UK is a member of the European Union, UK law now has to follow rules laid down by Europe.

Parliament can make law for the UK as a whole, and it does in a number of areas such as defence and foreign affairs. It does not make law for Scotland or Wales on the responsibilities that have been devolved to the Scottish Parliament and the Welsh Assembly.

To make or change law now, the agreement of all three parts of parliament is needed. The Queen's agreement nowadays is automatic.

ACTIVITY

1. What methods can parliament use to 'keep an eye' on the government? Which of these do you think would be the most effective? Say why.

2. Until quite recently, parliament could make any law it liked for the whole of the UK. Explain how and why this has changed.

How are laws made in parliament?

One of the major jobs of parliament is to make new laws or bring old laws up-to-date. The way this is done can seem more complicated than is really necessary, but is necessary to try to avoid making bad laws. Most of the ideas for new or amended laws come from the government. They are announced in the Queen's Speech at the state opening of each annual session of parliament.

A suggestion for a new law will be brought to parliament as a **bill**. Before a bill is presented, the government may have try to find out public opinion about the proposal in either a **green paper**, a **white paper**, or both, but it does not have to do this.

Government bills are known as **public bills** and are the most common type of bill. They change the law that applies to the general public. Government ministers put forward most public bills.

Ordinary MPs can propose bills and these are called **private members' bills**. Like government-backed public bills, they are designed to change the law that applies to the general public. Very few become law, but they are a very effective way of making the public aware of a particular issue.

HOW DOES A BILL BECOME A LAW?

This is a lengthy and complicated process that can take many months, though in an emergency, a bill can become law in 24 hours. Normally, a bill will go through a number of stages in both houses of parliament, and then receive the 'royal assent' to become a law.

1. **First reading** – the bill is introduced without any discussion.

2. **Second reading** – there is a general discussion of the bill.

3. **Committee stage** – a committee goes through the bill, line by line, to make sure it says what it is meant to say, so that amendments can be made.

4. **Report stage** – a further opportunity to discuss the bill and any changes the committee may have made. More amendments can be made at this stage.

5. **Third reading** – the final opportunity for discussion. More amendments can be put forward in the House of Lords but not the House of Commons.

When all these stages are complete in one house of parliament, it is sent to the other house and the process is repeated. Finally, the Queen will give her agreement and the bill becomes an **act of parliament**.

ACTIVITY

1. Describe how a bill becomes an act of parliament.

2. 'The way in which law is made in UK parliament takes too long and is far too complicated.' Do you agree?

3. Either:
   explain which part/s of the process could be removed without affecting the quality of lawmaking,
   or:
   explain why all the stages in the process are necessary to ensure good laws are made.

THE HOUSES OF PARLIAMENT

The House of Commons

The House of Commons is the most important part of parliament because its members, the MPs, are elected. So who are these elected people, how many of them are there, and where do they come from?

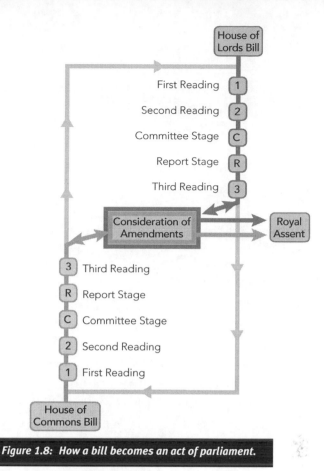

Figure 1.8: How a bill becomes an act of parliament.

(Source: www.parliament.co.uk)

There are 646 elected MPs in the House of Commons. Each MP represents a single **constituency** and is the only MP for that constituency. The average number of voters in each constituency is 68,500. Currently, of the 646 elected MPs:

- 529 represent constituencies in England;
- 40 represent constituencies in Wales;
- 59 represent constituencies in Scotland; and
- 18 represent constituencies in Northern Ireland.

Most of the elected MPs are members of one of the major political parties, though there are still a few who are independent. MPs come from a variety of different backgrounds. These can include teaching, business, law and local government.

But what do they do?

What do MPs do?

MPs really have two jobs, or at least two places of work for different parts of their job. They work in the houses of parliament at Westminster and in their constituency. This means that many MPs from outside London have to have two homes: one in London, and one in their constituency.

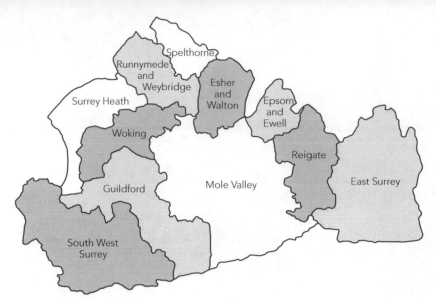

Figure 1.9: A map of the constituencies in the county of Surrey.

An MP has to represent everyone in their constituency, and that includes those who voted for other candidates in the election. At Westminster, an MP's day can involve speaking in debates in the Commons chamber, asking questions of ministers or sitting on a select committee to look at what the government is doing.

An MP's work in parliament is important, but so too is work in their constituency. After all, constituents are the people that an MP must rely on to re-elect them at the next election. Constituency work is about helping constituents with problems. Most MPs hold regular meetings, or surgeries, in their local area, for people to meet them to discuss any problems. The local MP is expected to support campaigns on local issues and to act as a spokesperson, speaking publicly on behalf of the constituency.

The House of Lords

The House of Lords is described as 'the upper house of parliament'. This does not mean that it is more important than the Commons. Since the passing of the Parliament Act in 1911, MPs have had the power to ignore the Lords if they choose. This gives it a lesser role in the process of law making.

Members of the House of Lords, or 'peers', are not elected by the public and do not have a constituency. Most are appointed for life. They use their specialist knowledge to check government policy. This is necessary because an important function of the House of Lords is to check government legislation. The House of Lords has more time to give to this process and frequently sends laws it does not agree with back to the House of Commons to be looked at again.

Some members of the government are deliberately selected as ministers because of their membership of the House of Lords. They are there to answer questions about government policy and actions.

Membership

Membership of the House of Lords has been a political issue for some time. Many members were **hereditary peers** who were in the House of Lords because they came from a noble family and their family was entitled to be there. Accident of birth did not seem to many to be a good reason to be part of parliament.

In 1997, the Labour Party won a large victory in the general election. Reform of the House of Lords was high on its list of promises (manifesto). A bill to abolish hereditary peers was announced in the Queen's Speech that autumn. In the end, 92 hereditary peers were allowed to remain. The House of Lords had 1144 members until 1999, when 666 hereditary peers lost the right to be members of the House of Lords.

Currently, most members of the House of Lords are **life peers**. These are nominated mainly by the prime minister. The House of Lords currently has 746 peers as members. You cannot be expelled from the House of Lords or resign from it.

ACTIVITY

1. 'The two houses of parliament do much the same job so they should be treated as equals.' Make a list of reasons why one of the houses is more important than the other.

2. 'If one house of parliament is clearly more important than the other, the less important house should be abolished.' Do you agree?

The electoral system

GENERAL ELECTIONS

The Parliament Act 1911 set the maximum length of a parliament to be five years.

This has only been extended twice when elections were suspended during the two world wars.

There are two ways a parliament can end. The first way is when it has reached the end of its five years of life. The second way is if the Queen, advised by the prime minister, dissolves it. The prime minister can advise the ending of parliament at any time during the five years. The dissolution of parliament causes a general election. A general election is an election involving all 646 constituencies in the UK.

WHY ARE GENERAL ELECTIONS CALLED?

The reasons for calling a general election can vary. As the prime minister picks the time, they may be influenced by an opinion as to whether the government can win the election and be re-elected for another five years.

Sometimes governments can be forced into an election to prove that the voters support what they are doing.

This is especially true if the government has lost the support of MPs in the House of Commons. For example, on 28 March 1979, the Conservative opposition put forward a motion in parliament: 'That this House has no confidence in Her Majesty's government.'

The vote in favour of this motion was 311 and the vote against was 310. The majority of MPs voted to say that they no longer had confidence in the Labour government. Because of this vote, the Labour government was forced to call a general election, which it lost.

After a dissolution of government has been announced, writs of elections are issued. These writs:

- are the official notices that an election is to be held;
- give the date on which parliament is to be opened;
- contain forms to complete to certify which person has been elected.

Throughout the election period, the government still runs the country. There are no longer any MPs and ex-MPs cannot enter the House of Commons during the election campaign.

BY-ELECTIONS

A **by-election** happens when a single constituency loses its MP during a parliament because of resignation, being expelled from the Commons, becoming a member of the House of Lords, bankruptcy, illness or death, but not because an MP changes from one party to another. Normally, by-elections take place within three months of a constituency losing its MP. If a general election is due, they can be left until the general election takes place.

ACTIVITY

1. What are the reasons for holding a general election?
2. 'The right for the prime minister to set the date of a general election gives the government an unfair advantage.' Do you agree?

HOW ARE MEMBERS OF PARLIAMENT ELECTED?

First past the post

First past the post is the electoral system currently used in parliamentary elections in the UK. It is a simple and straightforward system.

In first past the post, each constituency elects one MP. Voters are provided with a ballot paper that lists the names and parties of the candidates. They put a cross next to the candidate they wish to vote for. The candidate who gets the highest number of votes wins. The leader of the party with the largest number of constituencies then forms the new government. Quite often, if the votes given to the other candidates are added together they come to more than the number of votes for the winning candidate. This makes no difference to the result and some who feel that this system is unfair claim that all these votes count for nothing.

If it ain't broke, don't fix it!

First past the post is a simple system and, as a result, is cheap to run. Votes are easy to count and results can be given soon after the election has taken place. It produces strong governments who can run the country because it encourages large national parties. Usually, one of these parties wins an overall majority and can govern the country without having to ask for support from other parties. A party that wants to win and become the government must appeal to all kinds of people to vote for it. To achieve this, most parties put forward policies that most people can support. This makes it difficult for 'extreme' parties to get elected into government.

The first past the post system wastes votes, which puts people off voting

Only three MPs elected in the 2005 general election got more than 40 per cent of the votes of their constituents. In 2005, 70 per cent of votes cast were for losing candidates and counted for nothing. This meant that over 19 million voters 'wasted' their votes. This can persuade voters in a constituency where they know the candidate they most prefer has no chance of winning to vote negatively – they do not vote in favour of a candidate they like, but against the candidate they most dislike.

MPs are not elected in proportion to the actual number of votes their party wins nationally. In the 1983 general election, the Liberal SDP alliance won 25 per cent of the vote, but got only 3 per cent of the seats.

SINGLE TRANSFERABLE VOTE

No electoral system is perfect. There are a number of alternatives to first past the post, most of which are based on some form of **proportional representation**. Many people feel the single transferable vote system offers voters the best and most effective choice.

Under the **single transferable vote (STV)** system, each constituency elects a number of MPs. Each voter gets one vote but on the ballot paper they do not put a cross. At the side of their preferred candidate they put the number 1, for their second preference 2, then 3, and so on. To be elected, each candidate needs to win a share of the votes known as the 'quota'. If your first preference candidate has already got the quota when your vote is counted, it will be transferred to your second preference or, if necessary, your third. This should mean that very few votes are actually wasted.

Arguments used in favour of the STV system
- STV gives voters more choice and more power than any other system. Fewer votes are 'wasted'.
- STV offers voters a choice of MPs to approach after the election.

- As a result of STV, parliament is more likely to reflect the nation's views and therefore be more likely to respond to them.
- When voters have the ability to rank candidates, the most disliked candidate will not win, as they will not pick up second or third preference votes.

Arguments used against the STV system
- The multi-member constituencies needed for STV work best in areas where lots of people live – the towns and cities. In more remote areas, such as the Scottish Highlands, the small numbers of people who live there means that constituencies would cover an enormous area of land.
- In large multi-member constituencies, ballot papers can get rather big and confusing. This may affect some voters who may not fully understand the process. If the ballot is not filled in correctly, the vote may not be counted, leading to some 'wasted' votes. A voting system that allows voters to rank candidates is better only if voters actually have preferences, otherwise they may just list candidates at random.
- Because the ballot papers are complicated, the process of counting the results will take longer. Results cannot usually be declared on the same night that the vote took place.

ACTIVITY

1. Is proportional representation (STV) a fairer electoral system than 'first past the post'?

2. 'The simplicity of the current electoral system outweighs the disadvantages of the charge of wasted votes.' Do you agree?

THE RIGHTS AVAILABLE IN A DEMOCRACY

Unit 1.1 Rights and responsibilities traced the way in which human rights were eventually achieved. What are these rights that any citizen has in a democratic system of government?

The document that has had most influence on the modern approach to human rights was drawn up by the United Nations organisation after the Second World War. In 1948 it published the Universal Declaration of Human Rights.

The Convention for the Protection of Human Rights and Fundamental Freedoms, better known as the

European Convention on Human Rights, was agreed by the Council of Europe in 1950. This European response to the Universal Declaration of Human Rights tried to make these rights enforceable by the courts. The first Article makes every country which signs the Convention enforce these rights.

In 1998 the UK government passed a law listing what human rights were. It also allowed people to go to court if they believed their rights had been broken. There are 16 rights identified in the law and they are listed on the government website (see 'Websites' on page ii). They are:

- the right to life;
- freedom from torture and degrading treatment;
- freedom from slavery and forced labour;
- the right to liberty;
- the right to a fair trial;
- the right not to be punished for something that was not a crime when you did it;
- the right to respect for private and family life;
- freedom of thought, conscience and religion, and freedom to express your beliefs;
- freedom of expression;
- freedom of assembly and association;
- the right to marry and to start a family;
- the right not to be discriminated against in respect of these rights and freedoms;
- the right to peaceful enjoyment of your property;
- the right to an education;
- the right to participate in free elections;
- the right not to be subjected to the death penalty.

DICTATORSHIP

Dictatorship is a type of government that governs without the agreement of the people. It controls every aspect of people's lives. Dictators have no restrictions on what they can do.

Dictatorships usually show some or all of the following characteristics:

- no free elections or human rights;
- rule by decree not law;
- attacks on political opponents;
- the cult of personality.

Dictators usually come to power using force or fraud. They stay in power using intimidation, terror and the suppression of human rights. They use propaganda to encourage popular support.

Political parties

WHAT ARE POLITICAL PARTIES?

A political party is a group of people with similar ideas about how the country should be run. Their aim is to get their candidates elected to put their ideas into practice. Most candidates in elections, and almost all winning candidates, belong to one of the main parties. If an MP does not belong to a political party, they are known as an 'Independent'.

After a general election, the party with the most MPs forms the government. Its leader becomes the

Figure 1.10: *This 18th century cartoon shows how people viewed the parties then – how much has this changed?*

prime minister and the most important members of the party are given jobs in the cabinet and become ministers.

The second largest party becomes the official opposition. Its leader is the leader of the opposition and the party also forms a 'shadow cabinet', which mirrors the cabinet.

WHERE DO POLITICAL PARTIES COME FROM?

There have been political parties since at least the 18th century, though these were very different from modern political parties. The first identifiable parties appeared in the late 17th century when two groups of MPs were recognisable in parliament. These were the Whigs and the Tories.

The name Tory was a term of abuse used by the Whigs. It meant 'Irish Catholic Bandits'. Despite this, the name was adopted by the party. Generally speaking, the Tories wanted government to stay as it was. The successor to the Tories, although they still use the original name, is the modern Conservative Party.

'Whig' was also a term of abuse used by the Tories to try to discredit those who held different views. It meant 'Scottish rebels' and was first used in the reign of Charles II. Like the Tories, the Whigs adopted the name. Generally speaking, they wanted the way England was governed to change. The successor to the Whigs is the modern Liberal Democrat Party.

The Independent Labour Party was founded in 1893. Its major aim was the have Labour MPs in the UK parliament. This party became the Labour Party and began to grow, usually at the expense of the Liberal Party.

Since 1945, either the Conservative Party or the Labour Party has held power. The Liberal Democrats, the third biggest party in the UK, was formed when the Liberal Party merged with the Social Democratic Party in 1988.

HOW THE PARTIES WORK IN PARLIAMENT

The party system in parliament relies on a working relationship between the government and the opposition party.

Opposition parties help to make policy and legislation by putting forward sensible proposals for change. They oppose government proposals that they disagree with, and put forward their own ideas to improve their chances of becoming the next government.

Leaders of the government and opposition sit opposite each other on the front benches in the debating chamber of the House of Commons. Their supporters, called the 'backbenchers', sit behind them.

THE WHIP'S OFFICE

The people who make parliament work are government and opposition **chief whips**. Collectively they arrange the business of the House.

The chief whips and their assistants are appointed by the party leaders to manage their parliamentary parties. They keep members informed of upcoming parliamentary business. They make sure that MPs attend important debates. They also feed back backbench opinions to the party leadership.

WHAT DO THE UK POLITICAL PARTIES STAND FOR?

Below are statements adapted from the home pages of the three largest UK political parties (see 'Websites' on page ii).

The Conservative Party

Our Vision for Britain:

- Advancing opportunity. Giving people more opportunity and power over their lives.
- Nurturing responsibility. Making families stronger and societies more responsible.
- Protecting security. Making Britain safer and greener.
- Strengthening the ties that bind society.
- Protecting quality of life today and for future generations.

The Labour Party

Labour's achievements have revolutionised the lives of the British people. The values Labour stands for today are those which have guided it throughout its existence:

- social justice
- strong community and strong values
- reward for hard work
- decency
- rights matched by responsibilities.

The Liberal Democrat Party

- The Liberal Democrats exist to build and safeguard a fair, free and open society.

- We champion the freedom, dignity and wellbeing of individuals.
- The role of the state is to enable all citizens to attain these ideals, to contribute fully to their communities and to take part in the decisions which affect their lives.

ACTIVITY

1. What are the three main political parties in the UK? Briefly describe their history and what they now stand for.

2. 'The work of parliament would be seriously disrupted if there were no political parties.' Do you agree?

TAKING PART IN THE ELECTORAL PROCESS

Voters

In order to vote, you must register with your local electoral registration office. In England and Wales this is the local council, which compiles a new **electoral register** each autumn. Citizens over 18 are sent a registration form each year and completing and returning it will make sure your name is included in the up-to-date electoral register. This means that you can vote.

When an election is called, all registered electors are sent a polling card. This gives useful information such as the date of the election, the place where you should vote and the times at which you can vote. Polling stations are usually in local community buildings.

Electors are given a ballot paper which has the names of the candidates standing and the parties they belong to. They take the ballot paper into a polling booth to make sure their vote is secret. To vote, a cross is placed by the name of the candidate supported. Anything else written on the ballot paper may mean it will not be counted because it is a 'spoilt ballot'. The ballot paper is folded in half and put it in a locked ballot box.

It is possible to vote at an election by post. No reason has to be given but it must be arranged before the election.

Candidates

To stand for election a candidate must be:

- at least 18 years of age;

- a British citizen, a citizen of a Commonwealth country or a citizen of the Irish Republic.

Some people are not allowed to stand for election as an MP:

- convicted prisoners serving more than 12 months;
- peers who sit in the House of Lords;
- some employees of the Crown;
- bishops who sit in the House of Lords.

Candidates must be nominated by 10 electors registered in the constituency in which they wish to stand. No candidate may stand in more than one constituency. Candidates have to pay a deposit of £500 which will not be returned if they receive less than 5 per cent of the total votes cast.

Local government

WHAT IS LOCAL GOVERNMENT?

People are much more likely to come into contact with representatives and workers from a local council than central government. They are responsible for many of the things that make a daily impact on everyone's lives.

HOW DOES IT WORK?

In most of England, local government is split into two parts: county councils and district councils.

County councils cover large geographical areas and are responsible for most public services such as education and social services. Because they are so large, they are divided into smaller districts. The district councils provide local services such as leisure facilities and waste collection.

In large towns and cities in England there is one authority, which is called a unitary authority. Unitary authorities are responsible for all local services.

In some parts of England there are also town and parish councils, covering even smaller areas. They are responsible for very local services such as local halls and community centres.

WHAT DO THEY DO AND HOW IS IT PAID FOR?

Central government decides national policy, but the day to day implementation of these policies is the responsibility of local councils. Some of the things councils do are required by law; others can be provided if the council chooses to do so.

Local authorities spend almost 25 per cent of all public spending in the UK. This money is raised through government grants, council tax and business rates.

Central government provides grants to local authorities to pay for all the necessary services. There are two types of grant: general and specific. General grants allow local authorities to spend money as they wish. Specific grants are for particular activities.

Council tax raises 25 per cent of local funding. Households pay an amount that is dependent on the value of their home.

Business rates are a property tax on businesses. The rates are set by central government but collected by local authorities. Central government then divides the money raised and passes it back to local authorities.

WHO ARE MEMBERS OF LOCAL COUNCILS?

Local councils are run by councillors who have been elected by local people. Their job is to make decisions about local services. Each councillor is elected for four years, and they represent areas called wards. They are not council employees. Elected councillors make decisions which paid employees put into practice.

ACTIVITY

Describe the relationship between central and local government.

Active citizenship

Parliament makes laws and takes decisions that affect everyone's daily life. Many people feel that they have little or no control over these decisions. You only get to vote in elections every five years!

This is really an excuse, because there are many opportunities for people to contribute and be informed of what parliament is doing. Parliament needs this input if it is going to reflect the views of the people it claims to represent.

HOW CAN I INFLUENCE WHAT PARLIAMENT IS DOING?

The most obvious way is to vote in elections. This may sound simple but many voters never make the effort. Less than 7 in 10 people vote in general elections, and less than 1 in 3 vote in local elections and about 1 in 3 vote in European elections. What message does that send to the people standing for election about the interest their constituents have in what happens after the election?

Figure 1.11: Nice Treaty Referendum Posters in Dublin Ireland 2002.

You are entitled to contact your MP by letter, telephone or email, whether you voted for them or not. They can help you in ways you probably cannot imagine. They can raise your issue in a debate in parliament or question a member of the government about it.

They could put forward an amendment to a bill, or even attempt to introduce a private members bill to publicise the issue.

The public can contribute to the work of parliamentary committees by submitting evidence either in writing or by email.

The government publishes green papers and white papers, outlining policies and laws that are under consideration, inviting interested parties to contribute to the consultation.

If you are 18 or over you could always stand for election yourself and become one of the active citizens who help run the country!

ACTIVE CITIZENSHIP AND REFERENDUMS

If democracy is based on the active participation of citizens, one issue that currently causes some controversy is that of the role of **referendums** in a democratic system of government.

Governments claim to be democratic, but in practice they do not always act democratically. Once victory in a general election has given them the right to govern, they make all decisions without further reference to the electorate. The justification for this is that the people voted for the government's policies and therefore they have the right to put them into practice. Rarely – if at all – will they use referendums to fully find out what the public thinks about issues during the lifetime of that government.

ARGUMENTS IN FAVOUR OF REFERENDUMS

- Referendums are a very real form of direct democracy.
- They allow an active role in decision making that one vote every five years does not.
- Governments can be seen to act as 'elected dictatorships' until the next election, while referendums offer an answer to questions the government might be asking.
- They allow voters to give an opinion on major issues.

- If the government asks for people's opinions, it is more likely to be supported.
- Referendums allow controversial policies to be tested against public opinion, and important issues that were not issues at the election to be put to the electorate.

ARGUMENTS AGAINST THE USE OF REFERENDUMS

- Parliament is the body that has the power in the UK political system. Referendums would weaken this.
- It is not always possible to reduce complicated issues to a simple yes/no vote.
- Regular use of referendums could cause people to get bored with the process.
- Alternatives such as opinion polls and by-election results give information about the electorates' views.
- If only a few people voted, then how accurate would the result of a referendum be?
- When the result is close, does that give clear permission to go ahead or not?
- Who will pay for it?
- If a majority votes for an issue, is the government obliged to implement it?

ACTIVITY

1. 'The UK should use referendums on important issues between general elections.' Do you agree?

2. How would you phrase the question for the ballot paper in a referendum to lower the voting age to 16?

SUMMARY

This unit has explored the following points.

- The origins and meaning of the word 'democracy', different types of democracy and democratic practices.
- How democracy works in the UK and how laws are made.
- How MPs and governments are elected, what political parties are, what local government is and how they all work in parliament.
- How you can take part in the electoral process and what active citizenship and referendums are.

Unit 1.3 Judicial process in the UK

IN THIS UNIT YOU WILL LEARN ABOUT:

- the role of the law in protecting rights and resolving conflicts
- the difference between criminal and civil law
- the operation of the different judicial systems
- the due process of criminal law.

KEY CONCEPTS

Criminal law
Civil law
Trial
Legal precedent
Appeal

The law and the legal system may seem to be all about rules, telling you what you can and cannot do. When you think about the way laws restrict what people, particularly young people, can do, it is easy to understand why some people might take this view. Growing up seems to be a series of birthdays after which you can do more than you could do before. Or worse, that you have to do things that perhaps you would rather not.

Table 1.8: The ages at which you can do (or cannot do) certain things.

Age	What you can or cannot do
5	You must go to school (although you have probably been going to pre-school for 2 years).
10	You can be held responsible for committing crime.
16	You can get married – if your parents agree.
17	You can drive a car.
18	You are legally an adult and can do anything an adult can do.

This is only a small selection of the way people's right to do whatever they want is controlled. Like it or not, breaking these age limits is also breaking the law and a criminal offence which could lead to you being prosecuted.

You may remember the idea of 'freedom from or freedom to' raised in Unit 1.1 on human rights. Laws like the ones listed above are an attempt to put this into practice.

ACTIVITY

Do some research on the age at which you can do the following things:

- join the armed forces with and without parental consent for boys and girls;
- have a part time job whilst still at school;
- get a mortgage.

SO WHY DO LAWS SEEM SO RESTRICTIVE?

Laws probably seem so restrictive because they are about controlling people. They put the benefit of all above the benefit of the individual. They are also enforced by the police, judges and courts, which can lead to punishment, so they carry a threat.

There are limits on the type of laws that can be made. Laws should only be made for good reason. This is why law-making in parliament is such a lengthy and detailed process. It gives MPs, our elected representatives, the time to question whether the law is necessary, inside parliament. It also allows pressure groups outside parliament time to raise issues and to put pressure on MPs to change or oppose proposed new laws.

In a more positive light, laws could be described as the lubricant that keeps society rubbing along in relative peace and harmony. No one is above the law in the UK. Laws are fair and apply to everyone equally. Restricting what we can do at certain ages or at certain times, such as driving a car after drinking alcohol, tries to protect us from harming ourselves or others. This also sends clear messages about what is and what is not an acceptable way to behave. Finally to return to 'freedom from or freedom to' idea, laws are an important way of protecting our rights.

CRIMINAL LAW

A general definition of crime might be: 'An action forbidden by law or a failure to act as required by law'.

Crime is generally divided into two broad types: crimes against the person and crimes against property. Society's view of what actually is criminal has varied over time. More importantly, so has the punishment. The old saying 'might as well be hanged for stealing a sheep as a lamb' comes from a time when the punishment for stealing anything was hanging. In that case, the criminal would be encouraged to commit the bigger crime, as the punishment could not be any worse.

What is criminal also varies depending on where you are, as each country has its own laws. What might be perfectly acceptable behaviour in the UK could get you arrested in some other countries.

The idea behind criminal law is to support safe and orderly living for everyone. To achieve this, law-breakers can be prosecuted. **Prosecution** means an appearance in court and if found guilty could mean a fine, imprisonment or both.

The accused is assumed to be innocent until proven guilty. A guilty verdict can only be given if the evidence proves guilt 'beyond reasonable doubt'. This may seem, and in reality is, a difficult thing to prove. The reason behind it is that it is felt to be better to free some guilty defendants because of the benefit of the doubt, than to wrongly imprison an innocent person. This is not always achieved and **miscarriages of justice** do happen.

ACTIVITY

'The criminal justice system is biased in favour of the guilty getting away with their crimes, because you are innocent until proven guilty.' How far do you agree with this statement?

THE CRIMINAL JUSTICE SYSTEM

In England and Wales, the criminal justice system is made up of several agencies, departments and professionals. They have a responsibility to uphold the law and see that justice is done.

The police

The police are the most visible part of the system, and the one with which the public most frequently interacts. Their main roles are to prevent crime from happening, and catch the criminals if it does happen.

Figure 1.12: 'Stop and search' has proved a controversial idea in the UK. Some people think that it extends the police's powers too far. What do you think? Do you think it is necessary?

The **Home Office**, which is responsible for the police in England and Wales, describes the police on its website as a modern force that is responsible for building safer communities for everyone.

Police duties and powers are set out in the Police and Criminal Evidence Act 1984 (PACE). This Act tries to get the balance right between police powers and the rights and freedoms of the public. It is constantly reviewed and updated to take account of changing circumstances.

There are 43 police forces in England and Wales. They employ over 233,000 staff including over 140,000 police officers.

ACTIVITY

1. Find out more about PACE powers and procedures at the Home Office website (see 'Websites' on page ii).

2. PACE tries to get the balance right between police powers and the public's freedoms. How well do you feel it has succeeded?

The crown prosecution service

The **crown prosecution service** (CPS) is the government department responsible for prosecuting criminal cases investigated by the police in England and Wales. Its role is to:

- advise the police on cases for possible prosecution;
- review cases submitted by the police;
- decide on charges in all but minor cases;
- prepare cases for court;
- present cases at court.

In its Guide the CPS says the role of its service is:

> ' ... to prosecute cases firmly, fairly and effectively when there is sufficient evidence to provide a realistic prospect of conviction, and when it is in the public interest to do so.'

(Source: http://www.cps.gov.uk/about/index.html)

An example of how the CPS works is that the police catch, arrest and charge someone with a criminal offence. The CPS then makes the decision whether to prosecute or not by applying the statement above.

Solicitors and barristers

There are two quite separate groups of professionals in the UK legal profession. They have distinct and clearly defined roles in criminal cases. A **solicitor** is a lawyer who gives legal advice and does preparatory work for barristers. A **barrister** is a lawyer who is qualified to represent clients in the higher law courts in England and Wales.

Solicitors are usually the first contact for a suspect. They often become involved at a police station when an issue arises. They deal with the day-to-day administration of the case before it is taken on by a barrister.

The solicitor will contact a barrister about a case. The barrister considers the law and looks at similar cases to advise how to move the case forward. If the case goes to court, the barrister presents the case, cross-examines witnesses and argues the issues.

Magistrates

Magistrates, or **justices of the peace (JPs)**, are volunteers. They deal with around 95 per cent of criminal cases. They are not paid for their work. Anyone can be appointed between the ages of 18 and 70. Those over 65 are rarely appointed.

They are selected by being the 'right people for the job', and there is a positive attempt to include as many sections of society as possible. There is no requirement for any kind of paper qualification in the law or in anything else for that matter.

Magistrates sit in their local court dealing with criminal cases. They sit on a 'bench' of three consisting of an experienced chair with two other magistrates. They are supported by a trained legal advisor to give guidance on the law and sentencing options.

Crown court circuit judges

There are currently over 600 **circuit judges** throughout England and Wales. They are appointed to one of six regions of England and Wales and sit in the crown and county courts within their particular region.

To become a judge, they must have been a lawyer appearing in court as an advocate for at least ten years. They are appointed by the Queen, on the recommendation of the Lord Chancellor.

Unlike magistrates, judges are not representative of all sections of society. They are mainly male, middle class and white.

1. Make brief notes on the role of the CPS, barristers, solicitors, magistrates and judges.

2. Are they all necessary to make the UK legal system work?

Courts

If the CPS decides to proceed with a prosecution, all criminal cases are dealt with in court, but not all cases are dealt with in the same kind of court.

There are two types of criminal offence: summary offences and indictable offences. Summary offences are less serious and can only be tried in magistrates' courts. They carry a maximum sentence of either six months' imprisonment, a fine of up to £5000, or both.

All criminal cases start in magistrates' courts. Some cases begin in the magistrates' court and then, because of their serious nature, go to the **crown court** for **trial by jury**. Cases where a defendant is not entitled to trial by jury start and finish in a magistrates' court. Magistrates also deal with cases where defendants can choose trial by jury but decide to have their case heard in the magistrates' court.

Indictable offences are the more serious offences – for example, murder and robbery – and have to be tried in the crown court by a judge and jury. They cannot be tried in a magistrates' court because the maximum punishments allowed would not reflect the seriousness of the crime committed.

TRIALS

In the UK, a trial proceeds by what is known as the adversarial system. The prosecution tries to prove that the accused committed the offence, and the defence tries to prove that the accused did not commit the offence. Legal representatives, usually barristers, put forward the evidence for the prosecution and the defence.

At the start of a trial, an accused person is presumed to be innocent until they are proved guilty 'beyond reasonable doubt' by the prosecution. The burden of proof lies firmly with the prosecution – the defence does not have to prove the accused is innocent.

Criminal trials usually take place in an open court. This means that they are open to the press and public.

Figure 1.13: The Birmingham Six were involved in a famous miscarriage of justice. They were freed on appeal in 1991 after spending 16 years in jail.

The prosecution begins the trial by presenting the evidence to 'prove' the guilt of the accused. Witnesses will be brought into court to provide testimony to support the evidence. The defence has the right to ask questions of the witnesses to 'test' the reliability and truthfulness of their evidence. There are strict rules about how this should be done. When there is a disagreement about whether the rules are being properly observed, the judge acts as a referee.

The process is then reversed. The defence presents evidence that questions the case made by the prosecution and produces witnesses. The prosecution has the same right to question defence witnesses. Each of them is trying to persuade the jury, a panel of 12 ordinary men and women selected at random to make the decision about guilt or innocence, that their argument is correct.

When all the evidence has been heard and all witnesses have been questioned and cross-questioned, the judge plays the important role of summing up for the jury. During this, the judge will advise the jury about any points of law they should take into account.

After the summing up, the jury is sent to the jury room to decide on its verdict. Normally, verdicts are expected to be unanimous with all the jurors agreeing. In some circumstances, if all the jurors cannot agree, the judge can accept a verdict if at least 10 of the jurors agree.

If the verdict is guilty, the judge will sentence the offender. In deciding the sentence the judge must take several things into account, including the need to protect the public and help to reduce crime by preventing re-offending and also the need to punish the offender while at the same time encouraging them to make amends for their crime. Fines are the most common punishments. If a prison sentence is available, the maximum length is laid down by parliament.

Convicted offenders have a **right of appeal**. If the conviction was in the magistrates' court, the appeal can be against sentence, or conviction, or both. An appeal against conviction results in the whole trial being heard again at the crown court in front of a judge and two magistrates. An appeal against a sentence will be decided by a crown court judge. This could lead to an increase in the sentence, a reduction to it, or no change.

TRIAL BY JURY

Trial by jury is a legal process in which a jury is responsible for deciding the facts of a case. In the UK, the right to a jury trial is seen as a fundamental civil right. Most other countries do not share this view.

A jury is not part of the system of courts. It is made up of ordinary people, aged between 18 and 70, who have been randomly chosen from the up-to-date electoral register. They hear the case, listen to the evidence presented, decide on the facts, and agree a verdict of guilty or not guilty. They are advised and guided on the law by the trial judge.

Juries are used in the UK because it is believed that this is the best way to ensure a fair trial. The 12 jury members are from all parts of society and are expected to hear the case with an open mind. They do not have, and do not need, any knowledge of the law. Their common sense and life experience are what is needed to allow a fair trial to take place.

Some people are not allowed to sit on juries. They are excluded on the grounds of age, because they have recent criminal records, or are connected to the legal system. Around 200,000 people perform jury service each year.

The judge decides questions of law, sums up the case to the jury and either discharges or sentences the accused.

ACTIVITY

1. The jury is the only part of the criminal justice system that is not trained for its role. What reasons are given for allowing these amateurs to decide guilt or innocence?

2. 'Many countries do not use the jury system. All the proceedings, including determination of innocence and guilt, are in the hands of legally qualified judges. This ensures the process will be fairer for the accused.' How far do you agree?

CIVIL LAW

A general definition of civil law is 'law dealing with the rights of private citizens'. It is mainly concerned with disputes between individuals, businesses or organisations.

Civil law cases are referred to the county court. There are 228 county courts in England and Wales. The majority of claims concern the recovery and collection of debt. The next most common types of claim relate to recovery of land and personal injury.

Most civil disputes do not go to court at all, and most of those that do go to court do not go to trial, but are settled out of court. County courts also handle family proceedings, such as divorce, domestic violence and matters affecting children.

Many civil cases are dealt with through complaints procedures. Others are settled by mediation and negotiation. Cases too complex for the county court are sent to one of the three specialist divisions of the high court.

CASES IN THE COUNTY COURT

If a case is taken to court, the 'plaintiff' – the person bringing the complaint – sues the 'defendant' – the person being complained about. Cases are dealt with by a judge or a district judge. The judge will decide whether the defendant is 'liable' or 'not liable'.

The decision will be based on the balance of probability. This means the judge decides, after hearing the evidence, which party is most likely to be in the right. If the defendant is liable, they usually have to pay damages. This will be a sum of money to compensate for the difficulty caused. The amount awarded depends on the circumstances of each case but will not exceed £5000.

There is a right to appeal via the normal appeal procedures: firstly, the court of appeal, then ultimately to the House of Lords if the appeal is considered to be important enough.

ACTIVITY

1. Make a list of the differences between criminal and civil law cases.

2. 'The method of bringing a case in a civil case seems simpler than in a criminal case. The process for the criminal law should be simplified.' Do you agree?

The process of law making

STATUTE LAW

In the last unit we looked in detail at how law is made by the government and parliament. Law that is made in this way is known as **statute law**. It is by no means the only way in which law is made in the UK.

COMMON LAW

Common law is what we call the body of unwritten English law that developed from the 12th century onwards. It is called the common law because it was believed that English medieval law as applied in the courts was simply the application of the common customs of the country.

LEGAL PRECEDENT

As the court system became more organised during the reign of King Henry II (1154–1189), judges' decisions were recorded and the idea of **legal precedent** was accepted. This was the view that a judge trying a particular type of case should take note of the decisions made in similar cases by other judges. Over time these decisions became to be seen as legal precedents which gave them the status of guidelines to be followed.

Cases which raised new issues still allowed judges to create new rules or decisions, which themselves became precedent as they were accepted and used by other judges. This part of the common law is sometimes referred to as 'case law' or 'judge-made law'.

In common law systems the courts are in a hierarchy. This means that decisions are more important the higher up the system they are taken. Appeal court decisions are binding on trial courts.

EUROPEAN LAW

The law of the European Union (EU) is a legal system that operates alongside the laws of member states of the EU. EU law has direct effect within the legal systems of its member states, and overrides national law in many areas, especially in terms of economic and social policy.

It is estimated that about half of the laws enacted in existing member states stem from EU legislation.

Law making at EU level involves three bodies. The European commission is made up of a president and commissioners, who are appointed by the member states and approved by the European parliament. It puts forward proposals for new laws. Every proposal must be based on part of one of the treaties which all members of the EU have agreed to. This gives the right to make the proposal.

The council of the EU is the main decision-making body. It is made up of representatives of the governments of member states. The European parliament – the only directly elected body in the decision making process – shares with the council the power to make laws.

The parliament shares the power to make law equally with the council. If council and parliament cannot agree on a piece of proposed legislation, it is put before a conciliation committee, made up of equal numbers of council and parliament representatives to reach an agreement, so that they can adopt it as law.

EU law overides UK law. No UK law can operate if it is in conflict with EU law.

DELEGATED LEGISLATION

Delegated legislation is when parliament allows other bodies to make law under the authority of an act of parliament. There are three main types of delegated legislation: statutory instruments, by-laws and orders in council.

Statutory instruments allow government departments to make arrangements for areas under their responsibility. They allow ministers to make

technical changes to a law, such as altering the level of a fine. They are very useful and about 3500 statutory instruments are enacted each year.

By-laws are created by local authorities, and other bodies, to cover matters in their own area, such as litter, which must be approved by central government.

Orders in council are laws passed in emergencies by the government.

The main reason for delegated legislation is to stop the parliamentary timetable being swamped.

ACTIVITY

1. Briefly describe the different ways in which law is made in the UK.

2. 'Parliament is still in control of all laws made in this country.' How far do you think this is true?

SUMMARY

This unit has explored the following points.

- Why laws are needed.
- How the criminal justice system works in the UK.
- How the trial system works in the UK.
- What civil law is and how it works, and how laws are made outside of parliament.

Chapter 2
Issues of Economic Wellbeing and Financial Capability

Unit 2.1 The classification of economic activity and the nature of the modern economy

IN THIS UNIT YOU WILL LEARN ABOUT:

- the classification of economic activity
- the reason for the relative decline of primary and secondary industry
- changing global industrial patterns.

KEY CONCEPTS

Primary industry
Secondary industry
Tertiary industry
E-commerce

INDUSTRIAL ACTIVITY

Industry is the process or activity of making or creating a product or service. Industries are commonly divided into sectors. There have been three main sectors – primary, secondary and tertiary. Recently, the information industries have begun to be separated from the tertiary sector and are referred to as the quaternary sector.

PRIMARY SECTOR

The **primary sector** involves changing natural resources into primary products. These primary products are used as raw materials by other sectors. The sector involves raw material extraction, rearing animals, growing crops and catching fish. The sector employs around 2 per cent of UK workers. The main employment is in farming, mining, quarrying and fishing.

Primary industry is more important in less economically developed countries (LEDCs). In more economically developed countries (MEDCs), the increasing use of technology enables the primary industry to maintain output with a much reduced work force. This enables them to remain competitive against the products of LEDCs.

SECONDARY SECTOR

Industries in the **secondary sector** are those that take products produced by the primary sector and turn them into finished goods for sale. The sector involves turning raw materials into manufactured products. The sector employs around 22 per cent of UK workers. The main employment is in processing raw materials, manufacturing, construction and textiles.

The sector includes heavy and light manufacturing, food processing, oil refining and production of electricity and gas. Some of these industries use large amounts of energy to run the factories and machinery needed for manufacturing. The waste materials and heat they generate need to be controlled to avoid environmental problems.

TERTIARY SECTOR

The **tertiary sector** is also known as the service sector. It includes providers of services to businesses and individuals. It can be split into two general categories: wholesalers and retailers, and other services.

Wholesalers and retailers transport, distribute and sell producers goods to consumers. Wholesalers buy in bulk and sell to retailers. Retailers sell to the general public.

Other services include health services, transportation, education, entertainment, tourism, financial services, and personal services such as plumbers and hairdressers. The essence of these services is the personal interaction with people rather than making things. The biggest growth area in the tertiary sector over the last 25 years has been in financial and business services, where the number of employees has doubled to 20 per cent of the whole workforce.

QUATERNARY SECTOR

The **quaternary sector** consists of those industries providing information services. These are principally: information generation, information sharing, consultation, education and research and development.

The quaternary sector is sometimes included with the tertiary sector, as they are both service sectors. Between them, the tertiary and quaternary sectors form the largest part of the UK economy, employing 76 per cent of the workforce.

The aim of these services is to help companies to continue to grow. They will aim to cut costs and develop new markets and products, and this will include researching new production methods. This sector is best suited to MEDCs as it requires a highly educated workforce.

ACTIVITY

1. Write a brief explanation of the four sectors.

2. Do you agree that the tertiary sector should be split in two, or are services just services? Explain your answer.

Reasons for the decline of primary and secondary industries in the UK and EU

EMPLOYMENT STRUCTURES

The employment structure of a country is about how the workforce is shared between the employment sectors. These structures inevitably change over time.

When a country is in the early stages of development, most people live on the land and are agricultural or primary workers. Many will be **subsistence** farmers – peasants who grow purely for themselves. At this stage, most things that people consume they grow or make themselves.

As a country begins to develop, industry and manufacturing increase, which creates growth in the secondary sector of manufacturing.

This growth causes a structural change in the country's economy. A prime target for manufacturers is to increase agricultural machinery. The purpose of mechanisation is to do work more quickly than it can be done by hand. This means that far fewer people are needed to work on the land.

Figure 2.1: Robots and machinery have replaced people in the secondary sector, leading to a decrease in available jobs.

People begin to leave the land and are forced to move to the growing towns looking for work in the new factories. Some of these people move willingly, while many more are forced off the land. The process is inevitable and, if the country is to become more wealthy, an economic necessity. However, the cost in terms of human poverty and suffering is severe.

By the time a country achieves a more economically developed status, there is another structural change. This time, the secondary sector is most affected.

Mechanisation in the factories once more reduces the need for human labour. The tertiary sector grows and the increase in computers, machinery and robots replaces people in the secondary sector with the consequent decrease in secondary jobs. There is an increased demand for education to provide the more skilled workforce that is required by work in a tertiary economy.

ACTIVITY

Identify the cause of structural change in the economy. Explain how it caused the change from primary to secondary, and from secondary to tertiary.

THE IMPACT IN THE UK

One hundred years ago, the UK was the 'workshop of the world' and the world leader in manufacturing. The UK now imports most manufactured goods.

Fifty years ago, coal mining, shipbuilding and steel production were booming, and employed hundreds of thousands of workers. Coal mining and shipbuilding have almost disappeared entirely and, although there is still considerable steel production, this is now achieved with less than 10 per cent of its previous workforce.

There are now more people employed in fast food restaurants than in these three secondary industries put together.

Financial and business services now employ more than 20 per cent of all workers in the UK. This is a feature of the post-war growth in the service industries and the fall in manufacturing.

In 1980, 33 per cent of men worked in manufacturing. This fell to 20 per cent by 2000 and 14 per cent by 2008. The figures for women in manufacturing mirrored this fall. In 1980, 20 per cent of women worked in manufacturing, by 2000 this fell to 10 per cent and by 2008 to 5 per cent.

It would be reasonable to expect that as the number of people working in an industry decline, so will the production output. This does not always follow. Use of quicker and better methods of production can actually raise output with a smaller labour force.

ACTIVITY

1. What have been the changes in employment in the UK?

2. Do you think these have improved things for workers? Give reasons for your answer.

Overall trends

PRIMARY INDUSTRY

Employment in primary industry has seen a consistent decline, although this recently appears to have bottomed out. Output has shown a downward trend, but less than might be expected as a result of increasing use of technology.

In agriculture, farmers have improved crop yields by using improved seeds. New technology has helped to produce cheaper and healthier food. Computers control the growing conditions in greenhouses and calculate quantities needed for sowing, as well as fertiliser and pesticide usage.

SECONDARY INDUSTRY

As indicated in the survey of the impact on the UK, employment in all these areas has fallen, as has output. This has been less significant in energy production and construction. Increases in automation and changes in methods of working have maintained output, but overall, manufacturing output has fallen considerably but not consistently across all types of manufacturers.

Production of electrical and optical equipment, office machinery, computers and videos is growing. Production of wood products, such as containers, doors and veneers, is declining.

TERTIARY INDUSTRY

The tertiary sector has shown consistent growth. Output and employment have steadily increased, but there is not always a direct link between the two. For example, many jobs have disappeared in banking as a result of automation.

Table 2.1: Trends in UK employment 1700–2008.

Year	% employment primary	% employment secondary	% employment tertiary
1700	85	10	5
1750	80	20	5
1800	58	35	7
1850	40	50	10
1900	27	62	11
1950	20	57	23
1980	5	31	64
2000	2	22	76
2008	2	17	81

ACTIVITY

Explain how industries can lose workers but still make as much product.

Electronic commerce

It is possible that, in the foreseeable future, this new form of business could have an increasing impact on employment.

Electronic commerce, often called **e-commerce**, is the name given to buying and selling things using the Internet. It has become increasingly important in the last 10 years because of the increasing number of people who have an Internet connection, particularly high-speed broadband.

There are advantages in e-commerce for companies and customers. For companies, a website can be much more cost-effective than a shop. It can also enable them to reach a national, or even international market, rather than a purely local one.

Figure 2.2: Multinational corporations can bring benefits to less economically developed countries.

Customers can find products they want more easily than when they physically go shopping. They get more detailed product or service information from a website. Shopping can be done from home and in a more relaxed way. Goods have to be delivered but the cost of this is low and can be compensated by the time and money saved in physically going out to shop.

Some customers dislike shopping on the Internet because it lacks a human touch. They are also concerned about fraud when paying for goods electronically. Some people are concerned that products can be substituted inappropriately if the product they want is out of stock.

Changing global industrial patterns

MULTINATIONAL CORPORATIONS (MNCS)

Multinational corporations are global businesses that have interests in more than one country. They structure their operations so that different parts of the company are in the most appropriate location. For example, technical departments tend to be located in more developed countries that have the **infrastructure** and educated workforce needed. Manufacturing is done in less economically developed countries, because costs are lower.

THE BENEFITS OF MULTINATIONAL CORPORATIONS FOR LESS ECONOMICALLY DEVELOPED COUNTRIES

Investment

Generally speaking, governments want investment from these MNCs because they create jobs and incomes, and bring investment to countries that are not their own. If they choose to build production facilities, they will need to use local resources. This does not only mean labour, but also the land on which to build the plant, and local companies to provide the building materials for the construction.

Money spent in this way will work its way into the local area. The workers will spend their wages in local shops, and local employers will be looking for more workers who will then spend their wages in the local shops.

Technology transfer and skills training

MNCs bring with them new ideas and new techniques. These can improve the quality of production in a poorer country. As well as employing local labour, MNCs provide developing countries with training and new skills to help them improve productivity and efficiency. These skills can then be shared with other workers. This improves the supply of skilled labour in the area and makes the area more attractive to other potential investors.

Improvements in infrastructure

Having built a production facility in a developing country, the MNC may wish to transport goods to ports for export. This could lead the corporation to invest in additional infrastructure facilities like road, rail, port and communications facilities, which will provide benefits for the whole country.

THE DISADVANTAGES OF MULTINATIONAL CORPORATIONS (MNCS) FOR LESS ECONOMICALLY DEVELOPED COUNTRIES

Large, transnational corporations are becoming increasingly powerful. Many MNCs are large in relation to the national income of the countries in which they are located. This means that it is not as easy for the host governments to enforce national laws on MNCs. As profits are naturally the most important goal, damaging results can arise. These results include allegations that profit-motivated MNCs are trying to control entire economies. They are deliberately bankrupting local companies to create and exploit a monopoly position. They are exporting high-wage jobs from the USA and EU into low-wage countries. This perpetuates world poverty and potentially exploits child labour.

The expansion of MNCs is undermining the world's environment by exploitation of natural resources and by the **carbon footprint** left by the goods they ship over long distances.

MNCs increase the debt problems of developing countries by not allowing the host country a fair share of the benefits from the relationship.

Fair trade

There are alternatives for less developed countries to develop their economies without the interference of MNCs.

Fair trade is a market-based approach to helping developing country producers to develop themselves. Its central idea is to pay a fair price for goods and to support social and environmental standards in the production of a wide variety of exports from and to developing countries.

Its aim is to work with at-risk producers and workers in order to help them become economically self-sufficient. It also aims to help them achieve greater fairness in international trade.

In 2007, fair trade-certified sales amounted to approximately £1.8 billion worldwide. This is a fraction of world trade in physical merchandise – fair trade products form between one and two per cent of all sales in the products sold in Europe and North America.

In June 2008, it was estimated that over 7.5 million producers and their families were benefiting from fair trade technical assistance and community development projects.

STRETCH AND CHALLENGE

Fair trade supporters include many international development aid organisations, such as:

- Oxfam
- Amnesty International
- Catholic Relief Services
- Caritas International.

Research one or more of these organisations to find out more about fair trade and how they support it.

SUMMARY

This unit has explored the following points.

- How industry is classified into sectors.
- The reasons behind the decline in primary and secondary sectors in the UK and EU.
- How global industrial patterns are changing.
- The importance of fair trade.

Unit 2.2 Different types of work and methods of reward

IN THIS UNIT YOU WILL LEARN ABOUT:

- changing patterns of employment within the UK
- changes in technology, the organisation of work and the feminisation of the workforce
- the link between reward and motivation.

KEY CONCEPTS

Employment
Self-employment
Voluntary work
Full-time, part-time and flexible working

WHAT IS EMPLOYMENT?

Employment is a contract between an employer and an employee. An employer is a person or company who needs workers to provide labour to produce goods in return for payment. An employee is a person who works under instruction from his employer.

HOW DO I KNOW IF I AM AN EMPLOYEE?

If you are told by your employer how to do your work, and the work is provided by the employer, you are an employee. If you are paid at regular intervals, you are an employee. If your employer is responsible for finding someone else to do your work if you are not there, you are an employee. If your employer supplies tools, machinery and materials, you are an employee. If you are an employee, you are not self-employed. As we shall see, this is an important distinction as it has an impact on your employment rights.

ACTIVITY

Write a brief definition of the terms 'employer' and 'employee'.

WHY ARE THERE SO MANY DIFFERENT TYPES OF EMPLOYMENT?

There are different types of employees. These fall into four groups, which are identified by whether the employee is permanent or temporary, and full-time or part-time.

Table 2.2: Different types of employment.

Contract	Status and hours worked
Permanent full-time	Contract has a start date but no end date. Employee works the full business hours of the company.
Temporary full-time	Usually a fixed term contract with a start date and an end date. Employee works the full business hours of the company.
Permanent part-time	Contract has a start date but no end date. Employee works agreed hours which will be less than the full business hours of the company.
Temporary part-time	Usually a fixed term contract with a start date and an end date. Employee works agreed hours which will be less than the full business hours of the company.

As we shall see, one reason for this kind of flexibility in working practices comes from workers who want to fit work around family commitments. Employers were also interested in more flexible working, which would allow them to extend the business hours of the company, only pay for specific skills when they were needed, and increase staffing at busy times. Table 2.2 above gives a clear indication as to how this can be achieved.

THE PART-TIME WORKERS (PREVENTION OF LESS FAVOURABLE TREATMENT) REGULATIONS 2000

The Part-Time Workers (Prevention of Less Favourable Treatment) Regulations that came into force on 1 October 2000 made it unlawful for part-time workers to be treated less favourably than full-time workers. The purpose of the regulations, and the EU directive on which they are based, was to prevent the misuse of fixed-term contracts.

The regulations state that a fixed-term contract is one that ends for one of three reasons:

- the end of a specified period;
- the completion of a particular job;
- the occurrence of a specific event.

Employers are also not allowed to use rolling fixed-term contracts. If an employee is employed on fixed term contracts for four years, the contract becomes permanent.

These regulations define permanent employees as 'employees not employed under a fixed-term contract'.

Agency workers were not included in these regulations, but in June 2008 a new EU directive was agreed by the UK, which gives approximately 1.3 million agency workers the same pay and conditions as permanent staff after being employed for 12 weeks.

SELF-EMPLOYMENT

Self-employed workers are not employees because they do not have a contract of employment with an employer. They provide services for a fee and are in business for themselves. They do not have, or need, employment rights, because they are in charge and make their own decisions on everything related to the business such as pay, working hours and holidays. They do have legal protections, for example a safe working environment, if working for clients.

FLEXIBLE WORKING

In Unit 2.1 the survey of changes in patterns of employment within the UK concentrated on the shift from secondary-sector to tertiary-sector employment. Over the last 20 years of the last century, and particularly in the early years of this century, the direction of change has been less about the sector in which people work and more about how, when and where they work.

Changes in the UK's labour force over the last 30 years include the significant rise in the number of women in employment. In 1980, three million more men were in employment than women. By 2008, due to the rise of the service sector and changes in attitudes towards women who work, the number of men and women in employment is much closer. Flexible working has played an important part in this growth, as is demonstrated by the fact that almost 50 per cent of women's jobs are part-time.

Men and women still follow different career paths. About 25 per cent of female employees do administrative or secretarial work, while men are more likely to be managers, senior officials or working in skilled trades. Attitudes towards work, family and leisure have undergone significant change during this period. Probably the most significant reason for this was the large number of women who started work for the first time from the 1970s onwards. They wanted, in the main, part-time work, to allow them to manage the competing demands of work and family life.

This feminisation of the workforce – the largest growth in employment between 1990 and 2000 was mothers with young children – was achieved successfully. Employers accepted the need to introduce working arrangements that allowed women to work part-time. They quickly recognised the benefits a more flexible workforce could offer.

Flexible working quickly expanded to embrace not only how many hours were worked, but where and how the work was done. Flexible arrangements are still subject to legal controls on working time.

Some common types of flexible working opportunities offered are:

• part-time working;
• job sharing;
• working from home;
• working flexi-time.

Part-time working has already been considered. **Job sharing** is where two people split a job between them. Working from home once meant routine, low-paid jobs such as packing products. The growth of information and communications technology has opened much wider opportunities that will be dealt with below. **Flexi-time** requires all employees to be at work during the 'core time', usually between 10:00 am and 4:00 pm, and they can work the rest of their hours how best suits them within the normal business working day.

Work was once the centre of many employed people's lives. Now, spending time with family and taking part in leisure activities are juggled to achieve a 'work–life balance'. People expect to be able to have a life outside work to achieve this balance.

ADVANTAGES OF FLEXIBLE WORKING

It is argued that flexible working leads to better general health for employees, and this is supported by evidence from case studies. This means less sickness absence for employers – a better work–life balance reduces stress and absenteeism.

In a broader context, the ability to work at home means that employees do not necessarily have to resign from their company if they move location. This can save considerable amounts in recruitment and training costs, and as a result of a 'happier' workforce, productivity will often go up. Even the environment will benefit. Fewer people actually commuting everyday will cut both traffic congestion and atmospheric pollution.

DISADVANTAGES OF FLEXIBLE WORKING

There can be a financial cost to flexible working. To achieve a desired work–life balance might mean having a lower income. Some employees

Figure 2.3: *The feminisation of the workforce can even be seen in the House of Commons. This picture is of the female MPs working in Tony Blair's cabinet in 1997.*

might become isolated and out of touch with work colleagues if they do not meet them in a conventional work environment. Flexible working requires employees to be self-motivated and organised.

ACTIVITY

1. Describe the changes in the UK workforce that have led to the development of flexible working.

2. The phrase 'flexible working' is used to describe a variety of ways of working. List the major ways of working flexibly and identify the ways in which they differ from traditional ways of working.

3. Discuss the advantages and disadvantages of flexible working. On balance, do you think the move to flexible working is a good or a bad development for:
   - employees
   - employers?

THE RIGHT TO WORK FLEXIBLY

The UK government seems to support flexible working. In April 2003, the Employment Act allowed parents of young and disabled children the right to apply for flexible working.

From April 2007, this right has been extended to cover carers of adults. An application to work flexibly can cover hours, times and place of work. The employer does not have to grant this right but does have to take the application seriously and give clear business reasons for a refusal.

Only employees with a contract of employment can apply. Agency workers and members of the armed forces cannot.

THE FUTURE OF FLEXIBLE WORKING

Though many employers have taken to flexible working because of its beneficial effects, not all employers are convinced. In 2007, the Equal Opportunities Commission reported a two year investigation 'busting myths about new ways of working'. Its aim was to encourage employers to investigate more family-friendly methods of working. Its approach was to look at the arguments against flexible working and give examples of businesses that had succeeded.

Whether all employers have embraced this new way of working may not be the decisive factor. Recent research has identified in a study of more than 2500 people born after 1981, that those who took part in the research had very different attitudes towards work than their parents' generation. They were more concerned about achieving a work–life balance than high salaries. This group has been called **generation Y** and its members will make up the majority of the workforce within 10 years.

Some companies have already started to change the way they recruit to attract members of generation Y. They highlight the opportunity for flexible hours, the chance to work from home, up to a year of 'family leave' to look after children or elderly parents, and the promise of regular three-month periods of leave.

ACTIVITY

Flexible working is becoming an issue which employers must take seriously, not because of pressure from government but because the new workforce is not prepared to 'live to work' but is more interested in 'working to live'. Do you agree?

Why do people work?

Why do people work? The answer, of course, is obvious – they 'work to live'. They go to work because they can earn money, and that enables them to buy the things they need to live – that is their motivation.

Is it really that simple? There are people who choose to work not for money but because they want to contribute something. What is their motivation?

Why individual people choose to do what they choose to do is probably as varied as the people themselves – but there are theories that attempt to explain human motivation. Probably the most famous of these is Abraham Maslow's *Theory of Human Motivation*, written as far back as 1943.

MASLOW'S THEORY

Maslow suggests that human beings do things to satisfy their needs. The needs he identifies are usually shown as a pyramid with five levels. The bottom of the pyramid is concerned with basic needs, such as food and water. The needs become more personal as they rise up the pyramid.

Basic needs must be dealt with before any other needs can be satisfied. The first four layers of the pyramid are 'deficiency needs'. If they are not met, the individual feels anxious and tense. The deficiency needs are: physical, safety, social and esteem. The wish by an individual to achieve their potential is the final cause of motivated behaviour.

MASLOW AND EMPLOYMENT

Are Maslow's ideas relevant to what motivates people to work? Physical needs can be satisfied relatively easily by providing good working conditions and a salary sufficient to purchase the essentials of life.

Safety needs require a safe working environment and job security. Social needs are satisfied when the employee feels accepted and belongs in the work community.

Self-esteem comes from recognising workplace achievements and being given important work to do. This gives employees status and, in turn, makes them feel valued. Providing challenging and meaningful work that enables innovation and creativity helps employees to realise their full potential.

Although Maslow's hierarchy seems to make sense, there are concerns about its rigidity. Some societies appear to put social needs before any others. Many artists neglect their physical well being in pursuit of fulfilling their potential. It also appears to run contrary to individual experience to say that people are motivated by one need at a time. Most people appear to have multiple motivations for what they do.

ACTIVITY

1. Describe Maslow's theory of motivation.

2. Do you agree that this theory adequately explains why people work? Use information from other sections of this chapter to support your answer.

SUMMARY

This unit has explored the following points.

- What employment is and the different types of employment available.
- Changing patterns of employment in the UK.
- Why people work.

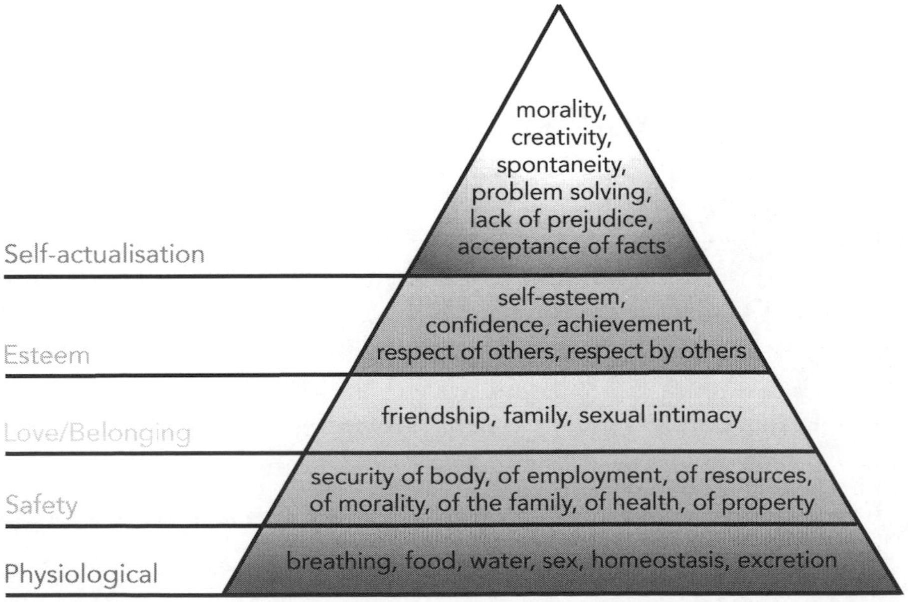

Figure 2.4: Maslow's pyramid of needs.

Self-actualisation — morality, creativity, spontaneity, problem solving, lack of prejudice, acceptance of facts

Esteem — self-esteem, confidence, achievement, respect of others, respect by others

Love/Belonging — friendship, family, sexual intimacy

Safety — security of body, of employment, of resources, of morality, of the family, of health, of property

Physiological — breathing, food, water, sex, homeostasis, excretion

Unit 2.3
Financial capability

MONEY MANAGEMENT

In 2003, the Financial Services Authority (FSA) commissioned research into young people and their finances. It chose to investigate the 15–19 age group because it identified that this is an age when young people begin to take more interest in financial services.

Unlike most previous research, it did not look at what was happening in formal educational settings such as schools and colleges. The FSA set out to discover what other more informal influences there are on how young people make financial decisions.

The FSA has a legal obligation to increase public understanding of the financial system. This understanding is seen as particularly important to the 15–19 year old age group both now and in the future. This group is at an age where life-changing events are happening:

- leaving school;
- starting a first job;
- going to university;
- leaving home.

For the first time, many of them are physically on their own. For the first time too they will be making decisions about their own finances.

It is also clear that this group is already involved with financial products (see Table 2.3).

Table 2.3: The financial products taken up by the 15–19 age group.

Age group 15–19	% take up
Current account	81
Savings account	39
Stocks and shares	2
Age group 18–19	
Credit card	18
Store card	12
Motor insurance	17

(Source: Young People and Financial Matters, FSA, 2004)

Simply because someone has a current account or a credit card, it does not mean they understand all the financial details that come with that product. Giving young people financial services without the knowledge of how to use them puts them at risk.

These concerns were supported by a report in 2008 by Reform and the Chartered Insurance Institute. This research concentrated on an older age group of people between 18 and 34. It showed that over 50 per cent of this group had debts, not counting mortgages, of up to £10,000. Another 20 per cent had debts of over £10,000. Their rate of saving is low, and 60 per cent have less than £1000.

The conclusion was that young people were happy to use financial products even when they did not fully understand them. Nearly 50 per cent did not know the rate of interest they were being charged on their credit card.

ATTITUDES TO FINANCIAL MATTERS

Parents of young people provide their children with most of the information about financial matters. This was because most young people felt that their parents know them best and have their best interests at heart. The vast majority of 15–19 year olds (88 per cent) identified the influence parents had on their decisions regarding money.

Parents try to set the right attitudes towards money matters, but their own behaviour with money is far more influential in informing young people's attitudes towards financial matters.

Saving is generally seen as a desirable, though not always achievable, objective. It is often undermined by the need to spend to make life enjoyable.

There is a relatively sophisticated attitude towards debt. Two kinds of debt are identified: debt that is unavoidable for modern living and cannot realistically be paid out of current income, including items like mortgages, car loans and student loans. The other from of debt is typified as 'overspending' on credit cards and overdrafts. The majority of young people are concerned that they might not be able to control their spending if their credit limit is not realistic.

Schools did not get a good press on financial education. Most young people had no recollection of effective coverage. To be effective, the teaching of financial matters needs to be interesting and relevant or, given the nature of the topic, it is unlikely to be remembered.

In contrast to the way young people usually shop around for the best deal, they do not shop around for the best deals for financial products.

ACTIVITY

1. What evidence is there to support the view that young people aged between 15 and 19 need more support and guidance with personal finance?

2. How far do you agree with this summary of young people's attitudes towards financial matters?

Income and expenditure

INCOME

Most people receive the majority of their income as either wages or salary. These are the two most common methods of paying people for working. There are a number of differences between wages and salary.

Wages are paid weekly, the amount being calculated on an hourly rate, which is only paid for time actually worked. Instead of a time rate, wages can also be based on a piece rate where workers receive a fixed amount for each product they complete.

Wages have traditionally been paid to manual and clerical workers.

Salaries are paid monthly and the employee receives the same payment for each pay period. Salaries have normally been paid to professional and supervisory workers.

The vast majority of workers in the UK have a legal right to a minimum wage. There is an annual review and increases are payable from October.

Table 2.4: The minimum wage rates from 1 October 2008.

Type of worker	Minimum rate per hour
Adults (22 and over)	£5.73
Development rate (18–21)	£4.77
Young people (older than school leaving age but under 18)	£3.53

TAXATION

Someone once said: 'There are three things in life that you cannot avoid – birth, death and taxes.'

The amount of income you receive is less than the amount of money you earn. This is because some of your earnings are taken by the government in the form of income tax.

Whether you are paid weekly or monthly you never see this money because it is taken out of your income using a method called Pay As You Earn (PAYE). Tax is used by the government to pay for the benefits we get, such as the health service and free education.

The tax system is progressive, which means the more you earn, the more you pay. There are currently two tax bands. In the lower band people pay 20 pence for each pound they earn. Once an individual has more than £35,000 of disposable income the higher tax band is applied. This is 40 pence for each pound earned.

BUDGETING

'Annual income twenty pounds, annual expenditure nineteen pounds ninety five pence, result happiness. Annual income twenty pounds, annual expenditure twenty pounds and five pence, result misery.'

These words were put into the mouth of Mr Wilkins Micawber, a fictional character in Charles Dickens's novel, *David Copperfield*, about life in Victorian England. The character was based on Dickens's own father, who was put into prison for failing to pay his debts.

The quote is a simple statement of how to avoid getting into debt. Put simply, Micawber is stating the blindingly obvious. If your spending is higher than your income it will lead to consequences that may not be very pleasant. The way to avoid this is to know what your income is and to plan your spending so that it does not exceed your income. This is the process of planning a **budget**.

Budgeting may not be exciting, but it is a clever thing to do, and not just when you are in debt. The really clever thing is to budget to avoid getting into debt in the first place. Budgeting is the process of actively managing your finances.

INCOME PER MONTH

Pocket money	£30
Saturday job	£50

OUTGOINGS PER MONTH

Bus fare to school	£10
Clothes	£25
CDs	£15
Food and drink	£20
Money left at month end	£10

Figure 2.5: Here is an example of what a monthly budget might look like.

You need to know what you are spending your money on. The way to do this properly is to keep a record of everything you spend for a month. This may seem excessive and time consuming, but it identifies those impulse buys that are not planned.

It will probably surprise you to discover how much you spend on things that do not cost much individually, but over a month add up to a significant sum. Once you have identified this you can do one of two things – stop buying them, or plan them into your expenditure. This is active management of your finances.

It is also important to check the items that cost the most. These may be unavoidable, but you may be able to shop around to get a better deal.

At the end of this process you should have a clear understanding of what you are spending your money on. This will enable you to identify the best way to cut your spending if that is needed.

Making a budget is fairly straightforward and, once done, only needs to be revised if there is a change in either your income or your expenditure.

COST BENEFIT ANALYSIS

This is the weighing-scale approach to making decisions. Once you have planned your budget, you may well be faced with the need to cut your expenditure. There may be a number of alternative ways of doing this, but which one should you choose? Equally, very few people are fortunate enough to have the money to do everything they might want, so how do they decide between competing options?

You could toss a coin or pick a solution at random, but this kind of decision making has the drawback that, at some point in the future, you may come to the conclusion that it was the wrong decision. Cost benefit analysis allows you balance the good and bad points of a decision and make the decision on a rational basis.

Cost benefit analysis also helps you understand the hidden costs of making choices. If you decide to spend your spare cash on a visit to the cinema, you may later regret this because you can no longer buy the clothes you also want. Applying cost benefit analysis would identify this future dilemma and allow you to spend your money on what you really want rather than what you fancy at a particular moment.

ACTIVITY

1. What do the terms 'income' and 'expenditure' mean?

2. Explain the reasons why budgeting is sensible for everyone.

3. What are the advantages and disadvantages of using a cost benefit model to organise a budget?

Debits, credits and bank accounts

There are two main types of bank account. Most banks offer more than two accounts, but they are simply variations on one of these.

THE BASIC BANK ACCOUNT

This is ideal for customers who require the facility for only a few basic transactions per month. It will allow them to set up standing orders to pay regular bills. A **standing order** is an instruction to pay someone a standard amount of money on a regular basis. Opening a basic bank account can be a first step towards opening a current account at a later stage.

A basic bank account allows customers to have their wages or other income paid directly into the account. Money can be obtained from cash machines with a cash card. Some banks let customers have a debit card.

CURRENT ACCOUNT

This is the most common type of account. It is similar to the basic bank account in that it allows the customer to manage their income and expenditure, but it provides more features. Often, accounts that offer these extra features require you to pay a minimum amount into the account each month. Some of these features could include:

- Internet banking;
- an **overdraft**;
- a debit card;
- cashback in some shops when using the debit card;
- monthly statements.

DEBITS AND CREDITS

Most accounts are currently free as long as the account remains in **credit**. This means that there is always money in the account. Money paid into an account is also called a credit. Any withdrawal from an account is called a **debit**.

If the total number of the debits over a given period is greater than the total number of credits, the account is said to be overdrawn. Accounts that are overdrawn are subject to charges. These charges will be at an overdraft rate of interest which will vary depending on whether the customer has agreed with the bank that the account can be overdrawn. This is called an authorised overdraft. If an account is overdrawn without an agreement, this is called an **unauthorised overdraft** and the charges will be higher.

ACTIVITY

1. What do the terms 'credit', 'debit' and 'overdrawn' mean?

2. Make a list of the advantages of having a bank account. Can you identify any disadvantages of having a bank account?

A range of financial products

SAVINGS ACCOUNTS

These accounts are for saving money in order to eventually buy a specific item, or simply to have money 'just in case' it is needed. Savings accounts pay interest on the money deposited in them. The rate of interest varies with the type of savings account.

Most banks have a range of savings accounts to meet the needs of individual customers. Examples of these different accounts are:

- Instant access. You can have your money when you want – but a lower rate of interest is paid.
- Tax-free **individual savings accounts** (ISAs). You can put in up to a fixed amount each year, and the interest is paid tax-free.
- Online savings accounts. These usually pay a higher rate of interest, as the bank saves money on administration costs.
- Fixed-rate term savings. You invest a lump sum for a fixed period of time with a guaranteed interest rate.

CREDIT CARDS

A credit card is a form of available borrowing. Credit cards are available from banks and building societies but only to customers over 18.

Providers tend to concentrate on the advantages of having a credit card, such as:

- a fast and convenient way to pay;
- no annual fee to pay;
- up to 56 days interest-free period;
- flexibility – online, over the telephone or at your local branch;
- free additional credit card – for partners or family members over 18.

If an application for a credit card is accepted, the institution that issues the card will set a credit limit, which is the maximum amount that can be borrowed.

A card holder can use the card to pay for goods or services. A statement is produced each month listing all transactions. Each month, the card holder must make a payment. This can be the minimum payment shown on the statement, the full amount shown or any amount between these two figures.

If the card holder pays off the full amount each month, no interest is charged and the card holder has benefited from an interest-free loan from the date of the transaction to the date when the payment is made.

If the minimum payment is made, the card holder will pay interest on the remaining balance. The rate of interest on credit cards is generally higher than on other ways of borrowing money. If the card holder pays off an amount between the total and the minimum amount, interest will be charged on the remaining balance.

Figure 2.6: Here is an example of a credit card statement showing the amount of interest payable for that month.

Date	Transaction	Description	Amount
		Balance from Previous statement	-£650.00
14/03/2009	001	CURRY'S	-£49.99
21/03/2009	002	SAINSBURY'S	-£23.26
23/03/2009	003	HILTON HOTEL	-£125.00
30/03/2009		Payment received	£400.00
01/04/2009	004	COUNCIL TAX (April)	-£136.00
01/04/2009	005	EDF ENERGY	-£85.74
30/04/2009		Interest	-£42.45

Total	-£712.44

A credit card may give you the freedom to buy things now and pay for them later – but there is a cost.

OTHER TYPES OF BORROWING

There are other ways to borrow money for the short- (1 year) to medium- (5 years) term. Personal loans, store cards and in-store finance are the most common.

To get this type of borrowing, an application form must be completed. The answers enable the lender to give a **credit score**.

Credit scoring awards points for the information provided. Lenders will also check information on an applicant on a credit report from a credit reference agency. The lender is attempting to calculate the risk it has in letting the applicant borrow money.

The lender has a minimum score that applicants need to reach to be offered credit. Failure to reach this might lead to either a refusal of credit, the offer of a smaller amount of money than has been applied for, or raising the interest rate to compensate for the higher risk.

Factors that count towards a credit score can include:

- length of time in a job;
- length of time at an address;
- the applicant's age;
- marital status;
- a good credit history.

Lenders use the electoral register – the list of people registered to vote, which is updated every year – to check applicants' names and addresses. If the applicant's name is not on the roll, the lender could refuse an application.

PERSONAL LOANS

Personal loans are available from banks and other financial institutions. An applicant borrows a fixed amount of money that is to be repaid in fixed installments at a fixed rate of interest over an agreed number of years.

The amount of the loan can vary between £1000 and £25,000. The interest rate will vary depending on the amount borrowed and the length of time over which it is to be repaid.

Generally, the higher the amount and the longer the term of the loan, the lower the interest rate will be, while lower amounts with shorter terms will give a higher interest rate.

Personal loans may incur a penalty for paying them off earlier than agreed, because the amount of profit the bank makes is calculated over the whole period of the loan and early redemption will affect this amount. Charges can also be incurred for late payment of installments. Most banks prefer loans to be paid by **direct debit** to minimise this risk.

Personal loans can be secured or unsecured. A **secured loan** is only available to home owners, as the home of the applicant is used as security for the loan. The advantage for the applicant is that the interest rate for secured loans is lower than the rate for unsecured loans. The potential disadvantage is that failure to keep up repayments could allow the lender to sell the applicant's home to repay the loan.

With an **unsecured loan**, the lender cannot repossess your home. Even so, you are legally obliged to pay back the loan as you agreed.

STORE CARDS AND HIRE PURCHASE

These financial products are offered by many big stores. Store cards have many similarities to credit cards. Two disadvantages are that they often charge higher rates of interest than other loans, including credit cards. Also, they are limited to a particular store and not accepted anywhere else.

Borrowing money through loans or credit cards means that the borrower immediately owns whatever is purchased. With a **hire purchase** agreement, a finance company owns the goods until they final repayment is made. The clue is the word 'hire'. If something is hired, paying the hire charge does not make it the hirer's property.

This has important consequences for a borrower. Although the method of repaying the money borrowed is almost identical to paying off a loan, the rights the purchaser has over the goods are limited.

As the goods are not the borrower's property:

- they cannot change them or sell them without the lender's agreement;
- the finance company can take the goods back if repayments are not made;

- they are liable for any damage during the contract period.

MORTGAGES

Mortgages are like any other kind of loan – money is borrowed and paid back with interest over a period of time. One important feature of a mortgage is that it is secured against property being purchased. This allows the lender to sell the property to recover their loan if payments are not kept up.

Loans for property purchases are based on how much the borrower can afford to repay and the value of the property being bought. The calculation of affordability is made by multiplying the annual salary of the applicant to produce a maximum figure that can be borrowed.

This multiplier varies from time to time and institution to institution. Over recent years, lenders have been prepared to have a higher multiplier and therefore lend more. This has led to some borrowers taking on debts that they struggle to repay.

Other differences between mortgages and other types of loan is the length of time the mortgage runs for. House purchase is probably the largest financial commitment most people will ever make. It cannot be repaid in the time scale applied to ordinary loans and mortgages tend to be taken out for 20 or 25 years.

The repayment process is similar to other loans, though unlike personal loans, the rate can vary and is usually linked to the Bank of England base rate.

There are two ways of paying a mortgage back – by way of a **repayment mortgage** or an **interest-only mortgage**. With a repayment mortgage, the monthly payment has two parts – interest and capital. Part of the payment clears the interest charge for the month and what is left is taken away from the amount originally borrowed. Over the period of the mortgage, the original loan will gradually be paid back.

With an interest-only mortgage, all the money that is paid to the lender is interest. The borrower then has to provide another way of paying off the original loan. This can be done through investments, which the borrower will pay for separately.

Interest-only mortgages were popular between 1970 and 1990. A problem was that some of the investments people made to offset their mortgage did not make enough money to pay off the original amount borrowed, leaving them with a problem at the end of the mortgage period. Repayment mortgages are now the preferred method of repayment.

There are various types of interest rates connected with mortgages. Two of the most common are:

- Standard variable rate, where payments move up and down with the lenders' mortgage rate, linked to Bank of England base rate.
- Discounted rate, where payments go up or down, but the borrower receives a discount on the variable rate for a set period of time, which reverts to the standard rate at its end.

STRETCH AND CHALLENGE

There are a large number of ways of borrowing money. Using the section 'A range of financial products' as a starting point, research the types of ways people are able to borrow money. You may want to look at the literature that banks, building societies and retail stores use to promote their financial products, either online or by visiting local branches and stores.

Write a report to identify:

- the most cost-effective ways of borrowing for specific purposes
- the least cost-effective ways of borrowing for any purpose.

Investments

Investors are taking what they hope is a calculated risk to increase the chance of getting higher returns on their money, especially over the longer term, which is usually five years or more.

When an individual invests, it is expected that the value of the investment will increase over time. This is not guaranteed and the value could fall, meaning that the investor does not get back the original amount of money invested.

It is unwise to make investments with money that the investor could not afford to lose. Investing is not like saving in a bank account. It is designed for the longer term and involves more risk.

There are four types of investments: **shares**, **bonds**, property and cash. People can invest directly in these. Increasingly popular are pooled risks, where

groups of investors join together to invest. Open-ended investment funds and life assurance bonds are examples of this.

Tax-free investment is also available. The independent savings account (ISA) is probably the best known of these.

ISAs

This is a 'tax wrapper' which can hold a range of different investments. The returns on these investments are tax-free. Other investments are subject to income tax or capital gains tax.

Because they are tax-free, there are strict limits on how individuals can use ISAs. There is a maximum investment of £7200 in each tax year. ISAs were simplified in 2008, and there are now two types of ISA: a cash ISA and a stocks and shares ISA, and any investor can open one of each in each tax year.

Investors can put £3600 into a cash ISA and the remaining £3600 into a stocks and shares ISA. Alternatively, they can invest the whole £7200 in a stocks and shares ISA.

Cash ISAs are similar to other savings accounts as there are different types – easy access, fixed-rate and notice accounts. Each type of account will have a different interest rate.

The common benefit of all ISAs is that taxpayers do not have to pay 20 per cent of the interest they gain in income tax, unlike other investments.

ACTIVITY

What are the advantages and disadvantages of investing money rather than simply saving it?

The financial implications of post-16 options

EDUCATIONAL MAINTENANCE ALLOWANCES.

In an effort to encourage young people not to leave compulsory education at the age of 16, the government has established a payment for 16 to 18 year olds called the educational maintenance allowance (EMA).

An EMA can pay up to £30 a week paid directly to the student. The amount paid depends on family income, but does not affect other benefits a family might be entitled to.

Table 2.5: The EMA rates for the financial year 2008–9.

Household income	Weekly payment
Less than £21, 835	£30
£21, 836 to £26, 769	£20
£26, 770 to £32, 316	£10
Over £32, 317	£0

These income levels are linked to the cost of living and change on an annual basis.

The payments are only made to those who attend regularly and work hard on their course. Earnings from part-time work make no difference to eligibility for the EMA. Bonuses can be paid to students who meet their targets.

Recent research suggests that individuals who obtain a qualification or new skill can improve their earning power by around £3000 a year.

HIGHER EDUCATION

The UK needs more highly skilled and educated workers. A higher education qualification can be the key to unlocking higher-paying careers. Graduates generally earn significantly more than people with a lower level qualification.

The latest figures from the Labour Force Survey, produced by the Office of National Statistics, show that the occupations with the highest weekly earnings for full-time employees are professional occupations. Managers and senior officials had the highest annual salaries. These are occupations that employ a significant proportion of graduates.

While still in their twenties, graduates earn on average 25–30 per cent more than those who did not go to university.

Graduates in their forties earn, on average, in excess of 60 per cent more per year than those without degrees of a similar age.

This financial benefit is one of the ways in which the government has tried to encourage able students from poorer backgrounds to go to university. Many young people balance this future potential prosperity against the immediate prospect of debt incurred by tuition fees and student loans.

ACTIVITY

How convinced are you that the possible financial rewards of higher education outweigh the student debt and lost earnings that going to university could create?

SUMMARY

This unit has explored the following points.

- How the 15–19 age group are involved with financial matters and money management.
- What income, expenditure and budgeting are.
- What financial services banks and others offer and what these services mean.
- What investment is and what options are available.
- What the financial implications of staying in education past the age of 16 are.

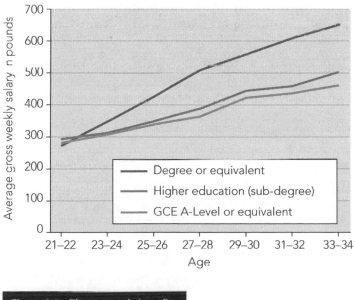

Figure 2.7: The economic benefits of being a graduate.

(*Source:* Graduate Market Trends Spring 2003, *Labour Force Survey*)

Unit 2.4 Rights and responsibilities at work

IN THIS UNIT YOU WILL LEARN ABOUT:

- the rights and responsibilities of employers and employees
- the importance of the contract of employment
- the functions of trade unions
- the ways trade unions seek to influence employers and the government.

KEY CONCEPTS

Employer
Employee
Contract of employment
Trade union
Negotiation
Arbitration

THE IMPORTANCE OF THE CONTRACT OF EMPLOYMENT

If you work for someone and are paid on a regular basis, you have a contract of employment. It may not be written but it exists. Your work and the payment you receive create the contract.

All employees, whether full-time or part-time, should receive a written statement from their employer within two months of their starting work.

This must give details about:

- the job;
- pay;
- hours;
- holidays;
- sick pay entitlement;
- pensions;
- notice and dismissal;
- disciplinary procedures.

Under this document, both sides have rights and obligations called contractual terms. As well as rights from the contractual terms, employees also have rights given by law.

Employers and employees can agree to any terms in a contract, but they cannot agree on less favourable rights than the law already gives. Any contract that does this is wrong and the legal rights apply. If the contract is more generous than the legal rights then the contract applies.

IMPLIED CONTRACTUAL TERMS

As well as the written contractual terms listed above, the employer and employee have responsibilities that are implied contractual terms. These are not negotiated and agreed but are expected to be implied in any contract.

Some examples of these terms could be:

- A duty of trust. The employee can be expected to keep their employer's business confidential and the employee can expect the employer to protect the employee's details.

Figure 2.8: *Displaying fire regulations where everyone can see them is an obligation of the employer to the employee.*

- **A duty of care**. The employer should provide a safe working environment for the employee and the employee should work safely in turn.
- To obey any reasonable instructions given by the employer. The employer should not give unreasonable instructions that might cause danger or break the law.

ACTIVITY

1. Why is a contract of employment important to:
   - the employer
   - the employee?
2. What is an implied contractual term?

STRETCH AND CHALLENGE

Using the Citizens Advice Bureau website (see 'Websites' on page ii), research the basic employment rights granted by law. Write a brief presentation of the rights you see as most important with reasons why you selected them.

The functions of trade unions

WHAT ARE TRADE UNIONS?

Trade unions are organisations that represent the people who work in a particular type of employment. They are formed, financed and run by their members.

In 1979, there were 446 trade unions representing 11.7 million workers in the UK. In 2008, the Trades Union Congress (TUC) claimed on its website homepage to have 58 member unions representing nearly 7 million workers. This sharp decrease in the number of unions is largely due to amalgamations. This is where small unions in related industries come together to form large unions in the hope they will have more influence with the government and employers.

There are three main types of unions:

- manual workers unions;
- white collar unions;
- managerial/professional unions.

These unions, as their names suggest, are divided by the work that their members do.

ACTIVITY

Given the information above, how important do you feel trade unions currently are?

WHAT DO TRADE UNIONS DO?

Trade unions do not only act on behalf of all their members, but also represent individual members when they have a problem at work. The two major areas where this might be necessary are if the employee has a **grievance**, or if the employer has an issue with the employee that might lead to **disciplinary action**.

Employers need to have disciplinary and grievance rules and procedures. These must be in writing and must meet the minimum standards of the statutory disciplinary and grievance procedures.

Grievances

Employees with concerns about their work, employment terms, working conditions or relationships with colleagues, can bring them to their employer's notice. The employer will need to look into and attempt to resolve the grievance.

There are three stages in this process. Firstly, the grievance must be put in writing. The grievance procedure should name the person to whom it should be sent. Secondly, a meeting is held to inform the employee of the outcome. This should be done as soon as possible. Employees must be told they have the right to appeal. Finally, an appeal meeting is held, if requested. If possible, someone more senior, and not previously involved, should deal with the appeal. After the appeal, the employee is informed of the decision.

The employee has the right to be accompanied at all meetings by a colleague or trade union representative.

If the employee is still dissatisfied, the grievance can be taken to an employment tribunal. Tribunals are bodies that check that employees and employers are following employment law. Cases are usually heard by a panel of three people: one legally qualified chairperson, and two 'lay members'. They are each independent of the employee's workplace. They listen to the employer's and the employee's arguments and then make a judgement about the case. Most cases are about pay, unfair dismissal, redundancy or discrimination at work.

Disciplinary matters

Disciplinary rules should be fair, clear and appropriate to the workplace. They should help employees understand the types of behaviour that are acceptable. It is impossible to give a complete list of all disciplinary situations, but examples should be included. **Gross misconduct** should be clearly identified as this can lead to dismissal without notice.

Informal disciplinary action

If an employer feels that an employee is not meeting appropriate standards under the workplace's disciplinary rules, the first step should be to try to help the employee improve.

At this stage, any action is informal. The employee should be informed of the issue and be offered support to resolve the problem. If this approach is unsuccessful, formal disciplinary action may be necessary.

Formal disciplinary action for misconduct

Before a formal disciplinary procedure begins, an employee's alleged misconduct must be investigated. If the employer is satisfied that there is 'a case to answer' then a disciplinary procedure will take place.

The meeting should take place as soon as possible. The employee must be told that it is a disciplinary hearing. The employer will state the case and the employee has the opportunity to question the facts. The employee will also have an opportunity to put across their point of view.

The employer will summarise the case and a decision will be made. The employee must be clear about the decision and whether they have received a disciplinary warning. They must be told about their right to appeal.

In most procedures, there are up to three warnings:

- Verbal: for less serious offences.
- Written: for a more serious offence or a repeat of a less serious offence.
- Final written: for a very serious offence.

Employees must be sent a copy of any written warning and be told how long it will stay on their file. If another disciplinary offence is committed while a previous warning is in force, the previous warning will be taken into account in deciding the new outcome.

Normally, dismissal is a last resort. Where an employee commits 'gross misconduct' they can be instantly dismissed. Gross misconduct could include violence, willful damage to property or being drunk at work.

The employee has the right to be accompanied at any meeting by a colleague or trade union representative.

Arbitration

Arbitration is when someone not involved in a dispute is asked to make a decision about the issue. There is no requirement on parties involved in a dispute to take part in arbitration, it is therefore a voluntary process and can only be used if both sides agree. Both sides should also agree to accept that any decision is binding before the process starts.

Arbitration is an informal process that avoids the formal procedures of a court or employment **tribunal**. It can often offer an alternative route to settling collective and individual disputes within the workplace.

The Advisory Conciliation and Arbitration Service (ACAS) is a government-funded independent body that can provide this kind of service. If employers and unions agree, ACAS can appoint an independent arbitrator to hear the dispute and make an impartial decision.

Information and advice

Unions are a major source of information that can be useful to their members at work. They can advise on a range of issues such as holiday entitlement, maternity leave and training.

ACTIVITY

1. In what circumstances might a trade union member require representation by their trade union?

2. Design flow charts to show the way in which

   - a grievance procedure
   - a disciplinary procedure

   would be carried out.

3. What are the advantages and disadvantages to employers and trade unions of using arbitration to settle disputes?

To join or not to join? That is the question

TRADE UNION MEMBERSHIP

In 2007, the rate of union membership in the UK fell by 0.3 per cent, to 28 per cent of employees. For the sixth year in a row, more women than men were trade union members. There was also a difference between workers in the private and public sectors. In the private sector, a fall of 0.5 per cent cut union membership to 16.1 per cent. In the public sector there was a rise of 0.3 per cent, which boosted union membership to 59 per cent.

There has been a steady decline in trade union membership over the last 30 years.

Table 2.6: Trade union membership 1980–2008.

Year	Trade union membership (millions)
1980	12.6
1985	10.8
1990	9.8
1995	8
2000	7.8
2005	7.5
2008	7.6

(Source: Annual Reports of The Trade Union Certification Officer*)*

A number of reasons are suggested for this decline. One is that the structural change away from secondary-sector manufacturing jobs, where trade union membership was historically strong, into new tertiary-sector industries, where there is no tradition of trade union membership.

Changes in the patterns of employment over the period since 1980 have seen the growth of part-time workers. Part-time workers are less likely to join unions. There has also been a growth in the number of small companies where unions find it more difficult to establish themselves.

Unemployment over the period from 1980 has been relatively high. Unemployed people do not tend to join unions. Conservative governments in the 1980s and 1990s passed laws making it more difficult for unions to operate.

Despite this, trade union membership is still significant. Recent figures suggest that the decline has slowed and may have come to an end. The TUC has promoted a number of initiatives to unionise the new industries. The success of this is perhaps indicated by the rise of women's numbers in trade unions in the first decade of the 21st century.

More people are joining trade unions because of the protection and benefits they provide.

ACTIVITY

1. Describe what has happened to trade union membership over the last 30 years. Use data to support your description.
2. Explain the reasons suggested for the changes in trade union membership.
3. What has the TUC done to address this situation? Are there any signs that it is being successful?

THE REASONS FOR JOINING, OR NOT JOINING, A TRADE UNION

Regardless of whether work colleagues are members or not, individual employees have the right to join, as well as not to join, a trade union. The choice is theirs and it is unlawful for an employer or employment agency to treat them any differently because of what they decide. Since 1990, it has been illegal to operate a 'closed shop'. A closed shop was where employees had to become members of a trade union or they would not be employed.

Trade unions can refuse membership to individuals, but only for very specific reasons. For instance, if the trade union is restricted to a particular group of workers or if a potential member does not have the necessary qualifications, membership can be refused.

WHY JOIN A UNION?

As it is not necessary to join a trade union to be employed, and as membership of a trade union is not free, why bother joining?

More than seven million workers in the UK are members of trade unions. This is a significant proportion of the workforce who presumably see some benefit to membership.

The benefits of collective bargaining and individual representation have already been touched on. For a cost of about half of one per cent of a worker's earnings, trade unions negotiate collective agreements that more than compensate their members financially.

Unions assist their members in claims for compensation for work-related illness and injury. They also often offer free legal assistance in areas that are not related to work, for example in providing free wills to members.

Collective bargaining achieves higher rates of pay for union members. The hourly earnings for union members averaged £12.74 in 2007, 15.6 per cent more than the earnings of non-members, who averaged £11.02 per hour. Traditionally disadvantaged groups also benefit from higher pay, most notably ethnic minority and women workers. Ethnic minority workers get the greatest benefit, earning 33 per cent more than their non-union colleagues.

Other benefits include pensions and job security. Employees are more likely to have a pension scheme as a result of their trade union's collective bargaining. Union members are also much less likely to be sacked – the risk is almost halved – and if they are dismissed, their compensation is likely to be higher.

Union members work in a safer environment. The presence of trade union safety representatives has been proved to have cut major injuries by half and raised general health and safety by 33 per cent. Sick pay is also likely to be higher with union membership.

Job-related training is more common in unionised workplaces. Increased skills enable union members to progress to more skilled and higher-paid employment. They also do better in terms of holidays. The average holiday entitlement for trade union members is 29 days, 6 days more than the average for non-union workers.

Women are better treated in unionised workplaces. This is because they are more likely to have equal opportunities and parental leave policies. These help women to make progress in their work and to work flexibly to balance work and family commitments.

Because most modern unions have large memberships, they can negotiate financial benefits at discounted prices for their members. These benefits range from cheaper insurance to discounted holidays. Some still offer financial help to members when they are sick or unemployed.

THE RIGHT NOT TO JOIN A TRADE UNION

Every worker has the right to refuse to join a trade union. They also have the right to resign from a trade union of which they have been a member. Employers are not allowed to treat employees who exercise these rights differently from other workers. Employers cannot insist that an employee joins a trade union.

Some people may object to paying the membership fees required to belong to a trade union. Others may be concerned about being 'expected' to take industrial action, such as striking, especially if they do not support the action. Employers cannot immediately sack striking workers, but they do not have to pay them either.

ACTIVITY

1. What are the advantages and disadvantages of being a trade union member?

2. 'Workers gain more from joining a trade union than refusing to join.' Do you agree? Give reasons for your answer.

The ways in which trade unions seek to influence employers and the government

NEGOTIATIONS WITH EMPLOYERS

Trade union representatives discuss issues that affect their members with their members' management. Typical topics for negotiation would be all aspects of pay, working hours and working conditions and, crucially, health and safety.

Where a business employs 21 workers or more, trade unions have the legal right to ask the company to agree their right to negotiate on behalf of their members. In many companies, the management is happy to make such agreements with the trade union, but this is not automatic. Sometimes, arbitration procedures are needed before negotiating rights are established. Once they are agreed, trade unions are recognised for the process of collective bargaining.

Collective bargaining involves the trade union in presenting the views of their members to management. Often, the employer may not share the view of the employees. The role of the trade union is to try to find a solution, through negotiation, that both sides can accept.

In 2007, 47 per cent of employees were in workplaces where there was a trade union presence, and 33 per cent had collective agreements regarding their pay and conditions. The difference between the public and private sectors was striking. Only 20 per cent of workers in the private sector were covered by collective agreements. This compares to 72 per cent of public sector workers covered by collective agreements.

Workers in organisations where unions are recognised are generally better paid and less likely to be made redundant than people who work in organisations that do not have this recognition.

INFLUENCING GOVERNMENT

Trade unions use their political power to try to persuade the government to pass laws that provide benefits and protection for their members.

They made good progress on these issues in times of economic prosperity in areas such pensions, unemployment payments, health benefits and holidays. Unions have also succeeded in establishing employment procedures that safeguard workers against unfair actions on the part of employers.

In more difficult economic times, trade unions' political agenda moves into defensive mode. The government is encouraged to take action to minimise the impact of an economic downtown. Programmes to create jobs and maintain income are the priority.

In recent times, trade union influence on government has declined. The laws passed by the Conservative governments between 1979 and 1997 seriously weakened trade unions' ability to take effective industrial action. Government was also not open to consultation with the trade unions.

This state of affairs continued, perhaps surprisingly, when the Labour Party returned to government in 1997. There have been some indications recently that the Labour government is once more interested in trade union views on government proposals for legislation.

ACTIVITY

1. Describe the role trade unions play in improving working people's lives by influencing:
   - employers
   - the government.
2. 'Trade unions are nothing more than pressure groups working for their own members' benefit. They have too much power to influence employers and the government.' How far do you agree? Give reasons for your answer.

SUMMARY

This unit has explored the following points.

- What a contract of employment is and the rights and responsibilities that come with it for the employee and employer.
- What trade unions are and what they do.
- How trade unions try to influence employers and the government.

Figure 2.9: Trade union officials at Number 10.

Chapter 3
Environmental Issues

CONTENTS

Unit 3.1 Climate change and its consequences

IN THIS UNIT YOU WILL LEARN ABOUT:

- the causes and impacts of climate change
- the historical development of climate change as an issue
- the difficulty of identifying future trends and the problems for planners
- controversies over climate change.

KEY CONCEPTS

Environmental issues
Sustainability
Climate change
Pressure group
Human environmental impact
Environmental legislation

The word **climate** describes a weather pattern established over a relatively long period of time – usually at least 30 years. It includes temperature, wind and rainfall patterns. It shows the conditions that can normally be expected month by month, throughout the year.

The climate of the earth is not fixed, and changes in climate are natural. They have happened since the earth was formed 4600 million years ago.

The geographical area that we now call the UK has gone through many different climates since it first appeared a little more than half a billion years ago.

Over this period it has been:

- a tropical rainforest – coal and oil was formed (300 to 350 million years ago);
- a desert – as part of a supercontinent (260 million years ago);
- a tropical rainforest – again;
- submerged (100 million years ago).

In the last 20,000 years, the UK has emerged from an ice age. In the last millennium, there have been significant variations in the climate. For example, eight hundred years ago, vineyards were common in the south of England. Four hundred years ago, there

Figure 3.1: This is a contemporary drawing of the fair held on the frozen River Thames.

was a mini ice age where the River Thames froze and people held fairs on it in the winter.

ACTIVITY

1. Explain the difference between weather and climate.

2. Make a brief timeline of the major changes in climate that have happened to what we now call the British Isles since it was created half a billion years ago.

WHAT IS CLIMATE CHANGE?

The term **climate change** has come to mean the rises in temperature that have been recorded in the last 100 years. Over this period, the average temperature of the earth has increased by 0.74°C. At the same time there has been a growing view that these changes are not due to natural events but are a direct result of human activity.

In 2007, the Intergovernmental Panel on Climate Change (IPCC), said:

'Most of the observed increase in global average temperatures since the mid-twentieth century is very likely due to the observed increase in man-made greenhouse gas concentrations.'

People have not been blamed for any of the previous climate shifts. For most of these events, people were not even around! So how and why did this very influential body come to the conclusion that the current climate change is the fault of man?

ACTIVITY

Produce a short definition of what climate change has come to mean.

Climate change over time

The interest in climate change goes back further than perhaps you suspect. In 1753, Joseph Black, a Scottish chemist working at the University of Edinburgh, discovered carbon dioxide. Seventy years later in 1827, Jean Baptiste Fourier, a French mathematician, suggested the existence of an atmospheric effect which kept the earth warmer than it would otherwise be. He described this effect as similar to the workings of a greenhouse and it was dubbed 'the **greenhouse effect**'.

In 1896, a Swedish chemist, Arrhenius, put forward a theory to explain ice ages. In his theory he suggested that changes in the level of carbon dioxide in the atmosphere could change its surface temperature. He did not suspect that the process might have already started.

Between 1890 and 1940, average surface air temperatures increased by about 0.25°C. Between 1940 and 1970, average surface air temperatures decreased by about 0.2°C. Scientists began to lose interest in the greenhouse effect. Some climatologists even predicted a new ice age.

In 1957, an American scientist began regularly measuring carbon dioxide levels in the atmosphere for the first time. The immediate results showed a year-on-year rise. An early computer simulation in 1967 calculated that average global temperatures could increase by more than four degrees Fahrenheit depending on carbon dioxide levels.

ACTIVITY

How important are the activities of the scientists described above in the development of our understanding of climate change?

Figure 3.2: As global temperatures have risen, the ice at the poles has melted. This has had a devastating effect on wildlife as this picture shows.

CLIMATE CHANGE IS TAKEN INCREASINGLY SERIOUSLY

The first world climate conference was held in February 1979. This conference led to the beginnings of the World Climate Programme with the dual aims of improving understanding of the climate system and applying that understanding.

The first major international conference on the greenhouse effect was in Austria in 1985. It predicted that **greenhouse gases** would, in the first half of the next century, cause the earth's temperature to rise by more than it had ever done before.

In 1987, an ice core from Antarctica showed an extremely close link between carbon dioxide levels and temperature, which could be traced back for more than 100,000 years. This was also the warmest year on record (although it has been exceeded since).

The United Nations set up the IPCC in 1988 which, in its first report in 1990, said the earth had warmed by 0.5°C in the 20th century and that only vigorous measures to limit greenhouse gas emissions could prevent serious global warming.

In 1992, the Framework Convention on Climate Change was signed at the Earth Summit in Rio by 154 nations, including the USA. This agreement set the target of reducing emissions to 1990 levels by the year 2000. It came into effect on 21 March 1994.

At the first meeting of the Framework Convention on Climate Change in Berlin in March 1995, industrialised nations agreed to negotiate real cuts in their emissions by the end of 1997. In November, the IPCC agreed that current warming was likely to be due to human influence.

The report predicted that if nothing was done, global warming by the year 2100 would be between 1°C and 3.5°C.

At the second meeting of the Climate Change Convention in 1996, the USA agreed for the first time to legally-binding emissions targets. Scientists also warned that most industrialised countries would not meet the targets set in the Rio agreement.

The Kyoto Protocol of 1997 agreed legally-binding emissions cuts for industrialised nations, averaging 5.5 per cent, to be met by 2010.

Scientists said in 1999 that the 1990s had been the hottest decade in the last millennium.

In 2001, newly-elected US President George W. Bush refused to sign the Kyoto Protocol. He questioned the science behind it and believed that signing it would damage the US economy. At the same time, international talks finally concluded the details of the Kyoto Protocol.

In 2002, parliaments in the European Union, Japan, and other countries, agreed to the Kyoto Protocol. It needed to be agreed by countries responsible for 55 per cent of emissions before it could come into force.

The summer of 2003 was the hottest summer in Europe for 500 years. The speed with which greenhouse gases grew continued to rise.

In May 2004, Russia agreed to sign the Kyoto Protocol. This meant that the 141 countries responsible for 55 per cent of greenhouse gas emissions pledged to cut the emissions by 5.2 per cent by 2012. The Kyoto Protocol came into force in 2005. Signatories also agreed to discuss emissions targets for the period beyond 2012.

ACTIVITY

1. Make a list of the organisations that were set up to look into climate change.

2. Make a brief comment on what they achieved.

3. Write a detailed account of how climate change gradually became an important issue.

Climate change – natural or man-made?

It is true that the world has had changes in climate without any interference from humans. Can the rise of 0.74°C seen over the last century be explained by natural factors? Can the earth's orbit in relation to the sun, volcanic eruptions and variations in the sun's energy account for the rises in temperature over the last 100 years?

This is a crucial question, because if the global warming currently taking place is the result of natural events, then to a large extent, it may beyond

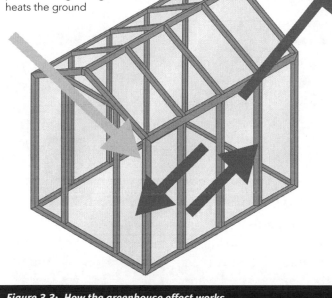

Visible energy from the sun passes through the glass and heats the ground

Infra-red heat energy from the ground is partly reflected by the glass, and some is trapped inside the greenhouse

Figure 3.3: How the greenhouse effect works.

human control. If it is the result of human activity then it can be dealt with – at a price.

The high-consumption lifestyles that **More Economically Developed Countries (MEDCs)** have become used to may have to be scaled back. **Less Economically Developed Countries (LEDCs)**, in the process of industrialising, cannot be expected to remain less economically developed to support the reduction in greenhouse gases from the developed world. This will inevitably mean that the MEDCs must bear a greater burden of reducing carbon emissions.

URBANISATION AND CLIMATE CHANGE

Climate change and urbanisation have in recent years become important issues. This is because one has an impact on the other. Moving into towns and cities changes the way in which we live and work. This has an impact on the pace of climate change.

In 1800 98 per cent of the world's population lived in rural areas. By 1950 30 per cent of the world's population was urban. In 2007 for the first time 50 per cent of the world's people were living in towns and cities. This growth in urbanisation is predicted

to continue. By 2030 75 per cent of the world's population are expected to be town and city dwellers and this could rise to 80 per cent by 2050.

Most of this growth will be in LEDCs, which have fewer resources than MEDCs, meaning that much of the development may lead to slums and shanty towns. Estimates suggest that there are almost a billion poor people in the world. More than 75 per cent of these poor people live in towns and cities without proper shelter or basic services.

In 1950 New York was the only city with a population of 10 million. It is predicted that by 2015 there will be 23 cities with a population over 10 million. Nineteen of these cities will be in developing countries.

Urban areas use 75 per cent of the world's total energy and give off 80 per cent of greenhouse gas emissions. Half of these emissions are caused by urban transport. Half are caused by the energy used to heat and cool buildings and run people's homes.

These two sources of emissions have to be the starting points for change in towns and cities. They must be addressed if cities are to avoid the problems that climate change could bring. The way cities are built will need to change to deal with the changing climate. The way we provide and use energy will need to change to reduce emissions.

INDUSTRIALISATION AND CLIMATE CHANGE

Over the earth's history climate has varied greatly. At the start of the Industrial Revolution in the 1780s the level of carbon dioxide in the atmosphere was about 280 parts per million (ppm).

We know this from analysis of three ice cores obtained at Law Dome, East Antarctica from 1987 to 1993. The air in these ice cores provides evidence of carbon dioxide levels from the 11th to the 20th centuries.

The evidence shows a major growth in atmospheric carbon dioxide levels over the industrial period.

This suggests that the global warming and climate change that concerns us today is probably the result of the large-scale use of fossil fuels to power the Industrial Revolution. Carbon dioxide levels rose, as did temperatures. The process was slow to start with but speeded up in the 20th century.

Table 3.1: The amount of carbon dioxide in the atmosphere from 1800 to the present day.

Year	CO$_2$ (parts per million)
1800–1870	280
1930	315
1970	330
1990	360
2008	380

This rise in CO$_2$ in the atmosphere has so far led to an increase in global temperatures of 0.75°C. If the change of 20 ppm in the last 18 years, which has not happened since the end of the last ice age 10,000 years ago, was to continue, by 2050 carbon dioxide levels would reach more than 500 ppm – twice as high as they were before industrialisation began.

Examination of the gases trapped in cores of polar ice show that levels of carbon dioxide in the atmosphere are now 35 per cent higher than they have been for 650,000 years.

The problem with this evidence is that such a seemingly small change in temperature does not seem significant when the temperature from day to day can vary by much larger margins. This convinces some people that daily temperature changes and global average temperatures on a year-on-year basis are not really related. It is interesting to note that the difference between today's average temperature and the average temperature during the last ice age is only 5°C.

THE GREENHOUSE EFFECT

The greenhouse effect was first identified by Jean Baptiste Fourier. It claimed that the earth is surrounded by a layer of 'greenhouse gases', mainly carbon dioxide and water vapour, which act like a blanket around the earth. This is a natural process that keeps the planet warm enough for people and animals to live on it. The blanket acts like the glass walls of a greenhouse. The sun's rays can reach the earth's surface, but the heat they create has difficulty escaping back out. The greenhouse gas effect keeps the earth around 30°C warmer than it would be otherwise.

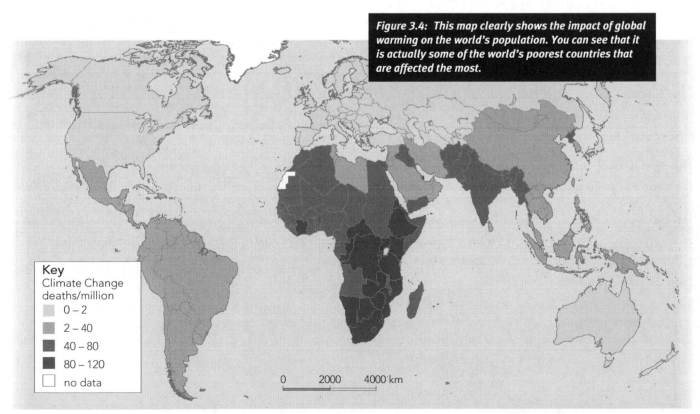

Figure 3.4: *This map clearly shows the impact of global warming on the world's population. You can see that it is actually some of the world's poorest countries that are affected the most.*

Key
Climate Change
deaths/million
- 0 – 2
- 2 – 40
- 40 – 80
- 80 – 120
- no data

0   2000   4000 km

(Source: World Health Organisation 2005)

The more gases there are, the more heat will be trapped, causing the earth's temperatures to rise, and the earth's climate begins to change unnaturally – 'global warming'.

Between 1800 and 1870, the first Industrial Revolution was taking place. This led to the burning of coal for developing industry, railroads and land clearance. A result of this development was an increase in greenhouse gas emissions. Better agriculture and sanitation led to population growth and growing urbanisation, again creating more greenhouse gas emissions. There is a natural process that enables carbon to be stored in forests, oceans and as mineral reserves such as coal, oil and gas. This is called 'the carbon cycle'. Carbon dioxide is one of the major greenhouse gases causing global warming.

The increase in human activity since the Industrial Revolution has produced more carbon dioxide by burning coal, oil and gas. It has also severely damaged the ability of the earth to absorb carbon into its carbon sinks through **deforestation**.

IS CLIMATE CHANGE ACCEPTED AS FACT?

It has taken a long time for the majority of people, especially those who are in a position to do something about it, to accept that global warming really is caused by human activity.

The Group of Eight (G8) is a body whose members set out to tackle global challenges through discussion and action. It consists of France, Germany, Italy, Japan, the UK, the US, Canada and Russia. The leaders of these countries meet face-to-face at an annual summit. The group represents the most powerful economies in the world. In 2005, it accepted that human activity was responsible for climate change.

In its answers to frequently asked questions about climate change that was published after the meeting at Gleneagles in Scotland in 2005, it stated:

'the view of the Intergovernmental Panel on Climate Change (IPPC) and more than 2,000 reputable scientists from across the world is that most of the warming seen since the middle of the last century is due to human activities ... mainly due to the burning of coal, gas and oil.'

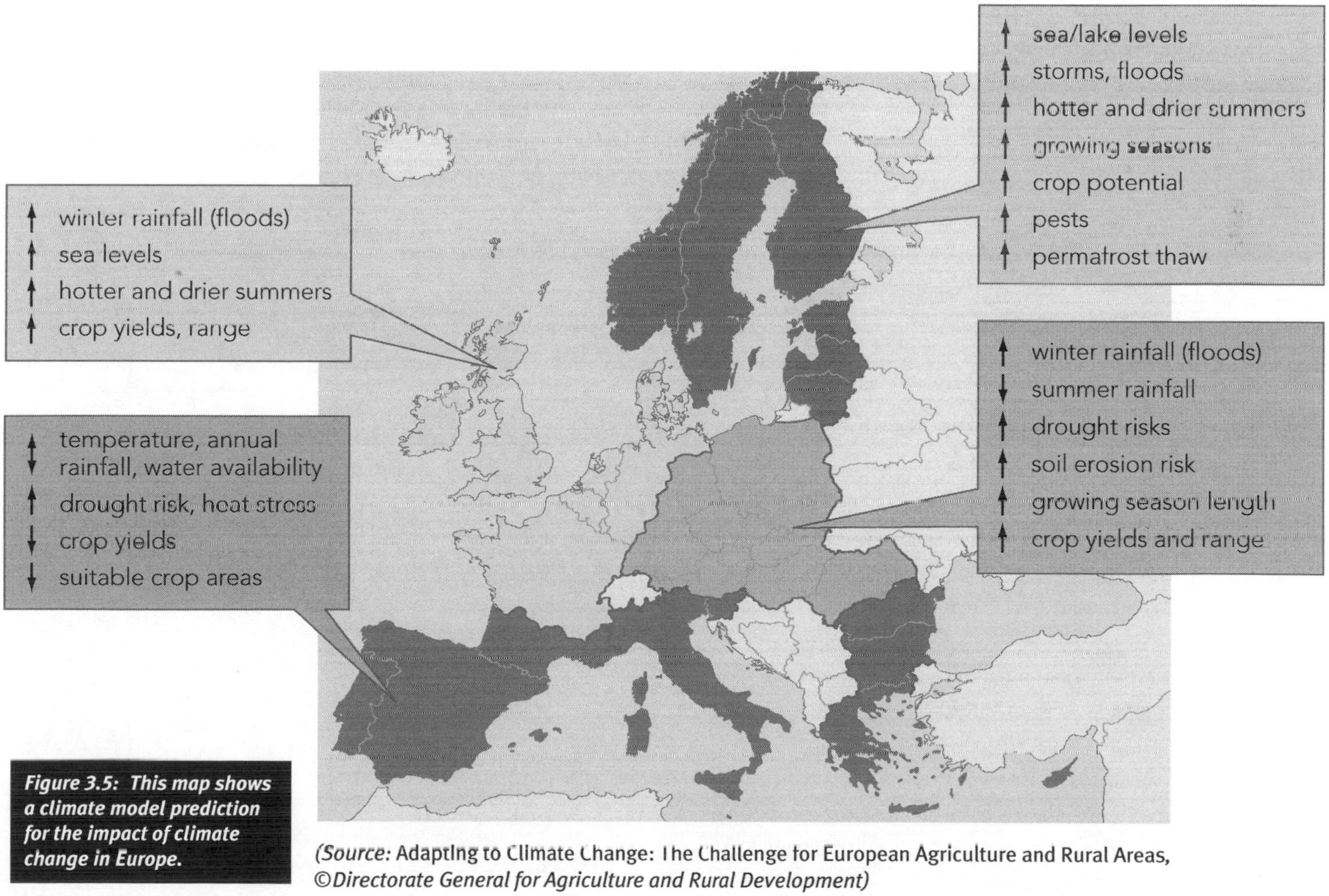

↑ sea/lake levels
↑ storms, floods
↑ hotter and drier summers
↑ growing seasons
↑ crop potential
↑ pests
↑ permafrost thaw

↑ winter rainfall (floods)
↑ sea levels
↑ hotter and drier summers
↑ crop yields, range

↑↓ temperature, annual rainfall, water availability
↑ drought risk, heat stress
↓ crop yields
↓ suitable crop areas

↑ winter rainfall (floods)
↓ summer rainfall
↑ drought risks
↑ soil erosion risk
↑ growing season length
↑ crop yields and range

Figure 3.5: This map shows a climate model prediction for the impact of climate change in Europe.

(*Source:* Adapting to Climate Change: The Challenge for European Agriculture and Rural Areas, ©*Directorate General for Agriculture and Rural Development*)

Using Table 3.2, assess who is making the more convincing case: the doubters or the supporters.

Table 3.2: The arguments for and against human influence in climate change.

Arguments made by those unconvinced about climate change	Arguments to answer those unconvinced by climate change
(1) Climate change is not really happening at all.	Temperature provides clear evidence that the climate is changing. Worldwide, the average temperature has risen by more than 0.7°C over the last 100 years.
(2) Even if there is some climate change, it is due to natural causes such as changes in the earth's orbit, volcanic eruptions and changes in the energy emitted by the sun, not human activity.	The 30% rise in CO_2 levels since the start of the Industrial Revolution has been caused by burning **fossil fuels** and deforestation. They are a direct result of human activity.
(3) The scale of the bad effects of climate change is often exaggerated and there is no need for urgent action.	If we continue emitting greenhouse gases, the warming will get worse: an increase this century of 2–3°C. This would mean that the earth will experience a larger climate change than it has experienced for at least 10,000 years. This is likely to result in an increased frequency and severity of weather events such as heat-waves, storms and flooding.
(4) Computer models which predict the future climate are unreliable and based on a series of assumptions.	Climate models can now recreate past and present climate changes accurately. They are not developed enough to present all the detail at regional or local levels. However, they do give us a reliable guide to the direction of future climate change.

In answer to the question 'How has the climate changed?', it said:

- temperatures have risen by 0.6°C in the past century
- the 10 hottest years on record have occurred since 1991
- the number of people affected by floods worldwide has already risen from 7 million in the 1960s to 150 million today
- in Europe alone, the severe floods in 2002 caused 37 deaths and had an estimated cost of US$16 billion
- 2003's heat-wave was linked to 26,000 premature deaths and cost US$13.5 billion.

Climate change was seen as a global problem requiring a global solution. All the G8 leaders agreed the aims on climate change: that emissions must reduce and countries move to low-carbon economies. And they agreed that it was urgent.

Why was the decision of the G8 on climate change at Gleneagles in 2005 an important event?

CLIMATE CHANGE DOUBTERS

It should not be assumed that everyone has accepted that climate change is either bad or caused by human activity. There is a strong body of opinion, particularly in the USA, which challenges this diagnosis.

The following is from a statement by the Director of Global Warming Policy, at the Competitive Enterprise Institute, based in Washington in December 2004:

'Potential global warming is much less worrying than the policies proposed to deal with it. The world cannot be put on energy rationing because around 2 billion people cannot hope to benefit from industrial civilization until they have electricity. This can only be achieved by using vast amounts of the cheapest form of energy – coal.'

This is a statement from Peter Calow, Director of the Environmental Assessment Institute, Copenhagen, Denmark, made in 2004:

'Climate change is worrying. Almost everybody agrees on that. How worrying, and how we should deal with climate change are more difficult questions, bedevilled by uncertainties. Here it is important to distinguish what we know from myths and prejudices.'

In June 2008, in *Global Warming Economics: Facts vs. Myths*, Iain Murray, of the Competitive Enterprise Institute, continued to criticise the generally accepted views on climate change:

'Temperatures have not risen in line with greenhouse gas concentrations. These have increased by 4 per cent since 1997. Temperatures have not; since 2001 they have either remained the same or fallen. No climate model predicted this.

'Researchers are now looking at other causes of warming. The Hadley Centre in the United Kingdom and the Liebniz Institute in Germany both have said recently that natural variations are currently more important than greenhouse gases as a cause of increased warming.'

He concludes that a sensible climate policy, rather than seeking to reduce the level of warming by a few degrees (which would not make much of a difference, anyway) should encourage policies that will allow the world's poor to improve their situation, which would enable them to deal with any problems that could arise from global warming.

Figure 3.6: *Protests such as this one by Greenpeace aim to raise awareness of climate change in order to influence government policy.*

Table 3.3: Climate predictions for the UK, graded into high, medium and low likelihood of actually happening.

Prediction	High likelihood	Medium likelihood	Low likelihood
The UK will continue to get warmer	By 2040, average temperature is expected to rise by 0.5–1°C. By 2100, average temperature is expected to rise by 1–5°C.	There is expected to be more warming in summer and autumn than winter and spring.	
Summers will continue to get hotter and drier	By 2040, average summer temperature is expected to rise by 0.5–2°C. By 2100, average summer temperature is expected to rise by 1–6°C. The number of days when buildings need cooling will increase.	By 2100, there is expected to be 50% less rain in the summer months.	
Winters will continue to get milder and wetter.	By 2040, average winter temperature is expected to rise by 0.5–1°C.	Large parts of the country will have long runs of winters without snow.	
Winters will continue to get milder and wetter	The number of days when buildings require heating is expected to decrease.		
Some weather extremes will become more common, others less common.	Heavy winter precipitation is expected to increase.	The number of very hot summer days is expected to increase. The number of very cold winter days is expected to decrease.	Winter storms and mild, wet and windy winter weather are expected to become more frequent.
Sea levels will continue to rise.	Global sea level is expected to continue to rise. The temperature of UK coastal waters is expected to increase but more slowly than air temperatures.	There is expected to be a greater rise in sea levels in the south of England than in Scotland. By 2100, storm surge events are 20 times more likely.	By 2100, sea levels around the UK coast could have risen by as much as 80 cm.

(Source: Adapted from the UK Climate Impacts Programme – UKCIPO2, ©Tyndall Centre and Hadley Centre 2002)

ACTIVITY

1. Using Table 3.3, how useful do you feel the predictions would be to planners charged with dealing with climate change? In your answer, try to take account of the level of confidence of the predictions.

2. 'Climate models are a useful tool in the battle against climate change.' Do you agree?

1. What are the doubts that are being expressed about climate change?

2. How important do you feel they are, given the other information you have seen?

MISLEADING STATEMENTS

Those who are unconvinced about the reality of climate change often put forward arguments which they suggest undermine the now generally-accepted view that current warming is caused by human activity.

Those supporting the opposite view have begun to address these 'misleading statements' on a point-by-point basis. One difficulty in this discussion is that while there is factual evidence of what has happened in the past, the impact this will have on the future is less certain.

Modern climate models are much better in predicting how the real climate 'works'. They use basic scientific principles and observations of the climate.

By creating computer simulations of how different parts of the climate system behave and interact, scientists have been able to reproduce the overall course of the climate in the last century. Using this understanding of the climate system, scientists can then project what is likely to happen in the future.

Computer models cannot exactly predict the future, but they can give a reasonably reliable guide to a variety of possibilities.

CLIMATE-MODELLING PROGRAMMES

Not all changes predicted by climate modelling simulations are made with the same level of confidence. Using their expert judgement and the results from climate-modelling simulations, predictions of changes in the future climate of the UK can be graded as having a high, medium or low likelihood of actually happening.

What do people think about climate change?

Considering the lack of certainty about the future of climate change, it would not be surprising if most people were confused by, or apathetic towards, the issue.

Figure 3.7: *This poster is for the film* An Inconvenient Truth *by Al Gore. It was widely shown in cinemas and has contributed to people's awareness of climate change and its impacts.*

The Department for Environment, Food and Rural Affairs (Defra) carries out regular surveys into attitudes to climate change. The most up-to-date research shows that awareness of climate change is increasing across the UK and that concern about the impact of climate change is growing.

Key findings from the latest adults' research include:

- awareness of climate change and global warming remains extremely high (98 per cent);
- the number of people who think they are taking action to tackle climate change continues to rise (73 per cent);
- 90 per cent of respondents felt the world's climate is changing;
- 80 per cent took personal responsibility for contributing to road transport emissions and carbon dioxide emissions.

Defra has also carried out surveys into youth attitudes to climate change. Key findings from the latest youth research include:

- 60 per cent are worried about climate change;
- 78 per cent think climate change is due to human behaviour;
- 33 per cent felt that the UK was already affected by climate change;
- 76 per cent felt that their home could use less energy.

PRESSURE GROUPS.

A pressure group is not a political party trying to get elected. It is an organisation of people who believe in the same cause that tries to change government policy to its advantage. The number of pressure groups runs into thousands.

'Pressure group' is a broad term which covers large scale organisations representing many members on a variety of issues, or a single issue campaign against a local problem. Some pressure groups use methods which are illegal and violent. Most try to use persuasion and the strength of their cause to advance their viewpoint.

Pressure groups allow people to take part in politics between general elections. Their activities can persuade government to change their mind. Often this is achieved through knowledge rather than protest. Many pressure groups become specialists in their particular field and their views are sought by government before making decisions.

Pressure groups use a variety of methods to exert their pressure. These range from letters to demonstrations and websites to the mass media to promote their message.

Some well known international pressure groups are Amnesty International and Greenpeace. Closer to home the Trades Union Congress (TUC) promotes the interests of workers, often finding itself in conflict with Confederation of British Industry (CBI) which promotes the interests of business.

ACTIVITY

1. How far do you agree with views expressed in the youth research on climate change?
2. Do you believe the individual can make an impact on climate change?

STRETCH AND CHALLENGE

Look at the evidence supporting the view that climate change is real and a result of human activity. Using books and the Internet research the evidence against this statement.

How far do you agree that climate change is happening, and how far is that down to the human race?

SUMMARY

This unit has explored the following points.

- What the climate is and what the term 'climate change' means.
- What international governments have done and said about the threat of global warming.
- The arguments for and against the idea that climate change is because of human activity and not a natural process.
- What climate modelling programmes can show and what their predictions are.
- What people's attitudes to climate change are and the involvement of pressure groups in the issue.

Unit 3.2 Resource management and the need for increased sustainability

IN THIS UNIT YOU WILL LEARN ABOUT:

- the impacts of sustainable lifestyles on developed and developing countries
- the economic and environmental implications of sustainable development
- the range of methods for managing waste
- the purpose and implications of Agenda 21.

KEY CONCEPTS

Renewable resources
Environmental footprint
Recycling
Finite resources
Environmental consequences of future economic development
Agenda 21

As the realisation grew that climate change was real and, in all probability, at least partly due to human activity, another strand of concern began to develop. This was a movement for a change in the way human development takes place to allow it to be sustained into the future.

In the same way that the awareness of climate change and its potential impact grew slowly over time, the movement for **sustainable development** gradually established itself.

THE UNITED NATIONS CONFERENCE ON THE HUMAN ENVIRONMENT

The United Nations Conference on the Human Environment, which took place in Stockholm, Sweden from 5 June to 16 June 1972, is generally accepted as the start of an awareness of global environmental problems and the need to address them. Representatives from 113 countries agreed a declaration stating 26 principles about the environment and development, and an action plan with 109 recommendations. Two of these principles are reproduced below:

Principle 2: The natural resources of the earth must be safeguarded for the benefit of present and future generations through careful planning.

Principle 3: The capacity of the earth to produce vital renewable resources must be maintained and, if possible, be restored or improved.

The conference also created the United Nations Environment Programme (UNEP), which was based in Nairobi, Kenya. This had the mission statement:

'to provide leadership and encourage partnership in caring for the environment by inspiring, informing, and enabling nations and peoples to improve their quality of life without compromising that of future generations.'

THE BRUNDTLAND COMMISSION

In 1983, the Secretary General of the UN set up the World Commission on the Environment and Development. The head of the commission was Gro Harlem Brundtland, a former Prime Minister of Norway, and the commission is more commonly known as the Brundtland Commission.

Sustainable development encourages the conservation and preservation of natural resources and of the environment, and the management of energy, waste and transportation.

The report of the commission is widely credited with producing the accepted definition of sustainable development:

'Development which meets the needs of the present without compromising the ability of future generations to meet their own needs.'

THE UNITED NATIONS CONFERENCE ON ENVIRONMENT AND DEVELOPMENT

The next step was the Earth Summit, which took place over 12 days in June 1992 in Rio de Janeiro. Its major aim was to build upon the findings of the Brundtland Report.

There was a tension at this meeting between the developed and developing nations. Developed nations wanted to concentrate on achieving environmental sustainability, while developing nations were more interested in being given the chance to catch up with the developed nations.

Three major agreements were adopted in Rio de Janeiro with the aim of changing the approach to development. These committed countries, including the UK, to be more sustainable, and drew up plans for a more sustainable future.

Agenda 21 is a programme for action across the world in all areas of sustainable development. The Declaration on Environment and Development sets out the rights and responsibilities of States for sustainable development. The Statement of Forest Principles is a guide for the sustainable management of forests worldwide.

Two legally-binding conventions with the aims of preventing global climate change and the loss of animal species were also agreed.

THE CONVENTION ON CLIMATE CHANGE

The Convention on Climate Change was established because the United Nations believed that whereas previously global climate changed human beings, now it was the other way round.

The aim of the Convention on Climate Change was to get countries to agree to stabilise greenhouse gas emissions. On 21 March 1994, the treaty took effect after 165 states signed up to it. It did have one great weakness, which was that it did not set specific, agreed limits on greenhouse gas emissions – they were only set in vague general terms.

THE CONVENTION ON BIOLOGICAL DIVERSITY

The Convention on Biological Diversity was agreed in June 1992 and came into force on 29 December 1993. By October 1998, more than 170 countries had signed up to it. Its three goals are:

- to conserve **biodiversity**;
- to achieve sustainable use of its components;
- to establish fair and equal sharing of benefits arising out of genetic resources.

THE KYOTO PROTOCOL

You can read about the Kyoto Protocol in Unit 3.1. You will know that some countries refused to sign up to the Kyoto Protocol. The most significant of these is the USA, which presented a major problem as they are the largest producer of greenhouse gases. They object that emissions from developing countries are not included, as well as claiming that signing will damage the US economy.

Most countries felt that the targets were challenging and would be difficult to achieve. Every country has to develop its own way to meet its targets, and many have already fallen behind. However, the agreement is legally binding, and there will be penalties for countries who fail to reach their targets. Any shortfall in 2012 will be added to their new target from 2012 with an extra 30 per cent added in this period.

For the latest progress on the Kyoto targets, look at the UNFCCC website (see 'Websites' on page ii).

THE WORLD SUMMIT ON SUSTAINABLE DEVELOPMENT

The World Summit on Sustainable Development was held in Johannesburg, South Africa, from 26 August to 4 September 2002. This conference was about sustainable development as a whole, and its aims included reducing world poverty and improving access to water and sanitation. Climate change also featured heavily in many of the discussions.

Water and sanitation. Around 1.1 billion people need access to clean drinking water. A target was set to halve this figure. Proper sanitation would significantly reduce diseases such as cholera.

Energy. It was agreed to take action to boost access to affordable energy. There was no agreement on targets for renewable power. These plans were opposed by some oil-producers.

Natural resources and biodiversity. It was agreed to cut the rate of extinction of animals and plants, but no targets were set.

The Worldwide Fund for Nature said the plan would not make a significant move forwards and might even prove a step backwards.

THE DELHI DECLARATION – OCTOBER 2002

This conference was supposed to work out the final details of the Kyoto Protocol before it took effect. Problems arose when developed nations asked developing countries to reduce their greenhouse gas emissions. Developing nations, led by China and India, refused, saying that the problem of greenhouse gases was caused when developed nations were themselves developing. It was therefore unfair, they argued, that poorer nations should be held back to deal with a problem not of their making.

A document was eventually signed by 185 countries. There was no requirement in the document for developing countries to limit greenhouse gas emissions. Some developed countries were disappointed with the final declaration.

DEVELOPING VS. DEVELOPED

'The United Nations Convention on Climate Change recognises that poorer nations have a right to economic development ... It acknowledges the vulnerability of poorer countries to the effects of climate change.'

The argument is simple and difficult to contest. It is difficult to fairly stop developing countries from developing. Developed nations have created the problem, and they should pay to sort it out, while agreeing that developing nations can continue to develop.

However, because climate change affects the whole world, the whole world needs to tackle it – another argument that is difficult to contest.

One possible solution to this disagreement might be a process of adaptation to climate change where everyone, developed and developing, uses environmentally friendly technologies.

Unfortunately, these technologies are much more expensive, and this could hold back the development of poorer countries.

The Convention is clear on this problem: it says that the countries that created the most greenhouse gases must take the lead to fight against them.

ACTIVITY

1. Make a timeline of the international conferences which have led to progress on the movement towards sustainable development.

2. Select two of these meetings which you feel were the most important in this process and explain why you chose them.

STRETCH AND CHALLENGE

There is tension between developed and developing countries over the pollution being caused by the rapid development of LEDCs. Using this unit, and your own research, put forward the arguments used by both sides to support their view.

Whose arguments do you find most convincing? Give reasons for your answer.

Adapting to climate change

That the earth's climate is changing is the increasingly accepted view from the IPPC and the 2000 reputable scientists from across the world that are part of it. The cause of climate change is also increasingly accepted to be an increase in carbon emissions caused by burning coal, gas and oil.

Global warming is expected to continue for the foreseeable future, fuelled by the emissions already released. Cutting future carbon emissions needs to be high on any list of actions to avoid further change. There is a need to take action to cut carbon emissions while, at the same time, changing or adapting behaviour to deal with what happens as a result of climate change. Such a change in behaviour is called 'adaptation'.

WHAT IS ADAPTATION?

Climate change will force people to adapt the way they do things. This does not only mean being prepared for the unpleasant effects of climate change but being able to make use of any benefits from climate change.

People have always adapted to variations in their climate, often by relying on past experience to deal with extreme situations. Because of climate change, past experience is no longer likely to be such a reliable guide.

The UK Climate Impacts Programme has identified possible future problems. The major ones identified are:

- an increase in the risk of flooding and coastal erosion;
- greater pressure on drainage systems;
- increased likelihood of winter storm damage;
- loss of habitat for wildlife;
- summer water shortages and low stream flows;
- increased risk of subsidence (in areas where subsidence is already a problem).

ACTIVITY

1. Give a brief definition of adaptation to climate change.

2. How serious do you think the changes identified by the UK Climate Impacts Programme are likely to be?

THE DEPARTMENT FOR INTERNATIONAL DEVELOPMENT

A country's ability to adapt to climate change is related to how developed it is and the resources it has at its disposal.

The challenges for the world's least developed communities will be the greatest, as they are more likely to be vulnerable to climate change impacts. To cope with this, adaptation must be central to all development policies.

The Department for International Development (DFID) is the UK government department which deals with aid to poor countries. It has two major projects relating to developing nations: the first is to achieve the Millennium Development Goals, and the second is to implement an action plan to deliver sustainable development in poor countries.

The Millennium Development Goals are United Nations targets to be met by 2015. They aim to reduce poverty and were agreed at the UN Millennium Summit in September 2000. Nearly 190 countries have signed up to them.

Figure 3.8: As extreme weather events increase, we will have to adapt our behaviour and infrastructure to cope with them.

The eight Millennium Development Goals are to:

- eradicate extreme poverty and hunger;
- achieve universal primary education;
- promote gender equality and empower women;
- reduce child mortality;
- improve maternal health;
- combat HIV and AIDS, malaria and other diseases;
- ensure environmental sustainability;
- develop a global partnership for development.

DFID will work with any organisation supporting the aim of finding a lasting solution to the problem of poverty.

The Sustainable Development Action Plan considers the economic, social and environmental aspects of what the UK supports in developing countries. It tries to:

- achieve a target of giving 0.7 per cent of the UK's annual earnings as development assistance;
- work with developing countries to build in sustainable development to poverty reduction;
- help developing countries to give water and sanitation importance in national development plans;
- share experiences of sustainable development with other countries;
- help developing countries adapt to climate change.

ACTIVITY

1. What is DFID trying to do through its aid to poorer countries?

2. Pick out three of the aims from the Millennium Development Goals and/or the Sustainable Development Action Plan. Explain the importance of the three aims you have chosen.

RENEWABLE ENERGY SOURCES

One of the major areas for adaptation is the expanding use of renewable energy sources. This offers a dual advantage. Carbon emissions can be reduced at the same time as reducing dependency on finite polluting resources like coal and oil. The main renewable energy sources are wind, water, geothermal and solar power. One potentially controversial addition could be nuclear power.

Geographically, the UK is well-placed to use renewable energy sources. Table 3.4 outlines the different types of energy source, which each have advantages and disadvantages.

ACTIVITY

Study Table 3.4. Which of the renewable energy sources do you think is most likely to make a significant contribution to reducing carbon emissions from fossil fuels?

NUCLEAR POWER

Nuclear power raises strong reactions both in its favour and against. Opinions are clearly divided over the issue of radioactivity and the potential disasters that could result from accidents at nuclear power stations.

Those in favour of nuclear power say that properly built nuclear power plants are extremely clean and generate considerably more energy than fossil fuel power stations. Those against it say that nuclear waste will remain a problem for hundreds of years, and transporting nuclear fuel can be risky.

ACTIVITY

1. Find out more about the arguments for and against renewing the UK's nuclear power plants.

2. Should nuclear power be part of a sustainable power policy? Give reasons for your answer.

THE CLIMATE CHANGE BILL

At the end of 2008, the UK became the first country to have a carbon emissions policy which people will have to follow by law. This is because the Climate Change Bill became law on the 26 November 2008.

To support this new law, the prime minister created a new government department in October 2008 – the Department of Energy and Climate Change. The new department will, as its name suggests, focus on solving the challenges of climate change and energy supply.

It is not enough for the government to be making progress, because 40 per cent of carbon dioxide emissions in the UK are the responsibility of ordinary people. This may seem a lot, but if you add up the emissions from using electricity in the home and driving cars, it becomes clear that ordinary citizens can, and should, make significant contributions to reducing their CO_2 emissions.

Table 3.4: Advantages and disadvantages of renewable energy sources.

Energy source		Advantages	Disadvantages
Wind farms		Environmentally friendly; emission-free; no long-term damage to physical environment; can be sited offshore.	Visual damage to landscape; noise pollution to those living nearby; they produce electricity that is expensive.
Solar power (in the form of solar panels)		Low energy bills in the long term.	Initial costs can be high.
Geothermal generators		'Heat from the earth'; pollution-free; heat pumps can be used almost anywhere; economical in the long term.	Geothermal resources are not available everywhere.
Hydro-electric generators		Pollution-free water power; safe once constructed.	Environmental disruption during construction; low output of electricity (2%).
Tidal generators		Work by using the gravitational pull of the moon; use turbines to produce energy from tidal rises and falls; promising source of UK energy and 5.5% of British energy could be produced with large site at Bristol.	Can be expensive to set up; disruptive construction process; concern of risk of river pollution.
Wave-power generators		Energy created by large waves (e.g. from North Sea); cheap once set up and environmentally friendly.	Collecting energy could be difficult and expensive; could pose problem for fishing industry.

RECYCLING

Nearly two thirds of all household rubbish can be recycled. Recycling saves a lot of energy and raw materials, and avoids waste going to landfill. This is important, because landfill sites are responsible for creating significant amounts of methane, one of the important greenhouse gases. This obviously helps to tackle climate change.

The recycling message has obviously made an impact with the general public, because they are now recycling three times more rubbish than they were 10 years ago. It is estimated that this figure could be doubled, or even trebled.

Recycling saves natural resources. It converts 'rubbish' into new products and avoids it ending up in a landfill. It also cuts down on the use of new raw materials. This protects habitat that might otherwise be destroyed by mining or forestry.

Processing recycled materials is less costly in terms of energy used than producing new products from raw materials. More energy is saved by not having to extract, refine, transport and process raw materials ready for industry.

Recycling is environmentally friendly. By reducing the need for raw materials, substantial air and water pollution is avoided. Greenhouse gas emissions are reduced by saving the energy that would be used obtaining these raw materials. This helps to tackle climate change.

It is estimated that recycling can save up to 18 million tonnes of CO_2 a year – equivalent to taking 5 million cars off the road.

ACTIVITY

1. Using the Defra, directgov and SITA websites (see 'Websites' on page ii), and others you may find, research the benefits and costs of recycling.

2. 'Considering the contribution recycling makes to the reduction of carbon emissions, it is not only reasonable to expect individuals to recycle – it should be made compulsory.' How far do you agree?

ENVIRONMENTAL FOOTPRINT

The 'environmental footprint' measures of the impact of human demands on the earth. It does this by comparing human demands on the earth with the earth's ability to meet this demand sustainably.

Across the whole world people are using about 25 per cent more natural resources than the planet can replace. In the UK we are using considerably more. If everyone lived in the same way as we do then we would need three planet earths to supply those demands.

Unless there is a drastic change in the way that people in the affluent parts of the world live there will be some serious consequences. A large amount (70 per cent) of the environmental footprint is caused by carbon emissions.

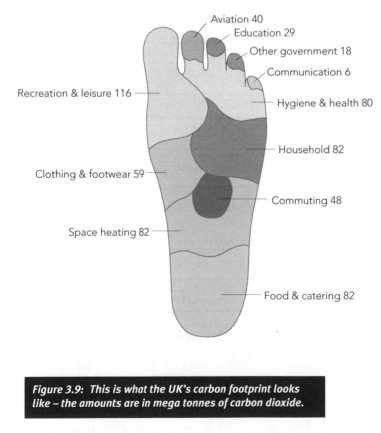

Aviation 40
Education 29
Other government 18
Communication 6
Recreation & leisure 116
Hygiene & health 80
Household 82
Clothing & footwear 59
Commuting 48
Space heating 82
Food & catering 82

Figure 3.9: This is what the UK's carbon footprint looks like – the amounts are in mega tonnes of carbon dioxide.

(Source: Reproduced from www.carbontrust.co.uk with kind permission from the Carbon Trust)

Finite resources

Crucial to the environmental footprint is the use of fossil fuels. Not only do they release carbon dioxide, adding to global climate change, but they are also non renewable. They are finite resources because the day will come when they run out.

Whilst there are currently still large reserves of coal, oil and gas, the demand for these natural resources is rising and the discovery of new reserves is in decline. The combination of these two trends will inevitably mean that the day when they run out is in the foreseeable future.

AGENDA 21

Agenda 21 was another initiative that came out of the 1992 United Nations Conference on Environment and Development in Rio de Janeiro. It asked for a commitment to sustainable development which was agreed to by many world governments. The number 21 was included as a reference to the 21st century.

The Agenda is monitored by the International Commission on Sustainable Development. Countries who have agreed to take part are expected to support Agenda 21 at local and regional levels within their own countries.

Agenda 21 focuses on the conservation and preservation of our environments and natural resources: a blueprint on how to make development socially, economically and environmentally sustainable in the 21st century. It provides a framework for tackling today's social and environmental problems. It is not simply for governments; all parts of society are encouraged to take part.

LOCAL AGENDA 21

It was decided that if sustainable development was to be achieved, it would have to come from a local level. There are 2500 action points in Agenda 21, and most are about local council actions.

Each local authority has had to draw up its own Local Agenda 21 (LA21) strategy after consulting local people for their views about priorities for their area.

Sustainable development is at the core of the local strategy because it is considered to be a local issue which should involve all members of the community. This is intended to produce enthusiasm for the process to ensure sustainable development is achieved.

Local authorities are allowed to share expertise and to join together to deal with large organisations on an equal footing.

LA21 believes that sustainable development can be achieved whilst maintaining the quality of people's lives. The price of this is that people begin to think and act in a more sustainable way.

ACTIVITY

1. Research the Local Agenda 21 for your local authority.

2. How well does the information you have found fit with what you would have expected from the information on Local Agenda 21?

SUMMARY

This unit has explored the following points.

- The idea of sustainable development and the history of governmental attempts to find a solution to the problem.

- Why we will be forced to adapt to climate change and how we can achieve this.

- What renewable energy resources are available and their advantages and disadvantages.

- What your carbon footprint is and how you can reduce it.

Chapter 4
Religious and Moral Issues

CONTENTS

Unit 4.1
The nature of God

IN THIS UNIT YOU WILL LEARN ABOUT:

- what religious people mean when they use the word 'god'
- the different beliefs religions have about God
- where God is
- why many people believe in God.

KEY CONCEPTS

Omnipotence
Theism
Atheism
Pluralism
Heaven
Creation

WHAT MAKES HUMAN BEINGS SO SPECIAL AND WHAT HAS THAT GOT TO DO WITH RELIGION?

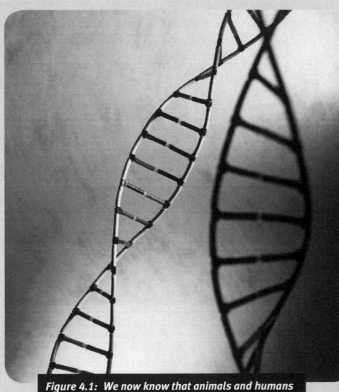

Figure 4.1: *We now know that animals and humans share many similarities, and over 90 per cent of their DNA, but there are important differences.*

As human beings are animals, many answers to what makes us special will focus on physical differences. However, there are two significant differences which relate to things other than the

physical. The first is the ability to question the world around us; to pose the questions starting:

- What?
- When?
- Where?

And, perhaps more importantly:

- Who?
- Why?
- How?

The second difference is to be able to anticipate our own deaths. This may seem a little morbid: all creatures die, but only humans are aware that, at some point, it is inevitable that they will die. This naturally raises the questions listed above, as well as a more difficult question – what, if anything, comes after death?

SO WHY IS THIS IMPORTANT?

The ability to ask questions leads human beings to wonder about the world around them. Many of these questions will be easy to answer: these will be the 'what', 'when' and 'where' questions, which can usually be answered from looking at the world around us.

Another characteristic of human beings, which is shared with many animals, is curiosity. This curiosity drives some people to think about the world around them and to ask important questions which cannot be answered by looking at the world around us. They will ask:

- Who are we?
- Why are we here?
- How did we get here?

When there is no obvious answer to a question, alternative answers must be found. A very popular and common answer throughout human history and prehistory has been to explain the unexplainable as the actions of a god or gods. This is when answers based on evidence we can see are replaced by belief.

ACTIVITY

1. Make a list of things that separate human beings from other animals.

2. What are the differences in using facts rather than beliefs to prove a point of view?

3. Is using facts better than using belief, or is belief better than fact? Give reasons for your answer.

What religious people mean when they use the word 'god'

Having used the word 'belief', it is important to consider what the word 'god' means in religious terms. The words that are used to describe religious belief can appear difficult, because they are based on the Greek word for god, which is *Theos*. So anyone who believes in a god is called a '**theist**', whereas someone who does not believe in a god is called an '**atheist**'.

Theists believe in the existence of at least one god. This belief does not depend upon:

- how many gods are believed in;
- how the term 'god' is defined;
- how the belief is arrived at.

Theism states that the existence and continuance of the universe is owed to one or more supreme beings, who are not part of creation.

Atheists do not believe in the existence of a god, or gods, and reject the idea that the existence and continuance of the universe is owed to one or more supreme beings. Atheists may simply not accept the truth of the belief, or may go further and actively oppose the belief.

ACTIVITY

1. What is the difference between a theist and an atheist?

2. Who do you think would be happiest: someone who believes there is a god, or someone who believes there are no gods? Give reasons for your view.

THE DIFFERENT BELIEFS RELIGIONS HAVE ABOUT GOD

Christianity

Christianity is a monotheistic religion, which means that Christians believe that there is only one God. However, to complicate matters, they also believe that God has three aspects. This is called **The Trinity**. The aspects are: God the Father, God the Son and God the Holy Spirit.

Christians believe that God is all-powerful (**omnipotent**), everywhere (**omnipresent**) and knows everything (**omniscient**): that 'God is absolute perfection'.

They believe that God is the creator of the universe and the one who keeps it going. God takes an interest in the universe by intervening.

Christians believe that they can have a personal relationship with God, who loves everyone unconditionally. They do this through prayer, worship and love. Christians believe that in the person of Jesus, God took on human form. Therefore, Jesus is worshipped and his teachings are followed to make sure that God is pleased and that they can go to heaven to be with God forever when they die.

Islam

The single most important belief in Islam is that Allah is the one and only God. He is unique and cannot be split into parts. This is why followers of Islam, called Muslims, reject ideas such as the Christian Trinity.

The Muslim name for God is 'Allah', Arabic for 'the' *al* and 'god' *llah*. Muslims believe that Allah is the all-powerful creator of a perfect, ordered universe. He is beyond knowing, and is not a part of his creation. He is most often referred to with names that emphasise his majesty and superiority. Among the '99 Beautiful Names of God' in the **Qur'an** are: the Creator, the Life-Giver, the Provider and the Lord of the Worlds.

Despite Allah being beyond knowing, the Qur'an does not teach that Allah does not know us, but that he is present everywhere and is close to man. Throughout human history, Allah has sent teachers or prophets to show people how they should live their lives. The last and greatest of these **prophets** was a man called Muhammad, who lived in Arabia 1400 years ago. Muslims respect Muhammad and his teachings but do not worship him.

Islam allows no images or pictures of Allah. Most Muslims believe that Allah has no body; therefore, pictures of Allah make no sense. Such images could lead to people worshipping the image rather than Allah and therefore should not be allowed.

Buddhism

Gautama was a spiritual teacher from ancient India and the founder of Buddhism. He is generally accepted by Buddhists as the Supreme Buddha. Whether the supreme Buddha is 'merely' human or an immortal, god-like being is not completely agreed.

Many believe that Buddha was born, lived and died a human being: a remarkable human being with supreme teaching skill and wisdom, but not immortal and therefore not contactable after he died. Mahayana Buddhism sees him as a human form of an eternal being, and therefore he can be worshipped. Images of the Buddha are put into shrines so that people can ask for his help in order that they too can become enlightened and reach nirvana, which for them is a kind of heavenly place.

Gautama does not teach that the universe was created by a god. He concentrates on the **Dhamma**, the teachings which lead to enlightenment through achieving true wisdom, compassion and freedom from suffering.

In some ways, Buddhism is an atheistic religion, because belief in a god is not necessary to lead a good life.

Hinduism

A specific belief about a god or gods is not one of the essentials of Hinduism. This is a major difference between Hinduism and monotheistic religions like Christianity and Islam.

Followers of Hinduism – Hindus – recognise one God, Brahman, who they believe is the eternal origin and the creator of all existence.

The other gods of the Hindu faith represent different expressions of Brahman.

Most Hindus are followers of one of the principal gods – Brahma, who creates the universe, Vishnu, who preserves the universe and Shiva, who destroys

Figure 4.2: In Islam, no images or pictures of Allah are allowed.

the universe. These are simply seen as different ways of approaching the Ultimate Brahman. Because God is in everything, a Hindu can worship a mountain or a river. A great hero from the past like Krishna can be thought of as being God in human form.

In Hinduism, God is neither male nor female and this idea makes depicting God in a statue or picture very difficult. Male and female forms of God are found in Temples, each one illustrating a special ability or characteristic of God which a person can pray to or pray for when it is appropriate to them.

Hindus believe in one all-pervasive supreme being who is both involved in life on earth and in the universe, but beyond everything that human beings understand.

Judaism

Jews – followers of Judaism – believe in a single, all-powerful God. This belief made them unique among other ancient peoples, and this belief has passed on to the religions of the entire Western world.

Jews believe God is the creator of the universe. The fact that the world exists is proof that God exists. God has no body, and is non-physical. This means that God is neither male nor female.

God has no beginning and no end but is eternal. God is everywhere, filling the universe and beyond, yet is always near. God is all-knowing, aware of all our thoughts and deeds, in the past, present and future. God is all-powerful.

God is forgiving. People can find their way back into God's favour by prayer and repentance. Prophets were people who were inspired or influenced by God to teach human beings where they were going wrong and how to lead lives that would be acceptable to God. However, they were not God and are not worshipped.

Sikhism

Sikhs believe that there is one God and that God is all powerful and created the universe for humans to enjoy.

People know about God through the teaching of **Gurus**. Humans need the Gurus to show the way to truth.

The Gurus are for everybody, they are messengers from God, God's servants and enlighteners. The Sikh scriptures – the **Guru Granth Sahib** – is thought

of as the final Guru, which can teach people how to realise that God is in all human beings: men and women, rich and poor, regardless of race or religion.

God created human beings. The cycle of birth and rebirth starts because humans desire material things, but this can be stopped by replacing desire with devotion to God.

Human beings are unique because they have a divine spark, but they struggle to live up to the divine.

Where is God and why do many people believe in God?

Religions put forward a number of ideas as to where God is. God is sometimes described as being in the universe interacting with human beings on earth, or as the opposite of this, the creator of the universe and therefore not a part of it.

Some Christians believe in God as a being, often described in human terms, with whom they can have a relationship through prayer and response to prayer. Others think of God as an impersonal force only understandable on its own terms.

Christians believe God is involved with life on earth but is at the same time beyond human understanding. Muslims share the view that he is beyond human understanding, while Buddhists do not believe there is a God.

Hindus see God in two parts: the soul of each person, but also the creator beyond human experience. Sikhs have similar views. Jews see God as all powerful but they feel they have a special relationship as the chosen people.

So why do people believe in God? Individuals will answer this question in different ways. Philosophers have grouped these reasons into different arguments for believing in God. We are going to look at some of them here.

THE DESIGN ARGUMENT

The design argument states that:

- The universe shows some evidence of design.
- This evidence shows not just evidence of design but of intelligent design or purpose.
- The best explanation for this evidence of intelligent design is that there is an intelligent designer who designed it.

WILLIAM PALEY'S WATCHMAKER ARGUMENT

William Paley's watchmaker argument is an attempt to identify what he believes are reliable indicators of intelligent design. It is paraphrased below.

> 'Suppose I found a watch on the ground and I questioned how the watch came to be there. I might say the watch had always been there. Would this answer be as believable for a watch as for a stone? No, because the way in which the watch has been made allows it to work, and without this intelligent design it would not work.'

There are two things about a watch that reliably indicate that it is the result of intelligent design. First, it does something that a person with intelligence would think was valuable: it tells the time. Second, the watch can only do this because of the way it is made. This tells us that the watch is made this way because some agency with intelligence designed it. This shows that the watch works in a complex way. It also clearly separates objects that have intelligent designers from objects that do not. The material universe shows the same kind of complexity as a watch; it is therefore reasonable to conclude that universe was created by an intelligent agent.

THE FIRST CAUSE (COSMOLOGICAL) ARGUMENT

Thomas Aquinas was influenced by Aristotle, and used Aristotle's findings to put forward the most important version of the cosmological argument. His idea of 'First Cause' was that the universe must have been caused by something that was itself not caused, and this he argued was God, and God caused the universe to come into existence.

According to his argument, the things we see around us are the result of previous causes, for example evolution. But these causes cannot go back in time forever; even the big bang had to be caused by something. There must be a First Cause. This First Cause was not itself caused by anything else. That First Cause is God.

The cosmological argument, putting forward a god as a 'First Cause', can be summarised in this way:

- Everything that exists or begins to exist has a cause.
- The universe exists and began to exist.
- The universe must have a cause.
- The cause of the universe is God.

THE MYSTICAL ARGUMENT

Religious people would say that sometimes something happens for which there can be no other explanation except that God was responsible. Sometimes someone prays for something, for example a person to recover from an illness. When this person recovers, and it appears that the prayer has been answered, they say that God has heard and answered their prayers and therefore God must exist.

Sometimes, when a person sees a beautiful sunset or experiences the silence of a forest or church, hears a wonderful piece of music or holds a newborn baby for the first time, they experience a feeling of awe and wonder, which cannot be explained or described. This convinces many people that God exists.

Figure 4.3: A watch is made to work. It has a creator.

SUMMARY

This unit has explored the following points.

- What different religions mean when they use the word 'god'.

- Where different religions believe that God is.

- The different arguments people use to support their belief in God.

Unit 4.2 The nature of belief

IN THIS UNIT YOU WILL LEARN ABOUT:

- the ways in which worship takes place in religious buildings and privately at home
- the meaning of important religious festivals
- ceremonies and beliefs associated with rites of passage
- beliefs about holy scriptures.

KEY CONCEPTS

Worship
Religious festivals
Ritual
Ceremony
Holy scriptures
Revelation
Authority

WHAT IS WORSHIP?

Do you believe in a god?

Do you show this belief in some way?

The answers to these questions are, of course, matters for the individual. However, the need for human beings in general to believe in someone or something is a very common feature of human societies, from the earliest times to the present day.

The focus of these beliefs has been varied from the forces of nature, to ancestors, to gods and goddesses – not necessarily in that order!

These beliefs have generally led to actions. People seem to need to show their ... what? Love? Fear? Respect? Whatever they need to show, the act of showing it very often gets called 'worship'. The word worship comes from an Anglo-Saxon word meaning 'honour' and was used by Anglo-Saxons to address people of high rank.

The act of worship strengthens and supports belief. This strengthened belief gives pointers on how to worship.

As common as belief and worship are and have been throughout human history, there is very little agreement on what worship is and how it should practised.

It can be unplanned with no set rules, and performed by an individual or a group, in public or in private.

It can be tightly controlled with set ceremonies and rituals, which should not be changed, which are part of belonging to a religion.

Often a holy place is used for worship. This may be a temple, church, mosque or any other religious building. It could just as easily be a house or somewhere outdoors.

During worship, the way people are feeling can sometimes be shown by what they do. Standing in human relations often indicates respect, kneeling can suggest submission – that the person you are kneeling to is more important than you.

Some religions require a qualified minister or priest; others do not.

When we look at worship in the major religions, we should not be surprised that there are differences between the religions or, more importantly, that not all people who claim to believe in the same **deity** (God) worship that deity in the same way.

CHRISTIAN WORSHIP

Christians believe that worship is at the centre of being a Christian. God created human beings, and gave them life. Christians show their thanks to God through worship.

Christian worship developed from Jewish worship. As Jesus was a practising Jew, this is not surprising. Unlike Judaism, whose holy day is Saturday, the Christian holy day is Sunday, the day on which Jesus rose from the dead.

Worship for Christians has always been closely linked to attendance at church services on Sundays. These services generally include singing, praying, readings from the Bible, preaching and meditation.

There is no standard form for Christian worship, though two major types can be identified. These are liturgical (formal) worship and non-liturgical (informal) worship. **Liturgy** means 'a form of public worship set out by a church or religion'.

So why is there no standard form of Christian worship?

The early Christian Church had some variety in worship, but also a great deal of worship that was common to all churches. Unfortunately, the unity of the early church did not last and disagreements appeared. Such a split often led to the group that broke away changing the way it worshipped, and created a new and distinct liturgy.

As a result, different Christian traditions, or **denominations**, have considerable differences in the way they worship, even though there are significant similarities. Holy Communion is a useful illustration of this situation. Most Christians remember the death of Christ in a service in which bread and wine are shared. Although most denominations keep this tradition, they give it different names. Roman Catholics call it the Mass, Anglicans the Eucharist, Protestants (such as Baptists) the Lord's Supper and the Orthodox Church calls it the Divine Liturgy.

Formal worship has a service book which sets out what the worshipper should do during the service.

Some people like this form of service because it is familiar and therefore comfortable. The service is predictable as the same rituals are followed at the same place in the worship. Many people enjoy ritual.

Informal worship is, as the name suggests, the opposite. There is no service book and worship proceeds in an unpredictable and spontaneous way. There is a lack of ritual.

Many people enjoy the variety and lack of formality.

ISLAMIC WORSHIP

The Qur'an teaches that human beings are worshippers and servants of Allah. Every part of a Muslim's life is following the will of Allah. The whole of a believer's life is therefore worship. **The Five Pillars of Islam** provide the framework to life that every believer must follow if they are genuinely submitting to Allah by putting faith first in everything they do.

1. Shahada
   The Islamic statement of belief: 'There is no god except Allah, and Muhammad is the prophet of Allah.'

2. Salat
   Five times a day – at dawn, noon, mid-afternoon, sunset, and before midnight – the muezzin climbs up to the minaret of a mosque and calls Muslims to prayer. Muslims can also pray individually at prayer time, wherever they happen to be.

3. Zakat
   Prescribed charity, to be used for the benefit of the poor, is calculated annually at 2.5 per cent of an individual's cash wealth.

4. Saum
   A dawn-to-dusk fast from all food and drink during the month of Ramadan, which is compulsory for all, from the age of puberty, unless they have a good reason for not fasting.

5. Hajj
   Hajj is a pilgrimage to Mecca which should be performed at least once during a person's lifetime by those who can afford it.

BUDDHIST WORSHIP

Buddhists follow the Buddha's example. They do not worship a God but look for personal enlightenment, the full realisation of the Buddha's teaching. They worship at a shrine in their home or in a temple.

All worship is focused on a shrine. A shrine will contain an image of the Buddha, candles and an incense burner. The light from the candles represents enlightenment. The smell of the incense, as it fills the shrine, represents the spread of dhamma, the teachings of the Buddha, throughout the world.

In Buddhist countries, there are many temples where people can make offerings of flowers and incense for the shrine and food for the monks. **Mantras** may be chanted either aloud or in their own head. Mantras are sacred words, chants or sounds which are repeated during meditation and are believed to have a spiritual effect on the individual.

During worship Buddhists may use prayer beads, wheels or flags. Prayer beads are used to count the number of times the mantra is repeated. Prayer wheels have mantras written down and placed inside the wheel. Spinning the wheel repeats the mantra. Prayer flags have mantras written on them. Prayers are repeated each time the flag moves in the wind.

HINDU WORSHIP

Puja – daily worship – takes place in a Mandir, or temple. Food, drink and prayers are offered to a picture or a statue of a god or goddess. Prayer involves the chanting of mantras. Yantras – diagrams of the universe – are used to aid meditation in Hinduism. The worship of the picture of the god or goddess is the most important part of the ceremony.

Worship can take place either at home or in a Mandir. These may range from a simple village hut to a grand building but all of them are called Mandirs. Many homes have a shrine, a ledge or alcove for a religious image, where the family worships. There is no formal service. Worship is individual rather than communal and involves personal offerings to the god.

JEWISH WORSHIP

Jewish worship consists of prayer, study of the **Torah** (the body of teaching in the Hebrew Bible) and the celebration of festivals. Prayer can be public or private. Devout Jews are expected to pray privately three times a day – in the morning, afternoon and evening.

Public worship takes place in the synagogue, usually on a Saturday morning. The Shema – the

Jewish statement of faith – is repeated twice daily, 'when you lie down and when you rise', and forms a major part of the prayers during the morning and evening services in the synagogue. Originally, the Shema was recited by the individual at sunrise and sunset.

The Sabbath (Saturday) is viewed as a most important observance in Judaism. This day of rest was ordered by God in the Ten Commandments to be a day for rest and worship without distraction from the world, when Jews forget the cares of their daily life and concentrate on their family and their faith.

SIKH WORSHIP

Sikhs can pray anytime and anywhere, but they believe group worship has benefits. They worship God in an abstract form. They do not have pictures or statues of God, as they believe God is visible in the congregation.

Any building where the Sikh scriptures, the Guru Granth Sahib, are kept, is a Sikh place of worship. They are called 'Gurdwara', which means 'the door that leads to the guru'.

Services in the Gurdwara are mainly held on Sundays in the UK. Readings from the Guru Granth Sahib are used with reciting and singing groups of hymns taken from Guru Granth Sahib, called 'Keertan'. At the end of the service, food is offered to the congregation.

Sikhs do not have priests. Any Sikh can lead the prayers, and recite the scriptures to the congregation.

ACTIVITY

1. Write a brief account of how the two major religions you are studying worship.

2. What are the similarities and differences in the way these two religions worship?

The meaning of important religious festivals

Religious festivals are events of special importance to members of a specific religion. They are usually celebrated on a yearly basis. Dates of the festivals can change each year because the calendar when they were first set was not accurate

CHRISTIAN FESTIVALS

Lent, Easter and Christmas are the main religious festivals of the Christian year.

- **Lent** is the forty-day lead up to Easter. It remembers the forty days that Jesus spent in the wilderness.
- **Easter** commemorates the death and resurrection of Jesus.
- **Christmas** celebrates the birth of Jesus.

ISLAMIC FESTIVALS

Islam has two major religious festivals:

- **Id-al-Fitr**, which is celebrated at the end of the month of Ramadan.
- **Id al-Adha**, which is celebrated at the end of the Hajj.

BUDDHIST FESTIVALS

The main Buddhist festival of the year is Wesak – the celebration of the Buddha's birth, enlightenment and death.

HINDU FESTIVALS

Some of the key Hindu festivals are:

- **Diwali**, often referred to as the Festival of Lights. Candles and lamps are lit as a greeting to Laksmi goddess of wealth. Gifts are exchanged and festive meals are prepared during Diwali.
- **Holi**, originally an agricultural festival to celebrate the arrival of spring, it now provides an opportunity for Hindus to misbehave in ways they normally would not.
- **Navaratri**, one of the greatest Hindu festivals, which lasts for nine days. It symbolises the triumph of good over evil.

JEWISH FESTIVALS

Festivals celebrate historic events that have played a significant part in creating the identity of the Jewish people. The major festivals are:

- **Passover**, commemorating the Jewish exodus from slavery in Egypt.
- **Shabouth**, commemorating the giving of the 10 commandments on Mount Sinai.
- **Sukkoth**, commemorating the autumn harvest festival.
- **Rosh Hashanah**, the Jewish New Year.
- **Yom Kippur**, the Day of Atonement. A day for fasting, confessing sins and asking God for forgiveness.

SIKH FESTIVALS

Baisakhi is the festival which celebrates Sikh New Year and the founding of the Sikh community, known as the Khalsa. Diwali is also celebrated by Sikhs.

Gurpurbs are Sikh festivals which celebrate the lives of the Gurus. The lives of ten Gurus are celebrated. The most important celebrations are:

- the birthday of Guru Nanak;
- the birthday of Guru Gobind Singh;
- the martyrdom of Guru Arjan Dev;
- the martyrdom of Guru Teg Bahadur.

ACTIVITY

1. What are the main festivals of the two main religions you are studying?
2. How are they celebrated?

Rites of passage

A **rite of passage** marks the movement from one stage of a person's life to the next. They are often associated with the transition from childhood to adulthood. Most world religions recognise this event with some sort of ceremony.

CHRISTIANITY

Many Christian denominations recognise Confirmation in the Roman Catholic, Anglican and Orthodox Churches, where infant baptism is the norm. It is an opportunity to take personal responsibility for the promises others made for them at their baptism. It signals that the individual is now a full member of the Church. The ceremony is normally conducted by a bishop and often involves 'laying on of hands' to symbolise the giving and receiving of the Holy Spirit. Other Protestant churches see Confirmation as a rite of passage to full Christian participation and not as a sacrament.

The age at which confirmation takes place varies. The Orthodox Church confirms infants immediately after their baptism. Western denominations prefer those being confirmed to be at least old enough to know what they are promising.

ISLAM

Islam is the largest single religious group to circumcise boys. In Islam, circumcision is also known as *tahara*, which means 'purification'. Most Muslims view circumcision as the introduction to Islam and a signal that the individual now belongs.

The age at which circumcision takes place depends on the family, region and country. Seven is a popular age, though it can vary from the seventh day after birth to the onset of puberty. Circumcisions are usually carried out in a clinic or hospital. The circumciser does not have to be Muslim, but must be medically qualified.

In some countries, boys have to recite the whole of the Qur'an before they are circumcised.

BUDDHISM
In some Buddhist countries, boys between the ages of 8 and 20 enter a monastery for a short time as a trainee monk, or novice, called a 'Samenera'. They help to run the monastery.

HINDUISM
The Sacred Thread ceremony, Upanayana, in the past took place when a boy left home to live with his guru. Today it marks the reaching of puberty. The boy's head is shaved and he is then presented to the household gods. He and his father make an offering and, he is given the sacred thread.

JUDAISM
When a child has reached the age of legal maturity, 13 for a boy and 12 for a girl, (girls are assumed to mature earlier), Bar Mitzvah and Bat Mitzvah respectively are celebrated. Their achievement of maturity means they take an active part in religious activity and are obliged to observe the Ten Commandments.

SIKHISM
When a Sikh boy reaches puberty (at around 14 to 16 years old), an initiation ceremony called the Dastaar Bandi (wearing of the first turban) is held. After this, he is allowed to join the 'Khalsa' – those who have been baptised as Sikhs.

He will also observe the Five Ks – symbols of his faith – in his everyday appearance (the Five Ks are uncut hair, steel bracelet, wooden comb, cotton underwear and steel dagger).

During the ceremony, a special solution of sugar and water, known as Amrit, is prepared in an iron bowl while prayers are recited.

ACTIVITY

1. All the major world religions have rites of passage. Why do you think religions see this as so important?

2. Explain why the rites of passage in the two world religions that you are studying are different.

Beliefs about holy scripture

REVELATION AND AUTHORITY
Revelation is the process of making something clearly understood through communication with God. It can come directly from a god through worship or direct personal experience, or through someone or something else such as a religious leader or **holy scripture**.

Holy scripture reveals what God is like and tells believers how they should live. For some these revelations are the actual words of God which can never be changed. Others accept that they were inspired by God but must be re-interpreted over time to adapt to change in the way the world is.

The fact that holy scripture is the revealed word of God gives it great authority.

CHRISTIANITY
The Bible is the Christian holy book. It is divided into the Old and New Testaments. Parts of the writing contained in the Old Testament are also sacred to Jewish and Muslim people.

Figure 4.4: A Bar Mitzvah, like other rites of passage, signals the beginning of adulthood.

The New Testament is unique to Christians. It explains that God sent his son, Jesus Christ, to renew the relationship between God and man, which had been damaged by man's evil.

Jesus was executed on a cross as a criminal by the Romans and, according to Christian teaching, rose from the dead after three days, before eventually ascending to heaven to sit on God's right hand.

ISLAM

Islam was founded on the ministry of a man named Muhammad, the last prophet to be sent by Allah. Other prophets who preceded Muhammad are recognised by Islam and include: Ibrahim (Abraham), Musa (Moses) and Isa (Jesus).

The Muslim holy scriptures are called the Qur'an. Muslims believe that the Qur'an is the actual word of Allah and was dictated to Muhammad. The only version of the Qur'an which is accepted as true is the original version, written in Arabic.

BUDDHISM

There are a large number of religious texts and scriptures in Buddhism, which are divided into two categories: texts believed to be the actual sayings of Lord Buddha, and texts which comment on the sayings of the Lord Buddha.

HINDUISM

The main Hindu scriptures are **The Vedas**, which describe the story of the Vedic gods. The Ramayana is a collection of epic poems about Rama, a hero worshipped as an incarnation of Vishnu and Sita, the wife of Rama, regarded as an ideal of womanhood; the Mahabharata, which tells about civil wars in the ninth century BC, and the Puranas, a collection of stories about histories, legends of gods and heroes.

SIKHISM

The collection of Sikh holy scriptures is called the Guru Granth Sahib. This is a collection of teachings and writings by Guru Nanak and other Gurus, as well as Sikh, Hindu and Muslim saints.

The text is not only the holy scripture for Sikhs, but is also seen by them as the living embodiment of the Ten Gurus, and therefore the living word of God. The role of Guru Granth Sahib, as a source or guide of prayer, is crucial.

JUDAISM

The most holy Jewish book is the Torah (the first five books of the Hebrew Bible), which was given by God to Moses on Mount Sinai. The Torah and the Talmud provide the Jewish people with moral rules for living. Following these rules is central to the Jewish religion.

STRETCH AND CHALLENGE

An 18th century author and philosopher François-Marie Arouet, better known by his pen name Voltaire, wrote:

'If God did not exist, it would be necessary to invent him.'

What do you think he meant by this? How far does the information about worship in this chapter support his statement?

SUMMARY

This unit has explored the following points.

- What worship is and why some people need to worship.
- How different religions practise worship.
- The importance of festivals in different religions.
- The importance of ceremonies surrounding rites of passage, in different religions.
- The beliefs of different religions about holy scripture.

Figure 4.5: All world religions have a collection of writings. Only some believe they are the direct word of God.

Unit 4.3 Religion and personal relationships

IN THIS UNIT YOU WILL LEARN ABOUT:

- the ways religious beliefs can influence relationships within the family
- religious attitudes towards marriage and divorce
- religious attitudes towards sexual relationships
- religious attitudes towards race, other religions and gender.

KEY CONCEPTS

Religious laws
Tolerance
Prejudice
Equality

THE CHRISTIAN FAMILY

The Book of Deuteronomy in the Old Testament identifies the importance of the family in religion and the part it should play in promoting and discussing belief in God.

> 'Love the Lord your God with all your heart and with all your soul and with all your strength. These commandments that I give you today are to be on your hearts. Impress them on your children. Talk about them when you sit at home and when you walk along the road, when you lie down and when you get up.'
>
> (Source: Deuteronomy 6:5-7, New Internation Version, Hodder & Stoughton)

The family is the place where people are taught about God and learn the basic beliefs of their religion. The family plays a vital role in God's plans, because it is here that belief in God is developed.

Because the family is the vehicle for bringing up children, introducing children to religion is a job for parents long before the Church gets involved. It is in the family that children learn how to behave in ways that are accepted by believers. Children of believers are more likely to become active believers themselves, because they see it as a 'natural' part of life.

Children born into a Christian family are therefore more likely to go to church. Their first visit might be for their baptism. During this ceremony, parents and godparents promise to bring the child up as a Christian. As part of this, the child will be taught to pray and may take part in religious ceremonies in the home.

As the child gets older, parents may choose to send them to a faith school. Faith schools place more emphasis on learning about Christianity and living a Christian life. This is intended to reinforce the messages from the family.

Attending Church will bring the family into contact with people who think the same way. Mixing with other Christians enables children to talk with, and learn from, others. Group worship can also strengthen individual belief and encourage people to put their beliefs into practice by actually becoming involved in the work of the church.

THE MUSLIM FAMILY

The structure of Islamic family life is based on four principles from the Qur'an and traditions from the life of the Prophet Muhammad. These are handed down from generation to generation. They are:

- That family life is the basis of Islamic society.
- That family life provides a wholesome outlet for the sexual desire.
- That family life is where the human virtues of love, kindness, mercy are taught.
- That without family life, society would be lawless.

Parents have a responsibility to bring their children up to be good Muslims. As a result, children are taught about Islam from a very young age. They hear stories about the life of the Prophet Muhammad and may learn short passages from the Qur'an. They will also learn how to pray, what to eat, how to dress and how to behave.

Family life is seen as a two-way process. Parents are required to provide for their children and, in return, children have a duty to respect and obey their parents for the whole of their lives. It makes no difference how old the children are – their parents remain their parents. A child's first duty is to Allah, the second is to its parents.

This emphasis on their duty towards parents means that as parents age, children have a duty to look after them. This results in extended families where families live close to one another, sometimes in the same house, to enable younger family members to care for the older family members.

The Muslim community reinforces the family. Children go to the madrasa (the mosque school) every day after they have finished at their state school. Here, they learn to read and write Arabic and to recite verses from the Qur'an.

The mosque can also provide help to the family. The Imam can give support in marital difficulties and financial support can be provided from the mosque Zakat fund in times of hardship.

OTHER RELIGIONS AND FAMILIES

Buddhism. Buddhism is not a family-centred religion, and does not have standard models of the family. As a result, Buddhist families reflect the cultural and religious values and customs of the society they live in.

Buddhism's main contribution to the family are the Five Precepts, which can be used to regulate family life. These govern marriage, roles and expectations, sexuality, children, and divorce.

Hinduism. The traditional family in Hindu society is the extended family. Older members of the family take important decisions and offer guidance to younger members. The extended family offers support for the elderly, the disabled and the less well-off.

Children are expected to look after their parents in their old age. Social trends suggest that the extended family is becoming less popular, especially outside India. Western values and the nuclear family are replacing the traditional Hindu family.

Sikhism. Most Sikh children live in an extended family with parents, grandparents, uncles, and cousins in one house. Sikhism likens the love of God to that of a mother and a protective and caring father.

Judaism. For Jews, the home is more important than the synagogue. Everything which is central to being a Jew can be found in the home. Prayers will be said three times a day, and before and after meals. Jews celebrate the Sabbath in their homes.

The home is so important for Jews because for many centuries, the Jews have been persecuted for their religion. They find security in the home and in the community. For many years, Jewish children were not allowed to marry anyone other than another Jew. The idea of family is still very strong today.

ACTIVITY

With reference to the two world religions you are studying:

1. Write down as many ideas as you can to show the relationship between religion and the family.

2. Describe the responsibility that parents have to children and the responsibility the children have to parents.

3. Make lists of the advantages and disadvantages of living in an extended family. Would you like to live in an extended family? Give reasons for your choice.

Religious attitudes towards divorce

CHRISTIAN ATTITUDES

Marriage is important for Christians, because they believe it is part of God's plan for human beings. It provides mutual support for men and women and it provides a supportive situation for children.

All Christians see marriage as being for life. Jesus taught that marriage was something agreed before God, and that man could not end it. Divorce was forbidden.

Unfortunately, it is a fact that some marriages fail. The Church needs to have a view on what to do if this happens. Most Churches, except the Roman Catholic Church, now accept divorce. The only way to end a marriage in the Catholic Church is to put forward reasons why the marriage should never have happened in the first place.

Remarriage has always been allowed if one of the partners in a marriage has died. Since 2002, the Church of England has accepted that in some cases, a divorcee can marry again in church whilst their previous partner is still alive. Most other Christian Churches have joined them in this view.

Under UK law, a vicar is able to marry a couple as long as there is no legal reason why the couple in question should not marry. They are advised by the Church to use this power with care and discretion, but ultimately the decision rests with the clergy member.

ISLAMIC ATTITUDES

Islam supports the principle of lifelong marriage but is realistic enough to realise that this is not always possible for all people. It also takes the view that there is no purpose to be served by making couples stay together in a failed relationship.

Islam allows divorce if there is no alternative, although it does not like the process, and divorce is highly discouraged. It should always be a last resort after strenuous efforts have been made to avoid it.

The grounds on which the Qur'an allows divorce are the failure of one or both parties to live up to their marital duties and to live with each other in kindness, peace and compassion.

The divorcing couple must wait three months, known as 'iddah'. There are two reasons for this. The first is to ensure that the woman is not pregnant. The second is to allow a member of each partner's family to try to bring about a reconciliation.

A man must support his wife until she remarries, unless she has divorced him through no fault on his part, in which case he does not have to support her and she must repay her wedding gift, which could be something of great value. In all cases, the man is still responsible for supporting their children.

OTHER RELIGIONS' ATTITUDES

Buddhism. The Buddhist idea of marriage is different from that of most other religions, as it is usually performed without the help of a priest at the ceremony.

Divorce is allowed in Buddhism because anything that might get in the way of enlightenment, like a broken relationship, should be removed. Divorce, in some cases, can therefore be viewed as a positive step in the path towards self-knowledge.

Any obstacles to divorce could be seen as working against the religious guidelines established by the Buddha himself.

Hinduism. The Hindu religion does not approve of divorce because it views marriage as a holy agreement which should not be put aside for personal reasons. In the past, women had few rights once they were married, and had to do what their husband's told them to do.

The Hindu Marriage Act allows legal divorce and sets out reasons, such as cruelty, adultery and desertion, which would be grounds for a divorce. Divorce rates in Hindu society are much lower than those in the West. This is not because marriages are better: many couples do not divorce because it is still seen as a shameful act bringing social disapproval.

Sikhism. As with the Hindu religion, Sikhs do not approve of divorce, and for the same reasons. As with Hindus, the law gives Sikhs the right to ask a court to grant a divorce.

Divorce is only reluctantly accepted and it causes great harm to a family's pride. Strenuous efforts are made by the family to prevent a split. Remarriage is allowed after a divorce.

Judaism. The Jewish attitude to divorce is that it is an unfortunate fact of life. Judaism accepts that divorce is preferable to the bitterness of a couple remaining together when their relationship has broken down.

This does not mean that Jews do not take divorce seriously. Jewish law discourages divorce and the process is complicated, to try to ensure that people do not divorce without good reason. Couples are forced to attempt reconciliation, but if that fails, they can split up.

Divorce is not something to celebrate, but equally it is not seen as shameful. People are encouraged to marry again.

Religious attitudes towards sexual relationships

Since the middle of the 20th century, attitudes to human sexuality have undergone major changes. This has placed a strain on the Churches in their role as guides to what is right and wrong.

The decline in Church membership has weakened the moral authority of the Churches and presented them with a dilemma. Do they persist in championing their long-held views about morality because its truth is everlasting and as relevant now as it was 2000 years ago? Or do they adapt their views to accommodate the requirements of a world unrecognisable from the one in which these laws were made?

Both arguments form part of the present attitudes of the different religions regarding sexual matters.

THE CHRISTIAN ATTITUDE

Christians believe that sex within marriage is a gift from God. Sex outside marriage is generally considered to be wrong, although there are variations in how different Christian denominations view this.

Christians are in favour of abstinence before marriage because of the risks of pregnancy and sexually transmitted infections.

The Roman Catholic Church has the most definite view on pre-marital sex. In its view, sex outside marriage is a major sin. Other Protestant Churches, such as the Church of England, though preferring couples to be married, are more tolerant of cohabitation.

Cohabitation – the practice of couples living together without marrying – is increasing. This causes ethical problems for the Churches. Many Protestant denominations tolerate it if it is seen as the first step towards marriage. Some liberal Christians even believe that pre-marital sex is acceptable if a couple has plans to marry.

There is more agreement on the other questions of sex outside marriage: adultery and promiscuity. Adultery – to have a sexual relationship with a partner outside your marriage – is totally unacceptable. This is specifically forbidden by one of the Ten Commandments given to Moses: 'You shall not commit adultery'.

Promiscuity – behaviour characterised by casual and indiscriminate sexual intercourse, often with many people – is totally unacceptable to Christians.

THE ISLAMIC ATTITUDE

Islam does not share the contradictions of Christianity. Muslims are clear that sex can only exist inside marriage: anything else is considered to be adultery. To maintain this, Islam does not allow couples who are not married to each other to have any privacy. Pre-marital sex is specifically forbidden by the Qur'an and is punishable by flogging.

Figure 4.6: Muslims of both sexes are expected to dress discreetly.

Dress is important in Islam. Muslims are expected not to dress provocatively or behave in a way that could be described as sexually suggestive. Clothes are baggy to hide the contours of the body. Many women cover their hair when they go out.

Once children reach puberty they are segregated from the opposite sex, and can only mix with them when they are chaperoned.

Muslims believe that promiscuity will cause a breakdown of society. If they are listening to Allah, they will know right from wrong and be able to resist temptation.

Muslims see adultery as the worst act that a person can commit. This is a major threat to the family and is difficult to forgive because of the enormity of the betrayal. There are punishments for adultery: a severe flogging is laid down in the Qur'an, but sometimes the death penalty is inflicted.

OTHER RELIGIONS

Buddhism. Buddhists believe that sexual urges should be controlled, or they will cause suffering. They do not believe in sex before marriage.

Hinduism. Hindus believe that sex outside marriage is wrong and can damage spiritual development.

Sikhism. Sex before marriage is forbidden. Sikhs try to avoid sexual temptations by segregating the sexes.

Judaism. Sex before marriage is forbidden. Sex is a gift from God, and is not just for creating children but also to express love.

Figure 4.7: Sometimes religious symbols have been used to promote prejudice.

Religious attitudes towards race, other religions and gender

Prejudice and discrimination are issues which challenge society. 'Prejudice' means to make your mind up about someone or something without good reason.

Most people have prejudices of some sort. It might be food we refuse to eat even though we have never tasted it, or a football club we do not like because they are the closest rivals to the club we do like. Neither of these is particularly damaging, though the second example could lead to problems for some people.

Discrimination takes prejudice to an active level. This is when people are treated differently or badly because of prejudice, for instance refusing someone a job, equal treatment or a civil right because of their race, gender or sexual orientation.

Religious attitudes to prejudice and discrimination come from religious teachings on equality and justice. Religions teach that all people are equal, and so have equal human rights.

THE CHRISTIAN ATTITUDE

To racism

Christian Churches base their position on prejudice and discrimination on the two ideas of creation and redemption. Christians believe that *all* human beings are made in the image of God. This means that there is only *one* human race. The modern idea of 'race' is nothing more than small variations on a single theme.

When Jesus was crucified, his sacrifice broke down the barriers between man and God. This is called redemption, and this process made trivial differences between human 'races' meaningless.

In the past, the Christian Churches have been racist, but the mainstream churches now clearly stand against prejudice and discrimination. This is not true of all Christian sects, and some still promote views of white supremacy.

To other religions

Christians in general feel that individuals should be free to follow their own beliefs through their own religion, or no religion at all.

The statement by St John's Gospel, quoting Jesus's statement: 'I am the way, the truth, and the life; no one goes to the Father except by me' causes some difference in the way individuals react to other religions.

Some Christians who take this statement as the literal word of God believe that, as no one who is not a Christian can go to heaven, they have a responsibility to try to convert non-Christians to Christianity.

Christians who do not take the Bible as the literal word of God see all religions as equal. None are superior, none are wrong and all will lead to God.

To sexism

Women have been almost invisible throughout much of recorded history. Men have dominated society and women have held second-class status. Religion has had a major role to play in this inequality.

Despite major reforms throughout the nineteenth and twentieth centuries, women are still a struggling against the 'glass ceiling' to achieve full equality. This is still evident in the Christian Church, where there is a major difference of opinion about the role of women in the Church.

The controversy, as usual, hinges around different quotations from the Bible, and how literally they should be taken. There are three major views.

Evangelical Protestant Christians believe that men and women should have different roles in the home and the Church. They believe the Bible is the word of God and is not to be interpreted, but taken literally.

This leads them to the belief that husbands are superior to wives, who should be homemakers who can attend church, but only men can lead the Church.

The majority of Protestants, like the Church of England, believe that men and women have equality in the Church and the home. Roman Catholics support this view of equality in life but not in Church leadership, where they refuse to allow women to become priests.

THE ISLAMIC ATTITUDE

To racism

The Muslim attitude to racism has marked similarities to the Christian attitude, and for very much the same reasons. They believe that racism is wrong because everyone is part of Allah's creation, therefore they should be treated with respect. This is an attitude confirmed in the Qur'an and by the Prophet Muhammad.

Today, Muslims include everyone who believes in Allah into the Ummah, the worldwide brotherhood and community of Muslims, regardless of gender, wealth or colour.

To other religions

Islam is tolerant of other religions even though its followers believe that everyone is born a Muslim. This is because they accept human free will, which allows people to choose other religions.

Muslims also believe that Islam is the only way to Allah and only those who accept Islam will go to heaven. This view is based on the belief that Qur'an is the third and final attempt by Allah to tell people how to lead their lives.

The previous attempts, which gave rise to the Torah and the Christian Gospels, have been distorted and changed. The Qur'an alone is the unchanged word of Allah. The prospect of hell for all those who do not believe prompts Muslims to perform the duty of attempting to help non-Muslims to learn about Islam, so that they too can go to heaven.

To sexism

Despite what many people may think, Islam sees women as the equals of men. This is because they were both created by Allah. The distinction is that equality does not mean that they are identical. They are physically different, and these physical differences define the different roles of men and women.

Women are expected to marry and have children. This probably means that women will stay at home, although the Qur'an does not forbid women from working. The needs of the family mean that women worship at home and do not have to attend the mosque. At the mosque, men and women worship separately but in the same way. Women are also expected to go on Hajj (the pilgrimage to Mecca).

Muslim men have equal responsibility with their wives for bringing up children to be good Muslims. Many help in the home.

OTHER RELIGIONS' ATTITUDES

Buddhism. Feeling superior to others is wrong. When enlightenment is achieved, there is no notion of male or female. The principles of 'Right Speech and Action' limit prejudiced speech and promote tolerance and consideration to others.

Buddhism believes in equality: Buddha allowed the ordination of women, and all races and nationalities are welcome in Buddhist communities.

Hinduism. Hindus have a duty to respect everyone, because all are created by God. Both sexes can achieve release from the cycle of rebirth.

Hindus are tolerant of other religions because of the diversity of their own religion. Hindu women can be educated and own property. It is believed that people prosper when women are properly treated, but not where they are badly treated.

Sikhism. Sikhs believe that all men and women are equal, as all are children of God. This makes it wrong to discriminate on any grounds.

As Sikhs believe that everyone worships the same God, they are tolerant of all religions. Women are respected because the future of the human race depends on them.

Judaism. Jews believe that God created everyone in his own image. Adam, the first man, was created from variously-coloured dust collected from all over the world, so the father of mankind represented all nations.

Social justice is more pleasing to God than religious ceremonies. Jews have for centuries been victims of persecution and genocide and this has led to an awareness of the need for racial and religious tolerance.

Men and women are regarded as equals, but in orthodox communities women cannot be Rabbis and have to sit separately in the synagogue. Progressive Jews believe women should be allowed to be Rabbis and families worship together.

ACTIVITY

With reference to the two world religions you are studying:

1. Explain why religion is opposed to prejudice and discrimination.

2. 'Religion has little problem in accepting other races and religions, but has more difficulty with the role of women.' How far do you agree? Give detailed reasons for your answer.

STRETCH AND CHALLENGE

The religions included in this unit were all founded hundreds of years ago when the society they served was very different from modern society.

How far are beliefs and religious regulations, which were appropriate for their time, still relevant to the 21st century?

SUMMARY

This unit has explored the following points.

- How religious belief can influence family relationships.
- The attitude of different religions towards marriage and divorce.
- The attitude of different religions towards sexual relationships.
- The attitude of different religions towards race, other religions and gender.

Unit 4.4 Religious beliefs about good and evil

IN THIS UNIT YOU WILL LEARN ABOUT:

- religious beliefs as to why there is suffering in the world
- the difference between natural and moral evil
- religious attitudes towards overcoming or coping with suffering
- how people cope with suffering through a belief in a better afterlife.

KEY CONCEPTS

Natural and moral evil
Human and animal suffering
Stewardship
Responsibility
Reward
Punishment

A quick look at a newspaper or a brief viewing of a news broadcast might make you feel that everything that is happening in the world is bad. Some of it appears to be positively evil. It would seem evident that this evil causes a great deal of the suffering in the world.

WHAT IS EVIL?

Like many words, 'evil' can mean many different things and refer to many different situations. Consider these questions:

- Is it possible to arrive at an agreed definition of evil?
- Is all evil the same – or is some worse?
- Where does evil come from – human beings, God, the Devil, or natural forces?

ACTIVITY

In small groups, discuss the questions above and prepare a brief report outlining the conclusions reached. More importantly, outline some of the problems that had to be resolved before conclusions could be reached.

WHY IS EVIL A PROBLEM FOR RELIGIONS?

Evil is a problem for religions because it asks the question:

'How can evil exist in a world created by an all-knowing, all-powerful and loving God?'

Atheists argue that the existence of evil should be impossible if God really exists: the fact that evil does exist proves that God does not. At the very least, religion requires an explanation of why God allows evil to continue in the world. Some of the questions raised by this are:

- Why does a good God allow suffering that is not good?
- A loving God would not let humans suffer – that would be the act of a cruel God, wouldn't it?
- An all-powerful God could stop suffering. If suffering exists, can God be all-powerful?
- An all-knowing God knows humans suffer, so why does God allow it to continue?

Figure 4.8: The suffering of innocents raises questions about the nature of God.

- How can God allow innocents such as children suffer?

Some suggested answers to these questions include the argument that evil is the price for humans to have **free will**. Suffering is something that is part of God's purpose, which is beyond human understanding. It is also an appropriate punishment for human wrongdoing.

St Thomas Aquinas, a 13th-century Roman Catholic monk, attempted to explain the presence of evil. He argued that God did not create evil when he created the world. He described evil as the absence of good, just as darkness is the absence of light.

As a result, evil is seen as something lacking goodness. As human beings are not absolutely good, they will do things that are not good, and this creates evil. Therefore, people create evil because God allows human beings free will, and some use this free will to create evil.

ACTIVITY

1. What are the problems that suffering causes believers in a good God?

2. What are the explanations for suffering in a world created by a good God?

3. Are you convinced by the explanations offered, or do you feel the problems raise a serious question about God? Give reasons for your answer.

THE DIFFERENCES BETWEEN NATURAL AND MORAL EVIL

Moral evil

Moral evil requires someone to do something which they know is not right. It is caused by an action, or lack of action, by a person, which causes harm to a third party. It is an event for which someone can be held responsible or to blame.

Not all moral evil is deliberate – some is accidental. Deliberate acts of moral evil can be caused by hatred, greed, selfishness and other emotions. Examples of the types of behaviour this can lead to are murder, rape, theft and war.

Accidental acts of moral evil can be caused by ignorance, laziness or thoughtlessness: for example, the driver who falls asleep at the wheel and kills others in a road traffic accident.

Moral evil is the most difficult evil for believers to come to terms with, because they ask why God would create a world where this kind of evil has a place.

Natural evil

Natural evil is not caused by the action or inaction of anyone. It only has victims, and is generally taken to be the result of natural processes. It is generally accepted that no one is to blame for such natural disasters, as they are simply a natural result of living on the planet.

Interestingly, insurance companies often refer to such events as 'acts of God' and exclude them from insurance cover!

Examples of natural evil could include diseases, such as cancer, and natural disasters, such as earthquakes and hurricanes.

Is there a real difference between moral and natural evil?

The difference between moral evil and natural evil is commonly accepted, but is it a real difference? People can be labelled evil because they have the free will to choose not to be good.

But nature has no choice. Natural disasters occur because that is what happens in nature. Natural events can be tragic and devastating, but are they really evil? The only way they can be seen as evil is if there is an all-powerful God who could stop them if he wanted.

Our growing understanding of the impact of human activity on the natural world has also called into question whether there is a real difference between natural and moral evil. If global warming is really the result of human activity, and as global warming causes natural disasters, is this natural evil or moral evil? If human beings choose to continue to emit climate-changing gases, is this not a deliberate action and therefore moral evil?

ACTIVITY

1. What are the differences between moral evil and natural evil?

2. Given man's impact on the natural world, is there any point in making a distinction between moral and natural evil?

Religious attitudes to suffering

IS THERE A POINT TO SUFFERING?

As suggested above, there are a number of reasons why believers are confused as to a loving God who inflicts suffering onto his people. These reasons are based on the idea that suffering is pointless and cruel.

There is another point of view. Some people, including believers in God, do not agree that suffering has no point. They believe that suffering can bring out the best in people, both individually and collectively.

Natural disasters frequently produce stories of individual heroism, where people risk their own lives to save others'. Individuals go to great lengths and often risk their lives to achieve personal goals.

Suffering can also be seen as a test. It is relatively easy to hold a principle when life is not difficult. When holding that principle is challenged and leads to suffering, it is only those with strong commitment who will remain faithful to their principles.

> ### ACTIVITY
>
> How convincing do you find the justifications for suffering as part of life?

Christianity

Christianity sees suffering in life as 'a cross we have to bear'. The difficulties we face and the hardships we endure are all part of the great plan and purpose of life itself and only God has a complete picture of this plan.

The most frequent explanation of suffering is free will. This is the belief that human beings are not simply puppets doing what God wants as he pulls their strings, and they are not robots following a pre-programmed path. They are free and have the ability to think and make decisions. They can decide to be good or not good. Human beings making conscious decisions to be bad cause much of the suffering in the world.

The basic method of dealing with the suffering of our earthly existence is to know that this existence is not the end, just the first step to a greater existence with God in the afterlife. The way people respond to this suffering could determine their situation in this afterlife.

Christians believe that God gave them the responsibility of caring for his creation. They were not to waste, exploit, or abuse his creation, but to care for it and use it in the service of God and fellow human beings. This idea is known as '**stewardship**'.

In the past Christians largely ignored animal suffering because they believed people were greatly superior to animals. Modern Christians think that unnecessary mistreatment of animals is both sinful and morally wrong.

Islam

Much like Christians, Muslims see suffering as part of life. Because of this, they consider it proper to try to make life better for themselves and others, but not to question the will of Allah.

Some Muslims see the suffering of life as part of the 'greater jihad' – the test of the way they live their life. It shows what kind of believers they really are: they will be judged by the way they respond to this test.

Muslims believe that Allah created the universe but not solely for people. They can use what Allah created but can never own it. Animals exist for the benefit of human beings but must be treated with kindness and compassion

Other religions

Buddhism. For Buddhists, suffering and misery are simply part of life in the same way as other emotions are part of life. The reason for this is desire. This is not evil desire, but any desire including the desire to live and even to breathe. This is something people are born with, and it stays with them throughout their life until it is overcome by following the Eight Fold Path.

That there is nothing in the religious texts and teachings of Buddhism that indicates that suffering is evil, or related to evil in any way.

To live in harmony with nature is a crucial Buddhist practice. If individuals harm other creatures or the environment they are really hurting themselves. They see humans and animals as closely related and believe that it is wrong to hurt or kill animals.

Hinduism. Hindus see the cause of suffering in life as being caused by human attachment to material things rather than the spiritual.

Suffering without an obvious cause is put down to sinful actions in a previous life. For a Hindu, the only things that are truly real are God and the soul. It is a Hindu's aim in life to realise this.

Hindus have great respect for the natural world. There are many specific teachings on environmental matters in Hindu scripture. The doctrine of ahimsa leads Hindus to treat animals well despite a general belief that animals are inferior to people.

Sikhism. Individuals who have too high an opinion of themselves behave selfishly, which leads to suffering. Despite God being in control of everything, he is not to blame for this suffering.

Sikhs believe that it is a mystery why God allows suffering to happen and why it seems to happen more to some people than others.

Sikhism believes God created the universe and the survival of all life forms are closely linked.

Judaism. Many Jews believe that suffering is a result of human free will. The prime cause of suffering in the world is the responsibility of Adam and Eve disobeying God. Suffering is also seen as a test of people's faith, punishment for sin and a part of God's purpose that is beyond human understanding.

Judaism teaches that the earth is God's. People are partners and co-workers in protecting the environment. Animals are part of this creation and should be treated with compassion. People must try to avoid causing pain to any living creature.

ACTIVITY

1. Make a brief note about the attitude to suffering of the two religions you are studying.

2. Compare this with the other major world religions. Identify where they agree and disagree.

Suffering and belief in an afterlife

For many believers, suffering is something to be endured because of the promise of a better life after death. There are a variety of different expectations both within and between religions.

THE CHRISTIAN VIEW

There are as many beliefs about the afterlife amongst Christians as there are types of Christians. However, some generalisations are possible. It is possible to say that the majority of Christians believe in the idea of heaven. In heaven, believers will be in the presence of God and free from suffering.

Most Christians also believe that they get to heaven because it is a gift from God, not something that is earned by good works. This belief is based on the words of St Paul: 'For it is by grace you have been saved, through faith'. Not all Christians believe this, and the belief that heaven is a reward for a good life is popular among Church members even in Churches that do not support it.

Figure 4.9: Pictures like this were painted inside churches to 'encourage' worshippers.

The alternative to heaven is hell – a place where sinners are punished. Fewer Christians believe in the existence of hell and some reject the idea completely.

Catholics believe that those who die with sins still unforgiven go to purgatory. This is a place of punishment where they stay until all their sins are forgiven.

Early Christians thought that those in heaven would be happy that sinners were being punished. This may explain why Christians today do not believe in hell. It does not sit comfortably with modern views of punishment.

THE ISLAMIC VIEW

Muslim beliefs have similarities to Christian beliefs, but they also have their own significant differences. On the Last Day – the Day of Judgement – resurrected humans will be judged by Allah.

The judgement will be based on how they have lived their lives. Where they are sent depends on the balance of the good and evil they have done in life. They will either be sent to heaven or hell. In heaven, they will enjoy eternal pleasures; in hell, they will endure torment.

On the Day of Judgement, all the resurrected will pass over hell on a narrow bridge in order to enter Paradise. Some fall, weighed down by their evil deeds. They will remain in hell forever.

OTHER RELIGIONS

Buddhism. Buddhists believe that after death, a person is either reborn into another life or enters nirvana. Reincarnation was described by the Buddha as the lighting of successive candles using the flame of the preceding candle.

Nirvana is the state of final liberation from the cycle of life and death. It is therefore the end of suffering. Is Nirvana a form of heaven, or simply the end of existence? The answer is not clear. Buddha said it was 'incomprehensible, indescribable, inconceivable'.

Hinduism. Hindus are most interested in bad karma which comes from things they should not have done. Bad karma will cause problems in the current life and the next.

Hindus therefore try to limit bad karma to achieve a better rebirth. The ultimate aim is to have no bad karma and to be released from the cycle of death and rebirth. This is known as 'Moksha'.

Sikhism. Sikhism follows the general Hindu belief in the cycle of rebirth. To Sikhs, life is not something to be endured, but it is an opportunity. Sikhs do not believe in a heaven or hell because they do not believe there is anywhere else to go or to be sent to. Human birth is the only way for a Sikh to find salvation.

Judaism. Unlike Christianity and Islam, Jewish literature has little to say about what happens after death. It does have views on the afterlife, but not one view which is officially agreed on.

In Judaism, the equivalent of heaven is the Garden of Eden. It is generally described as a place of great joy and peace. There is another view of a more spiritual garden with none of the pleasures of earthly life.

ACTIVITY

'Suffering in this life is compensated for by the promise of an afterlife.'

1. How far is this true for the two world religions you are studying?

2. How far is this true for the other major world religions?

SUMMARY

This unit has explored the following points.

- How different religions attempt to explain the existence of suffering in the world.
- Religious ideas about evil.
- Attitudes of different religions towards human and animal suffering.
- Attitudes of different religions towards beliefs about suffering and an afterlife.

Unit 4.5 Religious belief about modern dilemmas

IN THIS UNIT YOU WILL LEARN:

- religious and non-religious viewpoints about the origin of the universe and human beings
- differences both within and outside religion towards issues such as abortion and euthanasia
- religious and non-religious attitudes to war, violence and pacifism
- religious and non-religious attitudes towards the poor and needy.

KEY CONCEPTS

Science versus religion
Ethics
Warfare
Wealth
Poverty

RELIGIOUS VIEWPOINTS

Unsurprisingly, some religions that believe in a god also believe that their god had a part in creating the universe. These creation stories often describe creation as a deliberate act by one or more gods. Many creation stories have features that are similar.

The term 'creation myth' is sometimes used by people who do not believe the stories. 'Myth' implies that stories are fiction and made up. However, many believers do believe in the literal truth of what they see as the word of God.

CREATION STORIES

Judaism, Christianity and Islam

Judaism and Christianity have identical creation stories, as they share the book of Genesis in the Torah and Bible. Islam has a very similar story, with a few distinctions.

The story in Genesis describes how God created the universe in six days and rested on the seventh.

On day one God created day and night. The next day the sky and the water were separated. The third day saw the creation of the land and sea. On the fourth day the sun, moon and stars were created, and on the fifth day birds and fish were created. The last to be created, on the sixth day, were land animals and humans. Then God rested.

The Islamic story in the Qur'an is very similar to that of Christian creation but does not relate the events of creation to specific days.

The story of the creation of Adam the first man, and Eve the first woman, is almost identical. In both stories God made Adam out of soil and breathed life into him. Adam was taken to live in the Garden of Eden, or paradise.

God realised that Adam needed a human companion, so Eve was created from one of Adam's ribs. The couple were tempted to eat the fruit of a forbidden tree and were expelled from paradise to live on the earth.

Buddhism, Sikhism and Hinduism

Buddhism does not have a creation story and concentrates on achieving nirvana (nibbana), which is the state in which all suffering stops and the individual is joined with the world-soul like a drop of water falling into the sea.

Sikhism does not really have a creation story because Sikhs believe that God created everything with a single word. Before that word only God existed. God spoke once and there was creation.

Hinduism the best-known story starts with a giant cobra floating on the waters. Asleep on it is the Lord Vishnu. A humming sound – 'Om' – begins. Vishnu awakes. A lotus flower grows out of his navel. In the middle of the flower sits his servant Brahma. Vishnu commands: 'Create the world.' Brahma splits the lotus flower into three to create the heavens, the earth and the sky. Then he fills the world with plants and insects, fish, animals and birds.

SCIENTIFIC VIEWPOINTS

The big bang theory

Scientific research shows that the universe did have a beginning. Before that moment there was nothing; after that moment there was the universe. The big bang theory tries to explain what happened at that moment.

It is generally accepted that this moment occurred around 14 billion years ago. The universe is thought to have started as an extremely small, extremely hot, extremely dense, singularity. Singularities are events which our current understanding of physics cannot explain.

Where the universe came from and why is completely unknown. Once it was here it got bigger and as it got bigger it also cooled down. From an extremely small singularity, it expanded to the size of our current universe. It is still getting bigger and cooler.

The moment of the big bang is often assumed to have been an enormous explosion, probably because that is what you expect with a big bang! Scientists say there was no explosion but simply an expansion. Nor was the big bang a little fireball appearing somewhere in space. It could not be because according to astrophysicists, space did not exist before the moment of the big bang.

Does this theory rule out a god as the creator? No, because this event was outside the natural course of events – it was supernatural. It would seem that the universe has a definite beginning. That beginning must have had a 'first cause'. Was that God?

Evolution

The solar system was formed about 5 billion years ago as the matter released by the big bang cooled. Eventually life formed on the earth, but quite how this happened is not certain.

The theory of evolution was formalised by Charles Darwin when he published his book *On The Origin of Species* in 1859. Darwin's Theory of Evolution is the widely-held notion that all life is related and has descended from a common ancestor.

Complex creatures evolve from simple ancestors naturally over time. As random changes occur within an organism's DNA, the good changes are kept because they increase survival of the organism.

This process is called natural selection. Over time, good changes build up and the result is an entirely different organism which is not a variation of the original, but an entirely different creature.

ACTIVITY

1. State the main similarities in most religious creation stories.

2. State the main events of the big bang theory and evolution.

3. Identify the similarities and differences between the religious and scientific explanations of the origins of the universe and human beings.

Abortion

When we use the word 'abortion' we are usually referring to the deliberate ending of a pregnancy, resulting in the death of the foetus. Before 1967, women who wanted to end their pregnancies, for reasons other than those of serious damage to the mother's or baby's health, had to do it themselves or visit backstreet abortionists. Death caused by blood poisoning or bleeding was not uncommon.

In 1966, more than 100,000 illegal abortions were carried out. They were carried out by injecting poisonous solutions into the womb or inserting objects intended to dislodge the foetus. They were often carried out by untrained practitioners in unhygienic conditions.

The injuries and infections that followed these procedures often led to infertility and other problems. In the early 1960s, 40 women a year in the UK died from the complications of illegal abortions. To put an end to this situation, abortion was legalised by the Abortion Act of 1967.

More than 40 years later, opinion polls still indicate that the majority of people are in favour of legal abortion, but there is evidence to suggest that support is declining over time.

Abortion is legal in Britain up to the 24th week of pregnancy. However, doctors can now save the lives of premature babies born as early as 23 weeks. Only 27 per cent of people surveyed in 2007 thought the current limit on abortion should be maintained.

THE CHRISTIAN VIEW

There is no definitive Christian stance on the issue of abortion. Although all Christians believe abortion to be wrong, some denominations accept that in certain cases it is permissible and can be the lesser of two evils. Different denominations of Christianity have different views, although they may agree on many points.

The Church of England

The Church of England (CofE) is strongly opposed to abortion, but reluctantly accepts that in very exceptional circumstances, for instance where the life of the mother may be at risk, or the pregnancy is the result of rape, it may be better than allowing a pregnancy to continue. The sheer volume of abortions carried out each year in the UK causes great concern as the CofE views abortion as a major breach of moral law because the foetus has the right to live and develop.

A major aim of the CofE is to limit the types of reasons that allow an individual to have an abortion. It believes that the Abortion Act 1967 which legalised abortions has been put into effect in a way that allows a much greater number of abortions than was intended by the Act.

Another concern is the timing of abortions. The CofE believes that they should be carried out as soon as possible. Abortions after the 24-week period should only take place if the problem with the foetus would mean its survival after birth would be very limited.

The Roman Catholic Church

The Roman Catholic Church agrees that abortion is a grave moral wrong. It believes that human life begins at the moment of conception, the moment the egg is fertilised by the sperm.

The Church argues that at the moment of conception, the genetic code that will produce a unique individual comes into existence. Therefore, in their view, a new life begins at this point. The fertilised ovum is not a potential human being but a human being with potential.

Since the 16th century, anyone involved in the process of abortion has been excommunicated. This means that they are barred from being members of the Church. This hard line on abortion has not softened. In recent times, Pope John Paul II in 1995 wrote to all Catholics declaring that abortion was the deliberate killing of an innocent human being.

Abortion is the same as murder in the view of the Catholic Church. Some Catholics disagree with this view of abortion. However, even those who accept abortion see it as only the least bad moral choice in certain circumstances.

Despite the clarity of the Catholic Church's position, research shows that many ordinary Catholics are more practical in their approach to abortion. Even in strongly Catholic countries where abortion is illegal there are high levels of abortions.

THE ISLAMIC VIEW

All Muslims regard abortion as wrong but, like the CofE, accept that there may be circumstances where it might be allowed. As the pregnancy progresses, the wrong inflicted by an abortion increases.

The Qur'an, the Islamic holy book, has nothing to say on the issue of abortion. The Islamic attitude to abortion is therefore based on the belief about the sanctity of life and the general principle in Muslim law of choosing the lesser of two evils.

The main situations in which Islam allows abortion are:

- To save the life of the mother (it is assumed that the death of the mother would cause the death of foetus).
- If the foetus has a condition that cannot be treated, and which will cause a great deal of suffering, abortion is allowed for the sake of the baby.
- If the mother is the victim of a rape or of incest some would allow abortion others would not.

Abortion is not allowed after the foetus has been given a soul. However, there is some dispute about when this happens. The three main views on this are after 120 days, after 40 days, or when the baby moves in the womb.

Euthanasia

WHAT IS EUTHANASIA?

The word 'euthanasia' is originally from the Ancient Greek *eu*, meaning 'good' and *thanasis*, literally meaning 'a good death'. Its modern meaning refers to the practice of ending a life in a painless manner. This is currently illegal in the UK but some forms of euthanasia are legal in Belgium, Luxemburg, The Netherlands, Switzerland, the US state of Oregon and Thailand.

There are three main types of euthanasia.

- Voluntary euthanasia – also known as assisted suicide. Someone assists a person to end their own life when the individual has made it clear that they wish to die.
- Passive euthanasia – a patient is allowed to die rather than being resuscitated.
- Non-voluntary euthanasia – the patient is not in a position to make their views known: for example, a patient on a life support machine who is clinically brain-dead.

Figure 4.10: Is there a point beyond which life support is meaningless?

THE CHRISTIAN VIEW

In general terms, Christians are opposed to euthanasia because they believe that life is a gift from God. What God has given, only he has the right to take away. It also breaks the sixth commandment not to commit murder.

What does this mean in practical terms? Modern medical science has a number of ways of helping terminally ill people. Doctors can give drugs that will relieve a patient's suffering but at the same time hasten their death. This is known as the double or dual effect, and although its legal status is not totally clear in UK law, it is not classed as murder. Some Christians accept this process.

Many patients who, in the past, would have been declared dead can now be kept alive by the use of life support machines. This means that the long-accepted definition of death as stopping breathing – cardio-respiratory death – no longer applies. The standard now is the irreversible loss of brain activity – brain death. At this point, life support machines can be switched off with the consent of a court. Not all Christians would agree with this procedure.

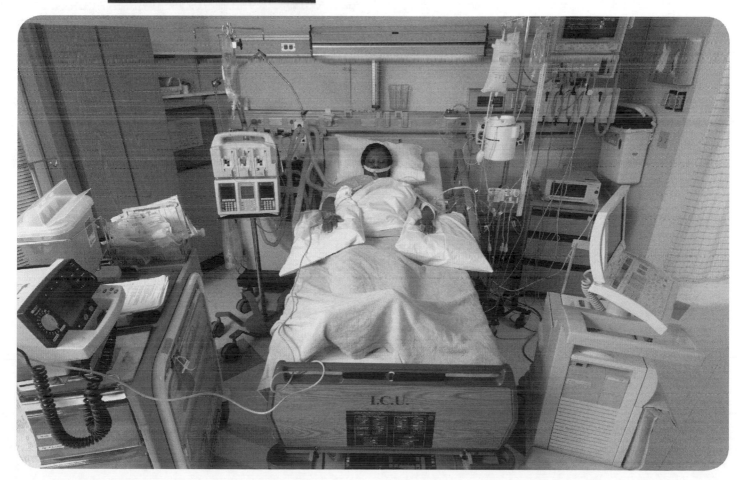

Doctors can prolong the life of a patient with no prospect of improving a poor quality of life or curing the patient. Some Christians would argue that this was an unnecessary interference – that doctors should not strive to keep alive those whose lives are already of a poor quality, or who would die soon anyway.

Some Christians believe that because God is a God of love, suffering and pain should be ended if medical science can do so as God would not want to see people suffer.

THE ISLAMIC VIEW

Muslims believe euthanasia is wrong. They have a similar attitude to Christians regarding the gift of life. They believe that Allah decides the length of a life and human beings have no right to interfere with this.

Muslims believe that life is a test from Allah, and that therefore any suffering has a reason. People who are suffering should be cared for, but pain is not a justification for euthanasia. Euthanasia can never be right because it changes Allah's plan for that person's life.

It is now considered acceptable not to treat a terminally ill person and to switch off a life support machine when the possibility of recovery is gone.

OTHER RELIGIONS' ATTITUDES TO ABORTION AND EUTHANASIA

Buddhism. The Five Precepts are the basic moral rules that all Buddhists should live by. The first of these is the simple statement 'Do not kill'. The accepted meaning of this is that they should not deliberately kill any living creature.

Following the first precept would stop Buddhists approving either abortion or euthanasia. This clear directive can be complicated by the belief that the solution to any situation should be the one that causes least pain.

Hinduism. The Hindu response to the question of abortion is to do what will cause the least harm to all those involved. This would include the parents, the foetus and wider society.

There is disagreement on the issue of euthanasia concerning its effect on individual karma. There are two views. The first argues that to end a painful life is a good deed, and therefore good karma. The second sees euthanasia as breaking the cycle of rebirth, which will attract bad karma for both the patient and the doctor.

Sikhism. Sikhs have a high respect for life because it is a gift from God. They also believe that life begins at conception. Therefore abortion, which destroys a life, is forbidden. For the same reason they would oppose euthanasia, preferring to see the timing of an individual's death left to God.

Judaism. Abortion is allowed in Judaism but only for serious reasons. It is opposed to abortion on demand. Cases are decided when they are looked at individually.

Judaism is opposed to euthanasia because maintaining human life is one of most important moral values of Judaism. It is therefore against anything that could shorten life.

ACTIVITY

1. What is the major reason for religions to be opposed to abortion and euthanasia?

2. Using the two major religions you are studying, explain in more detail their attitude towards abortion and euthanasia.

3. Do you agree that religion is right in its attitude to abortion and euthanasia? Give reasons for your answer.

War, violence and pacifism

A JUST WAR

Most religions are opposed to war. They believe that a war should only be fought if it can meet the criteria of a '**just war**'.

A just war is a war that must be fought, but only if certain conditions are met:

- it must be started by the government;
- there must be a good reason for the war;
- the aim of the war must be to achieve good;
- it should be a last resort after all other alternatives have failed;
- it should only use enough force;
- it should be winnable.

The purpose of the just war criteria is to identify the right way for countries to behave when there is the possibility of war. It attempts to resolve the conflicting beliefs that killing is morally wrong, but a state has the right to defend its citizens: that obligation can justify using force.

The just war criteria identifies the situations in which it might be considered right to go to war and how that war should be fought. A war can only be a just war if it meets these criteria. A war started for just reasons can fail to be a just war if it is not conducted in the proper way.

THE CHRISTIAN VIEW

Christians are not completely against war. Their aim is for a world of peace and justice. Ignoring injustice and the victimisation of innocent people can be seen as a greater evil than using war to do something about it.

However, the central message of Christianity is to use good works to overcome evil. Two examples of this come directly from Jesus himself. In the Sermon on the Mount, he declares: 'Blessed are the peacemakers'. He also changed the well-known saying 'Love your neighbours and hate your enemies' to 'Love your enemies', urging his followers to 'turn the other cheek' and not to respond to violence with violence.

THE ISLAMIC VIEW

Islam has clear rules to decide when it is morally right to go to war and equally clear rules on the way in which such a war should be fought. Muslims take part in the greater jihad and the lesser jihad. Jihad is an Arabic word meaning struggle. It is often translated into English as 'holy war'.

The greater jihad is a personal struggle to live life in a way of which Allah would approve. The lesser jihad refers to military struggle: war is allowed in self-defence, and to defend Muslims in other countries. It should be fought as a last resort, in a disciplined way to limit suffering and injuries to non-combatants, with minimum force and without anger.

PACIFISM

Pacifists are committed to peaceful means of resolving issues. They are opposed to war because they believe that killing is wrong and therefore, by definition, war must be wrong. **Pacifism** is therefore seen as a rejection of war and killing based on moral principles. Pacifists fail to see how war can ever be the right way to secure peace. They will often refuse to join the armed forces.

There was a growth in pacifism during the First World War because of the number of soldiers who were killed, and the fact that, for the first time, the British army was not made up solely of volunteers: conscription was introduced. This meant that all able-bodied young men had to join the armed forces and fight. As this was against the beliefs – or conscience – of pacifists, they became called conscientious objectors.

Pacifism can also be someone's whole approach to life. The ideal would be that all relationships are non-violent and peaceful, resolved by tolerance, patience and mercy instead of conflict. This might go as far as nonviolence towards all creatures, leading the pacifist to vegetarianism.

CHRISTIANITY AND PACIFISM

Christians who are pacifists believe that any form of violence is out of sympathy with the teachings of Christianity. They argue that Jesus was a pacifist, and he practised pacifism in what he said and did. They believe that Jesus's followers should follow his example. As God created all life, life is sacred, and to destroy part of God's creation is wrong.

In the same way that Jesus refused to use violence to avoid being arrested but then allowed himself to be crucified, the leaders of the early Christian Church forbade the use of violence even in self-defence. A clear example of this is the story of the martyrdom of St Stephen, who was stoned to death for his beliefs but did not resist, and at the point of death he forgave those who were stoning him.

This approach changed significantly after the Roman Emperor Constantine became a Christian and made the Roman Empire Christian. Christianity became the state religion. Warfare and violence were part of this process, and the Church began to justify this rejection of pacifism.

ISLAM AND PACIFISM

The word 'Islam' comes from the same Arabic root as the word 'peace' and the Qur'an condemns war as an abnormal state of affairs opposed to Allah's will.

However, Islam recognises that war is sometimes inevitable and is sometimes a positive duty in order to end oppression and suffering. If an aggressor is allowed to succeed – even if there is no fighting – peace is destroyed because of the impact this success has on others.

OTHER RELIGIONS AND PACIFISM

Buddhism. Buddhists see war as evil. There is no support for war in Buddhist teaching but Buddhists have taken part in war.

They have fought to defend their homes. This is not in itself wrong but if they hate their enemy while they are fighting this can be harmful to their karma.

Hinduism. Hindus believe that war is undesirable and should be avoided, because it involves killing. But it also recognises that there can be situations when war is preferable to accepting evil.

War is only justified in the fight against evil and injustice. It should not be used for aggression or to terrorise people.

Sikhism. Sikhs have always believed that war is, on occasions, a necessary part of life. Sikhs do not fight to defend Sikhs or Sikh concerns. They fight to defend the fundamental freedoms of all humans.

They see war as a part of life we have not escaped from.

Judaism. Judaism places a high value on each individual human life. It is therefore logical that Jews will be against war where loss of life is bound to happen.

Judaism hates war but does not forbid it. Some wars are considered to be necessary.

Before going to war, Judaism insists that all attempts to keep the peace are pursued.

ACTIVITY

1. Explain why religion has difficulty in saying that war is always completely wrong.

2. What is meant by the phrase 'just war'? How many religions would support this idea?

3. How practical would pacifism be in the face of a violent attack?

Figure 4.11: The religious belief in the value of the individual leads religions to help those in need.

Religious and non-religious attitudes towards the poor and needy

RELIGIOUS ATTITUDES

Most world religions have a number of beliefs which they share. All believe in justice. This is based on the belief that all people are valuable and so are entitled to be treated fairly. To fail to offer help to those in need is morally indefensible.

All religions believe it is proper to show compassion – the desire to do something about the suffering of others. This leads to an obligation to help those in need.

These views are largely based on the belief that the world does not belong to human beings but is given to them in trust by God. The wealth is given by God and they are accountable to him for the fairness of how they use it. This belief is known as 'stewardship'.

Christianity

When Jesus directed his followers to 'Love your neighbours as yourselves', he set the benchmark for the Christian attitude to the poor and needy. They needed not just sympathy, but action. It was not enough to feel sorry for them; it was necessary to do for them what you would do for yourself.

Jesus spelt out this message in his ministry in both words and deeds. He used the parables of the Good Samaritan and the Sheep and the Goats to underline the breadth of the idea of helping those in need. It not only applied to friends, but to enemies.

Jesus often spent time with people who were not model members of society: outcasts, the poor and sinners. This was even commented on by his disciples. However, it made perfect sense, because these were exactly the people who needed help.

Jesus's followers in the early Church tried to follow his example, and often sold their property to support the needy. Even in the modern era, some churchmen have the ability to make their fellows feel uncomfortable.

Desmond Tutu, a South African churchman, declared that a Church genuinely serving the poor could never be wealthy, because it needed to use its wealth to help the poor. This should give the leaders of some Christian Churches pause for thought.

Islam

Muslims are expected to be charitable, because they are using Allah's wealth. Charity in Islam is synonymous with doing things for the sake of Allah. When giving is done out of charity, this is called 'Sadaqah'.

The benefit of being charitable for the giver is that Allah sees everything. He will see the generosity as meeting part of the individual's test, and this will bring reward to the individual on the day of judgement.

Muslims are also expected to pay Zakat each year. This is the Third Pillar of Islam and is a tax that is used for almsgiving, that is, help for the poor and for others in need. It is an obligatory payment and is not, therefore, regarded as charity. It amounts to one fortieth (2.5 per cent) of an individual's wealth.

Other religions

Buddhism. There are four parts to Buddhist charity. The first is ahimsa, which means not causing harm. This becomes maitri, which means loving kindness. This leads to dana, which is the act of giving. The last stage is karuna, which means compassion. This is seen as perfection.

Hinduism. Hindus have a duty (dharma) to give and share. They are expected to give up to 10 per cent of their income to others. Generous giving helps the giver in the cycle of rebirth, thus giving benefits to both sides of the transaction.

Sikhism. Sikhs have a responsibility to the poor and needy because God's wealth had not been fairly shared out on earth. They are encouraged to give what they can, but have to give a tenth of their income (daswandh) to others.

Judaism. There is no word in Hebrew that translates as 'charity'. The word that is used comes from the word for justice or fairness.

Giving to the poor is not considered as generosity by Jews, but is the duty of those who are rich to help the poor. They are required to do whatever they can to get rid of poverty from society.

NON-RELIGIOUS ATTITUDES

There are many organisations and individuals that share a commitment to helping the poor and needy who do not need a religious justification for their actions. Below are the mission statements from two humanitarian organisations that work worldwide for those in need.

Oxfam International is an international group of independent non-governmental organisations dedicated to fighting poverty and related injustice around the world. The NGOs work together internationally to achieve greater impact by their collective efforts. Oxfam's beliefs are summarised below.

- Poverty and powerlessness are avoidable and can be eliminated by human action and political will.
- Basic human needs and rights can be met. These include the rights to a sustainable livelihood and the rights and capacities to participate in societies and make positive changes to people's lives.
- Inequalities can be significantly reduced both between rich and poor nations and within nations.
- Peace and substantial arms reduction are essential conditions for development.

Doctors Without Borders/Médecins Sans Frontières (MSF) is an international medical humanitarian organisation created by doctors and journalists in France in 1971.

Its work is based on the humanitarian principles of medical ethics and impartiality. The organisation is committed to bringing quality medical care to people caught in crisis regardless of race, religion or political affiliation.

ACTIVITY

1. Why do religions place importance on helping the needy?

2. Desmond Tutu suggests that Churches should not be wealthy because they should be serving the poor. Are there examples of wealthy Churches in your area? Do you agree with Archbishop Tutu?

3. Why do non-religious organisations place importance on helping the needy?

4. 'If religion was working properly, there would be no need for charity.' How far do you agree with this statement? Give reasons for your answer.

SUMMARY

This unit has explored the following points.

- Religious and non-religious viewpoints about the origin of the universe and human beings.
- Religious and non-religious attitudes towards abortion and euthanasia.
- Religious and non-religious attitudes to war, violence and pacifism.
- Religious and non-religious attitudes towards charity and the poor and needy.

Chapter 5
Issues of Health and Welfare

CONTENTS

Unit 5.1 Maintaining a healthy lifestyle

IN THIS UNIT YOU WILL LEARN ABOUT:

- the benefits and risks of health and lifestyle choices
- the consequences for physical and mental development of these choices
- the effect of toxic substances on human health
- the characteristics of emotional and mental health.

KEY CONCEPTS

Diet
Personal hygiene
Exercise
Stress management
Substance abuse

The World Health Organisation (WHO), says that by 2015 all people across society should have adopted healthier living patterns. They identified aspects of a healthy lifestyle as a way of living that:

- lower the risk of being seriously ill or dying early;
- help you enjoy more aspects of your life;
- help your whole family.

They were not suggesting that this could prevent all disease. However, scientific studies have shown that some types of behaviour contribute to the development of diseases like coronary heart disease and lung cancer.

There was also a positive emphasis that health is not simply about avoiding disease but also about promoting physical, mental and social wellbeing.

WHAT IS A HEALTHY LIFESTYLE?

Healthy living is the process of taking action to achieve optimum health. It is about taking responsibility and making sensible choices for today and for the future:

- healthy eating
- physical activity
- personal hygiene
- emotional wellbeing

are all part of this process of developing a healthy living plan.

The American Holistic Health Association developed a simple series of questions that were designed to help people identify areas of their life that need development to achieve a healthy lifestyle.

Wellness Quiz

Do you wake up with enthusiasm for the day ahead?

Do you have the high energy you need to do what you want?

Do you laugh easily and often, especially at yourself?

Do you confidently find solutions for the challenges in your life?

Do you feel valued and appreciated?

Do you appreciate others and let them know it?

Do you have a circle of warm, caring friends?

Do the choices you make every day get you what you want?

If you answered 'no' to any of these questions, congratulations! You have identified areas in your life that you may want to change. This can be valuable information.

(Source: Excerpt from Wellness From Within: The First Step *American Holistic Health Association* (http://ahha.org))

The British Medical Journal (Volume 326) reported that in 2007, British school children were 8 cm fatter around the waist than they had been in 1977.

Why is this important? A major reason is that larger waist measurements are linked to increased risk of coronary heart disease, type 2 diabetes, osteoarthritis and some forms of cancer. The future health outlook for many British young people is potentially very worrying.

In October 2008, a press release from the Government Department of Children, Schools and Families announced that Personal Social and Health Education (PSHE) will become a compulsory part of the curriculum from Key Stage 1 to 4 (ages 5 to 16). It said that all pupils in state schools should receive high-quality lessons in everything from first aid and personal finance to relationships and the consequences of drugs misuse.

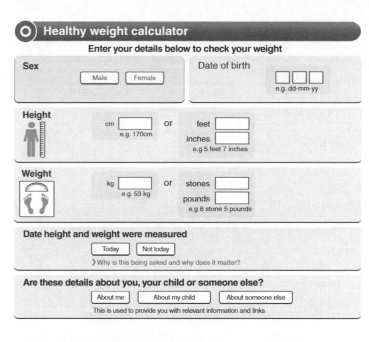

Figure 5.1: The healthy weight calculator can be used to find out if you are a healthy weight.

(Source: NHS website)

ACTIVITY

1. What do you understand the term 'healthy lifestyle' to mean?

2. How effective do you feel the introduction of compulsory PSHE will be in developing healthier lifestyles for people?

WEIGHT AND HEALTHY LIFESTYLE

A central issue in having a healthy lifestyle is maintaining a healthy weight. Healthy weight is calculated by working out an individual's **Body Mass Index** (BMI). This is done by taking the individual's weight in kilograms and dividing it by the individual's height in metres squared. For example:

Weight = 70 kilograms

Height = 1.8 m² (1.8 × 1.8) = 3.24

70 ÷ 3.24 = **21.6**

But what does this mean?

A BMI of 21.6 means the individual is a healthy weight.

A BMI of between 18.5 and 24.9 means a person is an ideal weight for their height.

Obesity, which is defined as being 20 per cent above the average weight for height and age, is considered by the WHO to be a global epidemic. WHO states that one billion people are overweight, with at least 300 million of these being obese. The health implications of these statistics are enormous.

ACTIVITY

1. Why is weight such an important component of a healthy lifestyle?

2. What is your opinion of the Body Mass Index method of calculating whether someone is overweight?

HOW TO MAINTAIN A HEALTHY WEIGHT

There are a number of recommended lifestyle changes that should help people.

Taking regular exercise is vital to keeping weight down. This does not necessarily mean going to the gym. Walking, swimming, housework and gardening can work equally well.

Thirty minutes of exercise a day that makes the individual slightly out of breath is the target. As exercise continues, fitness should increase, making

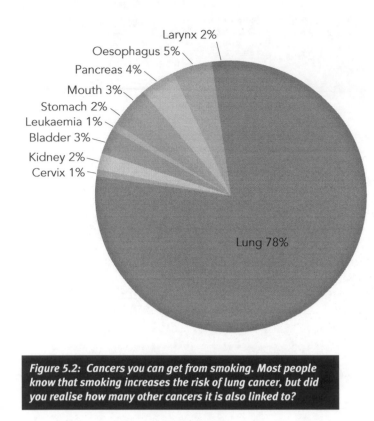

Larynx 2%
Oesophagus 5%
Pancreas 4%
Mouth 3%
Stomach 2%
Leukaemia 1%
Bladder 3%
Kidney 2%
Cervix 1%
Lung 78%

Figure 5.2: Cancers you can get from smoking. Most people know that smoking increases the risk of lung cancer, but did you realise how many other cancers it is also linked to?

it more difficult to get out of breath. This is a good indicator that fitness levels are improving.

A balanced diet, eating a wide range of foods, helps to keep weight down. Most people are already aware of the 5-a-day campaign, which recommends that at least five portions of fruit and vegetables are consumed, per person, per day. Fresh produce is healthier than processed food.

There is increasing evidence that too much alcohol makes it difficult to maintain a healthy weight. It also increases the risk of several cancers.

Quitting smoking is one of the most effective ways of improving health. Smoking carries a significant risk for a wide range of cancers and other diseases.

ACTIVITY

'Sticking to a healthy lifestyle takes all the fun out of life!' Write as many statements as you can to agree with this point of view, and as many statements as you can to disagree. Finish by writing a conclusion based on the evidence you have collected.

DOES ADOPTING A HEALTHY LIFESTYLE REALLY WORK?

Apparently it does. Scientists from Cambridge University found in a study that people increased their life expectancy by changing their lifestyles in just four ways: stopping smoking, taking regular exercise, drinking sensibly and eating five portions of fruit or vegetables a day has the potential to add up to 14 years to people's lives.

Those who cannot manage all four changes are advised to give up smoking, as the study found this has the biggest impact on an individual's health.

PERSONAL HYGIENE

Hygiene refers to behaviours associated with ensuring good health and cleanliness.

Personal hygiene takes these behaviours to the individual level. Children should be introduced at an early age to the routines and importance of hygiene.

Personal hygiene should include teeth cleaning, washing, toilet hygiene and hair care as well as looking after wounds and preventing infections. Keeping a high level of personal hygiene is not only important in maintaining health; it can also help people to feel good about themselves.

A lack of hygiene can have effects for the individual beyond increasing the risk of becoming ill. Many people prefer not to associate with people with poor personal hygiene, for understandable reasons. It can also make it more difficult for individuals trying to get a job. Employers are not anxious to have employees who present a poor image of themselves and therefore the company.

The effects of toxic substances

ATMOSPHERIC POLLUTANTS

Atmospheric pollutants are caused by human actions. They are chemicals, biological materials and other matter which are released into the atmosphere and are harmful to living things. They also have the potential to damage the natural environment.

Atmospheric pollutants include carbon monoxide, nitrates, sulphur dioxide, ozone, lead, tobacco smoke and particulate matter. Particulate matter is made up of solid and liquid particles within the air. These come from a variety of sources:

- vehicle emissions and road dust;
- power generation and industrial combustion;
- smelting and other metal processing;
- construction and demolition activities;
- forest fires, volcanic emissions and sea spray.

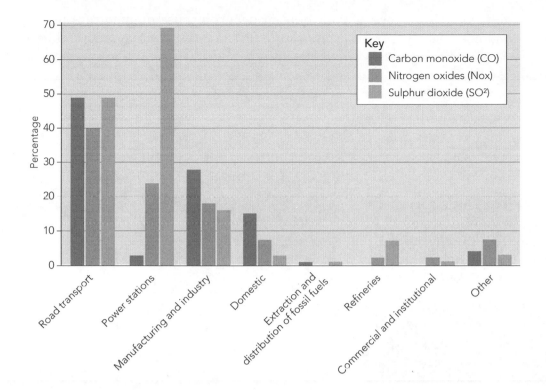

Figure 5.3: This chart shows where air pollutants originate – as you can see, a lot comes from human activity.

(Source: UK Statistics Authority)

Primary pollutants are directly released by a process, for example carbon monoxide from vehicle exhausts or sulphur dioxide from factory chimneys. **Secondary pollutants** are formed in the air when primary pollutants react or interact, for example ground-level ozone.

There are many health effects caused by atmospheric pollutants. The major effects are on the respiratory system and the cardiovascular system, which can cause heart and lung disease. Such effects range from small-scale physical changes to difficulty with breathing and aggravation of existing lung and heart conditions. The result can be an increase in the use of medication, hospital admissions or even premature death.

ACTIVITY

'Using less of the world's natural resources would not only be good for the planet but also for the lifestyle of the people who live on the planet.' How far do you support this statement?

RADIATION

Radiation is a form of energy that is present all around us. It is released into our environment and can be measured in units called 'curies'. The amount of radiation that a person receives is measured in units called 'rem'.

People are exposed to radiation every day, both from naturally occurring sources, for example cosmic rays from the sun, and man-made sources, including some electronic equipment such as microwave ovens and televisions.

The amount of radiation from natural or man-made sources to which people are exposed is usually quite small.

How does radiation cause health effects?

Radioactive materials produce ionising radiation. This has sufficient energy to break some chemical bonds. The tissue in the human body can be damaged by ionising radiation. The body attempts to repair the damage, but sometimes the damage is too severe or widespread. Also, the effects of mistakes made in the natural repair process can lead to cancerous cells.

The most common forms of ionising radiation are alpha and beta particles, or gamma and x-rays. In general, the amount of radiation exposure and the period of time over which that exposure occurs determines the type and severity of the effect on health. There are two broad categories of health effects: long-term low-level exposure and short-term high-level exposure.

Long-term low-level exposure (stochastic) effects

Cancer is the primary health effect from radiation exposure. A simple definition of cancer is 'the uncontrolled growth of cells'. Radiation can damage the natural process of controlling the way cells grow and replace themselves. This allows cells to grow out of control, and they become cancerous.

Radiation can cause **mutations**. It changes a person's DNA, the code that produces a perfect copy of the original cell. If the body does not repair these mutations, they can become genetic and these will be passed on to any children.

Short-term high-level exposure (non-stochastic) effects

Short-term, high-level exposure to radiation is referred to as 'acute exposure'. Health effects from acute exposure to radiation usually appear quickly, and include burns and **radiation sickness**.

Figure 5.4: The number of deformities in children has risen 83% since the Chernobyl disaster. Increases in the number of cases of cleft palate, Down's syndrome and deformed limbs and organs are the most common defects from the fallout. Even the areas where the fallout was light have had an increase of 24% in deformities.

Radiation sickness can cause premature aging or even death. The symptoms are nausea, weakness, hair loss and skin burns. If the dose is high enough to cause death, this will usually happen within two months.

Table 5.1: The impact of different levels of radiation exposure.

Exposure to radiation measured in rem	Symptoms	Time for onset of symptoms
Stochastic exposure		
5–10	Changes in blood chemistry	
50	Feeling sick	Hours
55	Feeling tired	
70	Being sick	
75	Loss of hair	2–3 weeks
90	Diarrhoea	
100	Bleeding	
Non-stochastic exposure		
1000	Destruction of stomach lining; internal bleeding; death.	1–2 weeks
2000	Damage to central nervous system; loss of consciousness; death.	Minutes or hours to days

ACTIVITY

Radiation has always been part of life. The amount of radiation in the modern world has the potential to cause major risks for human beings. Do you believe that the benefits from increased use of radiation are worth the potential risks?

Alcohol and drugs

ALCOHOL

In 2004, the WHO produced a Global Status Report on alcohol. It stated that alcohol had both health-related and social effects. The social effects of alcohol include negative behaviour of individuals and negative interaction with others.

It is believed that the social effects of alcohol have a significant impact on the wellbeing of individuals and society. It is accepted that this impact can be difficult to quantify.

The health effects of alcohol are both physical and mental. Alcohol can affect nearly every organ of the body, and has been linked to over 60 diseases.

The amount of alcohol drunk and the way in which it is drunk, for instance **binge drinking**, creates:

- effects on cells and organs in the body;
- intoxication;
- alcohol dependence.

The effects of alcohol cause:

- chronic disease;
- accidents and injuries;
- short- and long-term social consequences.

A considerable number of diseases are identified as being caused solely by alcohol. These include diseases affecting the nerves, the heart, the stomach and the liver. Alcohol also causes an increased risk of developing cancers of the lip, tongue, throat, oesophagus and liver.

Intoxication is strongly linked to accidents, injuries, deaths, domestic conflict and violence.

Alcohol is a depressant. There also appears to be a link between **alcohol dependence** and other mental conditions. The exact relationship between these conditions is unclear.

ACTIVITY

1. Certain drugs are classed as dangerous and are therefore illegal. Discuss what the effects of a drug should be that you feel are enough to get it classified as dangerous.

2. List the effects alcohol has on society and individuals. Write a short statement to explain why you would or would not make alcohol an illegal drug.

Alcohol and young people

In 1999, the British Medical Association (BMA) published an article called 'Alcohol and Young People'. This article reported the findings of a survey on alcohol and young people. It looked at:

- what they drink;
- how drinks are marketed to them;
- how this marketing is monitored;
- current laws and their enforcement;
- education.

The survey identified a number of issues that gave rise to concern from the medical profession, including:

- a rise in the number of 11- to 15-year-olds who drink alcohol regularly;
- an increase in the amount being consumed;
- high-strength alcoholic drinks being targeted at teenagers;
- designer drinks appealing most to 13- to 16-year-olds;
- unhealthy teenage drinking could that could lead to addiction in later life;
- the dangers of casual sex when intoxicated.

The chairman of the BMA's Board of Science and Education said that the government needed to tackle these problems through effective laws to monitor the drinks industry and particularly the way it advertises drinks to young people.

Figure 5.5: Binge drinking doesn't just affect the individual. The use of ambulance services and police to tackle the problem creates significant costs to society.

Figure 5.6: Who are these adverts designed to appeal to?

The number of 11- to 15-year-olds who admit to drinking has remained fairly constant at around 60 per cent. By the age of 13, the number of those who drink is higher than the number of those who do not. The amount they drink has doubled since the 1990s from 5 units a week to 10.

Young people drink for a variety of reasons. Adolescence is a time when they prefer to associate more with friends than parents and family. They may feel pressure to 'fit in' or 'go along with the crowd' in order to be accepted socially.

Although young people may drink in an uncontrolled way at times, most will not go on to develop serious alcohol problems. However, there is evidence to suggest that alcohol and anti-social behaviour are linked. Nearly 20 per cent of school-age offenders said that they had been drinking prior to their offence.

ACTIVITY

1. Why is underage drinking seen as a problem by the government?
2. Is there any evidence to suggest that the problem is growing?
3. Is there any truth in the statement that the long-term impact of underage drinking is probably less serious than the short-term consequences?

Government action

In December 2008, the government announced measures to control alcohol-fuelled crime and disorder. An independent review reported that many retailers were not following the voluntary standards for responsible selling and marketing of alcohol. As a result, the government announced plans to impose a compulsory code of practice on all alcohol retailers.

A government consultation on these conditions will include:

- bans on 'all you can drink' promotions in pubs and bars;
- bans on promotions to specific groups, such as women, in pubs and bars;
- bans on supermarket price discounts only available on bulk purchases.

Money will be allocated to some areas to help control alcohol sales to underage customers and to confiscate alcohol from under-18s.

ACTIVITY

How successful do you feel the measures outlined above will be in controlling alcohol-fuelled crime and disorder?

ILLEGAL DRUGS

A drug is a chemical that you take into your body, which changes your mood and the way you feel. Drugs change how you view things.

Why do people take illegal drugs?

There are many reasons why people might take illegal drugs. Young people may feel it makes them look more mature. As with alcohol, some will do it to fit in with their friends. It is something that is forbidden, which of course makes it more appealing. The effects of taking drugs may appear to be enjoyable. It can also be an escape from problems at home or school.

There are always risks involved taking any kind of drug. Even taking drugs prescribed by a doctor or bought over the counter in shops can have side effects that people need to know about.

Taking illegal drugs carries serious health risks because they are not controlled or supervised by medical professionals. Many illegal drugs are imported into this country from other parts of the world, and may be mixed with substances to increase the quantity, which allows illegal drug dealers to make more profit. Quite often, what the drug is mixed with is more harmful than the drug itself.

ACTIVITY

1. Make a list of the reasons people decide to take illegal drugs and a list of the dangers associated with taking them.

2. Argue a case claiming that the reasons for taking drugs outweigh the risks of not taking them.

OTHER DRUGS

Drugs change the way you see the world. They affect how your brain works, including your memory. They cause a variety of potentially serious or fatal physical conditions.

Table 5.2: How different drugs can affect your health.

Drug	Some typical reactions/problems
Steroids	Addiction Higher risks for hearts attacks, strokes and liver problems Acne and hair loss Hostility and aggression
Marijuana	Psychological dependence Mild to severe anxiety Increased risk of respiratory problems Damage to the immune system
Cocaine	High risk of addiction Irritability and anxiety with depressed mood Damage to the nasal membranes and nasal septum Higher risks for heart attacks, strokes and seizures
Amphetamine	Very high potential for addiction Headaches, increased heart rate and blood pressure Stroke, convulsions and irregular heartbeat and respiration Weight loss, paranoia and hallucinations and delusions
Ecstasy	Long-term damage to nerve cells in the brain Dehydration Dangerous increases in heart rate and body temperature Heart attacks, seizures and death
Hallucinogens	Sound and visual perception can become distorted Anxiety, confusion and depression Mental health problems Decreased awareness of pain resulting in injury
Depressants	High potential for dependence Slows activity in the central nervous system Tolerance can develop Accidents or injury due to side effects
Narcotics	About half of users develop a dependence Tolerance can develop

As well as health risks, there is also a legal risk in taking illegal drugs. Possession of **Class A drugs** can mean up to seven years in prison. Supplying Class A drugs has a maximum sentence of life imprisonment.

ACTIVITY

Looking at the list of illegal drugs and the potential risks or problems associated, is it reasonable to argue that some ought to be legalised?

Table 5.3: Penalties for possession and dealing and classification of illegal drugs.

		Possession	Dealing
Class A	Ecstasy, LSD, heroin, cocaine, crack, magic mushrooms, amphetamines (if prepared for injection).	Up to 7 years in prison or an unlimited fine or both.	Up to life in prison or an unlimited fine or both.
Class B	Amphetamines, cannabis, methylphenidate (Ritalin), pholcodine.	Up to 5 years in prison or an unlimited fine or both.	Up to 14 years in prison or an unlimited fine or both.
Class C	Tranquilisers, some painkillers, gamma hydroxybutyrate (GHB), ketamine.	Up to 2 years in prison or an unlimited fine or both.	Up to 14 years in prison or an unlimited fine or both.

(Source: Home Office website)

Emotional and mental health

WHAT IS EMOTIONAL AND MENTAL HEALTH?

Many people view their emotional and mental health in a negative way, describing it as being free of mental health problems. It is more positive than this and is not simply being without depression or other psychological problems. It is made up of positive characteristics.

Emotional health is about an individual's psychological wellbeing. A description should include positive statements about how an individual approaches life. A number of bodies have produced lists of characteristics of people who are emotionally healthy. These lists usually include some or all of the following:

- they are self-confident and feel good about themselves;
- they have their emotions under control;
- they can make and keep good relationships;
- they can laugh at themselves and with others;
- they can deal with stress and life's disappointments.

A lot of people give little consideration to their emotional health until something goes wrong with it. Physical health takes time and energy to achieve. The same is true of emotional health.

Even where there is obviously an emotional problem, individuals and society still see emotional and mental problems differently from they way they see medical problems. There is a feeling that all the individual needs to do is 'to get a grip' or 'pull themselves together'.

Break your arm and it's off to casualty you go. No problem! Become depressed, and many people are too embarrassed to get the professional assistance that they need.

Ironically, it is not a sign of weakness to seek help, but a sign of strength – a positive action by a strong individual who has the self-confidence to know when a problem is beyond their own ability to resolve.

RESILIENCE

Being emotionally healthy is not the same as having a magic wand. It does not mean that nothing will ever go wrong for that individual. What it does mean is that individuals with good emotional health have a greater ability to deal with difficulties and stress.

This is sometimes described as resilience. Resilient people have methods of coping with difficulties without becoming negative. They remain positive and creative at all times.

Two important elements of this resilience are the ability to recognise and deal with your emotions, and also to have support from people you can trust.

PHYSICAL HEALTH AND EMOTIONAL HEALTH

Being physically fit and healthy makes a major contribution towards being emotionally healthy. Improving physical health not only strengthens the body but also releases endorphins – powerful chemicals that make people feel better.

The activities that people take part in each day affect the way they feel physically and emotionally. These include:

- getting enough rest;
- eating well;
- exercising;
- limiting alcohol;
- avoiding cigarettes and other drugs.

STRESS MANAGEMENT

What is stress?

Stress is what an individual feels when they are being asked to do something they feel is beyond their capabilities. A common reaction to this is to feel that they are no longer in control of their lives. The worst part of this loss of control is the belief that there is nothing they can do about it.

Regaining control is the essential first step in managing stress. Crucial to taking control is accurately identifying what is causing the stress. Often individuals concentrate on the external stressors, ignoring the way they deal with these.

Many people adopt coping strategies that ignore the causes of stress but make them feel better in the short term. They may smoke, drink or take out their stress on others. In the longer term this does not change the underlying problem and will not reduce the stress.

If the way people deal with stress does not improve their emotional and physical health they may need to change their coping strategies. This can mean changing either the situation causing the stress or their reactions to that situation.

It would be foolish to suggest that there is a magic bullet that will work in any circumstances. It is important to concentrate on things that help an individual re-assert control.

ACTIVITY

1. What are the similarities and differences between physical and emotional health and people's attitudes towards them?

2. Explain why asking for help should be seen as a sign of strength and not of weakness.

3. Identify the strategies essential to help people to be resilient and manage stress effectively.

SUMMARY

This unit has explored the following points.

- What a healthy lifestyle is and how you can achieve it.
- What toxic substances are and how they can affect your health.
- How alcohol and drugs can affect your health.
- What emotional and mental good health is and how you can achieve it.

Unit 5.2 The importance of sex education for social, moral and cultural development

IN THIS UNIT YOU WILL LEARN ABOUT:

- the purpose and focus of sex education in the UK
- the sources of sex education and its effectiveness
- the joint responsibilities of parents, medical authorities and voluntary agencies for sex education
- the debate about where primary responsibility lies
- the importance of sex education for women and men.

KEY CONCEPTS

Responsibility
Partnership
Conception
Contraception

SEX AND RELATIONSHIP EDUCATION GUIDANCE 2000

The Department for Education and Employment (DfEE) issued a guide to sex and relationship education (SRE) in 2000, which stated in its introduction that effective education is vital to young people making responsible and well-informed decisions in their lives. Personal, Social and Health Education (PSHE) should support young people through their physical, emotional and moral development and teach them to respect themselves and grow up confidently.

Schools are expected to deliver SRE by developing age-appropriate programmes from which pupils learn about human reproduction, **contraception**, **Human Immunodeficiency Virus (HIV)** and **sexually transmitted infections (STIs)**, and high-risk behaviours. They should be taught about the health risks associated with early sexual activity and pregnancy, where and how to seek advice, and the importance of marriage and stable relationships.

The programmes developed must be available for parents to inspect. Parents have the right to withdraw pupils from those elements of SRE which are not a part of the National Curriculum.

Some sex education is compulsory for all pupils because it is part of the Science National Curriculum. This includes the biological processes of reproduction, human anatomy, puberty, contraception and information about STIs and HIV and **Acquired immunodeficiency syndrome (AIDS)**.

QUALIFICATIONS AND CURRICULUM AUTHORITY (QCA) GUIDELINES 2005

The effectiveness of SRE was called into question when the QCA issued guidelines to encourage schools to focus sex education on relationships rather than biology. Understanding the human reproductive system and how conception occurs is not enough for young people to make informed choices.

This follows criticism of schools for teaching the mechanics of sex education through science but ignoring the more difficult issue of exploring personal relationships.

The new guidelines have been issued alongside advice on how to teach pupils about managing their health and finances. These new guidelines have been added to existing guidelines on drugs and alcohol to create a new PSHE curriculum.

Schools do not have to teach PSHE as it is not part of the compulsory National Curriculum. Many have tried to deliver more appropriate sex education. These have often been hampered by unenthusiastic delivery by teachers who lack specialist training and are not really comfortable with the subject matter.

This aspect of the guidelines was highlighted by experts outside of schools. Their concern was that unless SRE became compulsory, it would be impossible to ensure a consistent approach that would help all students.

Table 5.4: Teenage pregnancy rate 1998–2008.

Year	Under 18 pregnancies	Under 18 pregnancy rate per thousand females aged 15–17
1998	41,089	46.6
2001	38,461	42.5
2004	39,593	41.6
2006	39,003	40.4

(Source: Office for National Statistics Teenage Pregnancy Unit, 2008)

Figure 5.7: *Unwanted pregnancy is not a new problem, as this early 20th century postcard shows.*

WHAT! HERE AGAIN.

ACTIVITY

1. How far do you agree that parents should have the right to withdraw their children from sex and relationship education that is not a part of the National Curriculum?

2. Should schools be forced to teach more than the science based mechanics of human reproduction?

THE SOCIAL EXCLUSION UNIT REPORT ON TEENAGE PREGNANCY 1999

This report stated that Britain had the worst record of teenage pregnancies in Western Europe, with approximately 90,000 teenagers becoming pregnant every year. The report set two main goals:

- to reduce the rate of teenage pregnancies to half the rate of 1998 for under-18s by 2010;
- to get more teenage parents into education.

A national Action Plan was developed which included better prevention education in and out of school.

THE REVIEW OF SEX AND RELATIONSHIP EDUCATION (SRE) 2008

This review of SRE in 2008 included teachers, academics, PSHE advisers, school nurses, young people and representatives from all faith groups. The group investigated how SRE was being delivered through the school curriculum. The review included evidence from Ofsted, as well as surveys of young people and teachers.

Its major recommendation stated that PSHE should be made a statutory subject in schools in all four key stages. The government accepted this recommendation. Other recommendations were accepted in principle, subject to further work to implement them.

These recommendations included improving the skills and confidence of teachers who teach SRE. A new training course to enable teachers to specialise in PSHE was to be developed.

Schools were to be encouraged to use support from outside professionals and agencies in order to improve the delivery of SRE. Further guidance and support programmes were also to be provided to schools. Young people were recommended to take part in the development of school SRE programmes, and school leaders were advised to have their awareness raised on the value of SRE.

The sources and effectiveness of SRE

THE SOURCES OF SEX EDUCATION

The guidance issued in 2000 made it clear that the delivery of SRE is not seen as simply the responsibility of schools. Parents are seen as the key people in teaching their children about sex, relationships and growing up.

This view is informed by research which shows that young people prefer to receive their early sex and relationship information from their parents. Unfortunately, a lot of parents are uncomfortable talking to their children about sex and relationships. Fathers, for instance, rarely take responsibility for giving sex and relationship education to their sons.

Parents may need support in their role as sex educators. Schools have an obligation to work with parents, especially with consulting them on the content of sex and relationship education programmes.

People in the wider community can offer a great deal to SRE. Health professionals, social workers, youth workers and visitors bring different points of view and specialised knowledge, experience and resources to the subject. Schools need to work effectively in partnership with parents and others in the wider community.

THE EFFECTIVENESS OF SEX EDUCATION

Perhaps the most important people with a view on this are the students, the target audience. A number of surveys of young people have been carried out, and their conclusions have been remarkably consistent.

The views of students

The UK Youth Parliament published a report in 2007 based on a questionnaire that had been completed by more than 20,000 young people.

The main finding was that 40 per cent of young people described the SRE at their school as 'poor' or 'very poor'. Another 33 per cent said it was 'average'.

Other key findings were:

- 43 per cent had not been taught anything about personal relationships.
- 55 per cent of 12- to 15-year-old females said they had not been taught how to use a condom.
- 50 per cent had not been told where their local sexual health service was.

The Sex Education Forum, an organisation which aims to make sure all young people receive SRE, was commissioned to produce a more detailed survey for the 2008 review of SRE. Its findings were as follows.

- Significant numbers of young people did not feel that the SRE they had received was adequate: 34 per cent rated it as poor and a further 43 per cent said it was only OK.
- There was a strong view that SRE was too biological. Broader aspects of SRE were taught least well, including skills for coping with relationships, and feelings and emotions that are experienced during relationships.
- Other key criticisms of current SRE delivery included that it was not relevant to young people's real lives, it was not given sufficient curriculum time, it was delivered by untrained teachers, and it was not inclusive of lesbian, gay, bisexual or

transgender (LGBT) young people or those with disabilities.

One very telling comment from one of the young people surveyed perhaps sums this up:

'I understand the science side pretty well but it seems a bit like a pencil – I know it's made from wood and soft graphite that gets broken off, but does that tell me how to write?'

The views of teachers

Perhaps surprisingly, most teachers agreed with the findings of the surveys. This was the response of one PSHE teacher:

'Many members of staff feel uncomfortable when teaching SRE, whilst others are fine with it. This means that provision is mixed. All pupils get the bare essentials, but there are others who receive a more detailed approach ... depending on the teacher that is delivering the work.'

Lack of training was seen as the biggest problem: 75 per cent of teachers thought that they could not provide what young people really needed, because they were concerned about negative reactions from parents. Most teachers felt that the factual aspects of SRE were taught well, but that the teaching of the relationships aspect was generally weak.

The views of parents

The role of parents in the process of SRE is probably the most problematic. Teachers are concerned about parental attitudes to SRE in schools, particularly on what might be considered sensitive issues. However, this view is not supported by any evidence.

Surveys of parents consistently show that they do want schools to teach SRE. They believe it will:

- provide information that is factually accurate;
- be taken more seriously by their children;
- help their children understand risks.

This can result in parents who rely on schools to deal with relationship issues, because they feel they lack the knowledge or confidence themselves. Parents want their children to be aware of a wide range of issues that they are not prepared to discuss with them themselves.

When parents do get involved in SRE in schools, there is surprise at how limited it can be. This surprise extends to how little of SRE is compulsory.

ACTIVITY

1. Summarise the views of students, teachers and parents about the effectiveness of SRE teaching.

2. What conclusions could you draw from your summary of these views?

THE JOINT RESPONSIBILITY FOR SEX EDUCATION

As has already been stated, the Guidance on SRE issued in 2000 clearly indicated the multidisciplinary nature of its expected delivery.

This expectation was reinforced and heightened when the government published its green paper, 'Every Child Matters' (ECM). The Children Act of 2004 passed into law the principles of ECM, which set out a new approach to the wellbeing of children and young people from birth to the age of 19.

All the organisations involved with providing services to children are expected to work together and share information. The expectation is that this will enable them to work in a more effective way to protect children and young people from harm and help them achieve what they want in life.

Obviously, these expectations could not be incorporated in the guidance which pre-dated the Act, but have been recognised in the 2008 review. In the foreword to the report, the authors specifically identify the following points.

- SRE needs to complement the wider provision of information, advice and support to young people on sex and relationships, led by parents and supported by high quality and accurate advice and support by schools, help lines, websites, peer educators and other professionals whose work involves supporting children and young people's personal development.

- Schools should work in partnership with external professionals in health and wider children's services, both to bring expertise into SRE delivery and to ensure that young people have access to advice and support on sex and relationships outside the classroom, building on the opportunities provided through Extended Schools.

THE DEBATE ABOUT WHERE PRIMARY RESPONSIBILITY LIES

The government decision to accept the recommendation of the 2008 Review of SRE – to make SRE compulsory as part of PSHE – has brought the received view of the role of parents into question.

Part of the justification for this is that young people are growing up in an increasingly sexualised society, where parents may find it hard to discuss sex and relationship issues. Without compulsory school-based SRE, young people may remain confused by the conflicting messages they are exposed to and emotions they are experiencing.

While acknowledging that parents need more support, the suggestion is clearly made that parents may lack up-to-date knowledge on issues such as contraception. It is suggested that parents should work in partnership with schools to ensure that playground myths are counterbalanced by accurate information.

It concludes that although parents have views on SRE, the government can no longer allow individual schools to decide on the role and delivery of SRE in PSHE. To receive only the biological aspects delivered by science through a series of collapsed days or relying on cross-curricular teaching is seen as insufficient by Ofsted.

The firm recommendation is that compulsory, statutory PSHE is the only way to provide all young people with the quality sex and relationship education they require.

ACTIVITY

1. List the reasons that led to the government decision to make SRE part of a compulsory PSHE requirement.

2. Consider the objections you might have if you were a parent, teacher and student to this recommendation.

The importance of sex education for men and women.

It would be useful if all human beings came equipped with a set of detailed instructions

Figure 5.8: The Silver Ring Thing is a programme that has grown in popularity in the USA. It aims to teach young people that abstaining from sex is the best option, and participants wear a silver ring to show that they believe in abstinence. Do you think such a programme could be popular in the UK?

about sex which automatically switched on at the appropriate time in their development. Unfortunately, they don't.

Nonetheless, there is no doubt that sex is something about which most people have at least a passing interest. There is equally no doubt that sex seems to be everywhere in modern society, especially the media. Much of this is not helpful to teenagers trying to make sense of their own feelings and emotions on a tidal wave of hormones.

One major contribution that sex education can make is to help people make sense of what they actually think and feel about sex, and what, if any, sexual activity they are ready for.

It can also raise awareness of the consequences of sexual activity. Some of these can be physical, like pregnancy and STIs. Others can be emotional, and perhaps more difficult to handle.

BEING READY FOR SEX

Abstinence, just like most things in life, really is down to personal choice. The problem is that there are pressures that can make the individual feel they ought to choose one way or the other.

These can be the media pressures already mentioned, but, perhaps more persuasively, peer pressure – the belief that everyone else is doing it and you are missing out! There seems to be general belief that everybody is having sex all the time, and anybody who is not is a loser. This is far from the truth.

WHAT DO PEOPLE WANT FROM SEX?

This is where the stereotypes click in. 'Men want sex all the time, whereas women want relationships but are not really interested in sex.' Neither of these statements is true for all men, or all women, all of the time.

There is no list of things that men and women want from sex. Like so many other things, it comes down to a personal decision.

PLAYGROUND MYTHS ABOUT SEX

One major benefit of sex education is that it provides factual information that can dispel the sort of stories that can cause a great deal of anxiety for many young people. Typical of these myths are the ways to avoid getting pregnant, such as the following.

- 'You won't get pregnant standing up, as sperm can't swim upwards.' Wrong – they can, and do.
- 'You can't get pregnant on your first time.' Wrong – you can.

RELATIONSHIPS

Young people who are in a relationship are probably thinking about sex. *Thinking* does not necessarily mean *doing*. In our society, there has been some confusion between sex and love. The two words do not mean the same thing.

It is just as easy to have sex without being in love as it is to be in love without having sex. Beware the partner who tries to put pressure on you to have sex because they claim it will demonstrate that you really love them. If they really loved you, they would not ask.

ACTIVITY

1. The real value of SRE education for young men and women is that it provides facts on which individuals can make sensible decisions. Give examples to show how true you feel this statement is.

2. Do you feel that SRE is meeting the needs of young men and women? Give reasons for your answer.

SEXUALLY TRANSMITTED INFECTIONS (STIs)

A surprisingly high and increasing number of young people already have STIs.

Practising safer sex by using a condom can drastically reduce any risk of infection.

STIs are a major cause of ill health and can cause infertility in both sexes. Large increases have been seen in the number of young men and women diagnosed with STIs since 1998. The women were mainly in their late teens the men in their early twenties.

Treatment is readily available for individuals concerned as to whether they have an infection. A family doctor (GP) can provide treatment and cannot inform parents, even if the patient is under 16, unless they are convinced that the patient does not understand the treatment. Anonymous treatment is available at specialist clinics called Genito-Urinary Medicine (GUM) clinics which are usually based in local hospitals. Most STIs are treatable with antibiotics.

There are 25 types of sexually transmitted infection. Some can be caught without sexual contact, though most are usually passed on by sex with an infected person. As a result anyone diagnosed with an STI will be encouraged to inform their partner or partners so that they can be tested and treated as well.

PROTECTED SEX

Protected sex has a double meaning because, as should have become fairly obvious, there are two things to protect against when having sex. The one which probably dominates most young people's thinking is protection against pregnancy. Protection against STIs tends to come a distant second.

This is particularly interesting as recent statistics suggest a decline in teenage pregnancy but a rise in infection with STIs.

When using condoms the most important step in preventing pregnancy is using the condom correctly – so that it doesn't break or slip off and it is in place before there is any physical contact. They are cheap, or even free from family planning clinics, and readily available in many outlets including vending machines.

Condoms have an added benefit. They are the most effective contraceptive method for reducing the risk of infection from the viruses that cause AIDS, other HIV-related illnesses and other STIs. Condoms are intended for one-time use.

There is a female equivalent to the male condom with all its advantages but it is much less popular.

The contraceptive pill is 99 per cent effective in protecting against pregnancy, but gives no protection against STIs. It works by affecting the hormones that prepare a woman's body to receive a fertilised egg. There are some side effects from the pill but not all women suffer from them. One major drawback is that to be effective it needs to be taken every day.

The other major forms of contraception place a mechanical and/or chemical barrier in the way of conception. They are not popular with women except for those who do not like to take the contraceptive pill for long periods of time. These methods are effective protection against pregnancy but do nothing to protect against STIs.

STRETCH AND CHALLENGE

Much of the thinking which is driving forward changes in SRE is based on the statistics on teenage pregnancy and STI diagnosis. How far do you feel that this thinking will make an impact on these statistics?

SUMMARY

This unit has explored the following points.

- The debate on what sex and relationship education should contain, and how the content can be improved.
- How parents, teachers and students feel SRE should be delivered and who should be providing the information.
- The importance of sex education for men and women.

Unit 5.3 Health and safety at work and in the environment

IN THIS UNIT YOU WILL LEARN ABOUT:

- the potential risks to health and safety in the workplace
- the ways of reducing health and safety risks in the home
- the purpose, focus and effectiveness of health and safety law
- the case for and against the law to reinforce voluntary codes.

KEY CONCEPTS

Protection
Prevention
Legislation
Voluntary code

HEALTH AND SAFETY LAW

Before 1970, UK health and safety law was confused. There were around 500 separate acts of parliament enforced by nine different government departments. Despite this large number of laws, a review by the Robens Committee concluded there had been no significant reduction in the numbers of people killed and injured at work.

A new act was passed. The Health and Safety at Work Act 1974 is the primary law covering health and safety at work in the UK. The Health and Safety Executive (HSE) has the duty of making sure the act is enforced.

In addition to the primary act, there are what are called statutory instruments or regulations. These cover specific subjects relating to health and safety made under other acts of parliament, for example the control of asbestos at work. The HSE and local authorities work together to enforce these regulations consistently.

The HSE helps businesses to implement changes in occupational health and safety law. Since 2005, all changes in UK law are implemented on only two dates each year, 6 April and 1 October. Changes in European health and safety law are also implemented on these dates whenever possible.

The HSE publishes a range of free and priced information to inform businesses of health and safety law.

ACTIVITY

1. What is the Health and Safety Executive?

2. What improvements did the 1974 Health and Safety at Work Act introduce?

The risks to health and safety in the workplace

Under health and safety law, the main responsibility for controlling risks to health and safety at work falls on the employer. This is the employer's 'duty of care' to employees. This duty of care also covers anyone else on the premises, whether they are visitors or customers.

Implementation of this duty of care should start with a **risk assessment** to identify possible dangers. A practical way to do this might be to:

- assess the risk;
- decide what is needed to control the risk;
- put the control in place;

- train the workers;
- monitor the solution to ensure it works.

Workers are expected to take care of their own health and safety and always be aware of how their actions might affect others. Health and safety legislation requires employees to cooperate with employers.

Businesses with five or more employees have to keep a record of risk assessments and draw up a formal health and safety policy.

All employers, regardless of the size of their company, have a general duty to make the workplace safe and prevent risks to health as far as is reasonably practicable. This will mean doing some very practical things like making sure machinery is safe to use and workers are trained to use it safely. Others will be more theoretical, like preparing an emergency plan to evacuate the premises if there is a fire and making sure all workers are aware of the plan.

Workers, as well as cooperating with the employer to work safely, should also keep the employer informed of anything that might affect their ability to work safely, for example someone who is working with machinery or driving while taking medication that makes them drowsy should inform their employer before a risk is posed.

ACTIVITY

1. Explain the employer's duty of care.
2. What responsibility does an employee have towards their own safety and that of other workers?

Ways of reducing health and safety risks in the home

'The safest place to be is at home.' This is not true if the statistics are to be believed.

From 1976 to 2002, the Department of Trade and Industry funded the Home Accident Surveillance System. The purpose of the system was to collect information to inform accident prevention policy to improve consumer safety. This was discontinued in 2003 and so the last data relates to the year 2002.

The figures from 2002 indicated that there are 2.7 million home accidents each year leading to hospital treatment. Nearly half a million of these are to children under 5.

There were almost 4500 deaths due to home accidents in 2002. This figure, higher than the number of people killed on the roads, was made up of nearly 2500 male and 2000 female deaths. Almost 2000 of those who died were aged over 75 years and most were victims of falls.

The cost of these accidents in lost education, working time and hospital costs was estimated at £25 billion per year.

There were less than 300 deaths and nearly 137,000 serious injuries as a result of accidents at work in 2007. On the roads there were fewer than 3000 deaths and less than 28,000 serious injuries in 2007.

Figure 5.9: Government campaigns such as this have greatly increased awareness amongst the public and have led to a reduction in the number of road deaths.

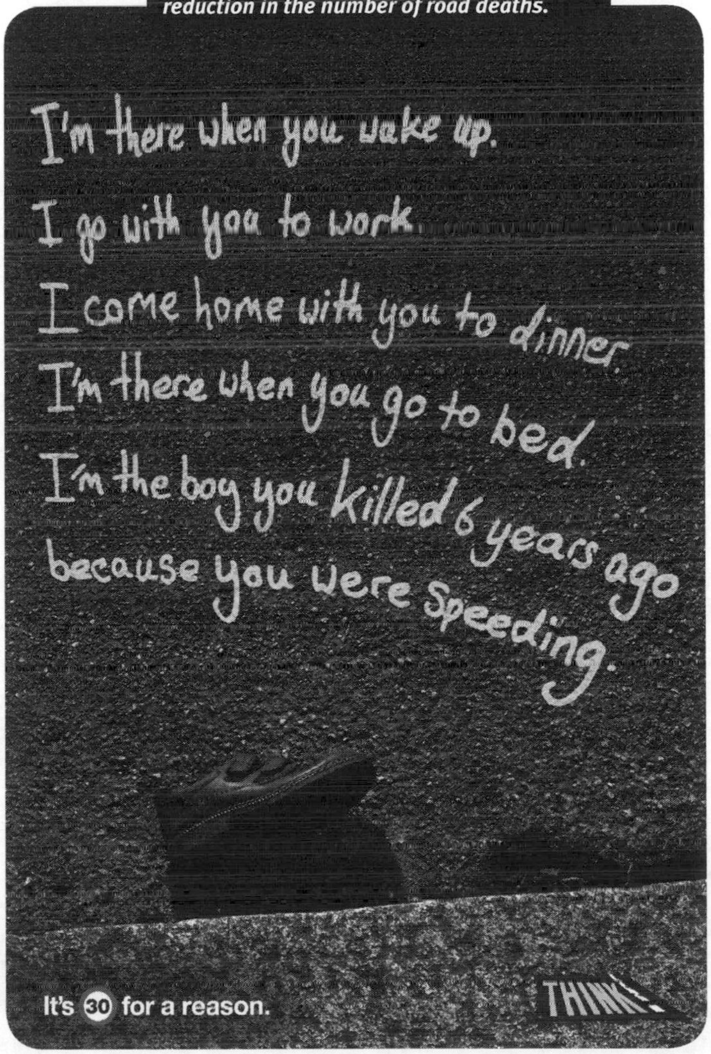

I'm there when you wake up.
I go with you to work.
I come home with you to dinner.
I'm there when you go to bed.
I'm the boy you killed 6 years ago because you were speeding.

It's 30 for a reason. THINK!

The Royal Society for the Prevention of Accidents (RoSPA) believes the figures for home accidents do not attract attention because the events happen behind closed doors. Workplace and road traffic accidents are declining because they are public and, as a result, have been targeted with reduction strategies.

In 2002, RoSPA published a policy document called 'Can the home ever be safe?' This was a policy statement recommending improvements in the design and specification of both new and refurbished homes.

The document advocated 10 improvements, ranging from more use of fire guards and second handrails for elderly people, to greater awareness of keeping medicines and chemicals out of children's reach and the dangers of DIY and gardening.

Despite limited implementation, these suggestions achieved some success in accident reduction in the home. When revising this policy in 2005, RoSPA commented that as long as the measures remained optional the impact on home accidents would be limited.

THE MAIN HEALTH AND SAFETY RISKS IN THE HOME

In its information sheet on preventing accidents in the home, RoSPA identifies eight main areas of risk. They are:

- fire safety;
- electrical safety;
- heating and cooking;
- safety glass;
- safety with medicines and cleaners;
- DIY and garden safety;
- child safety;
- safety of older people.

Most of them are fairly obvious and self-explanatory.

ACTIVITY

Choose two risks from the list above and explain what the risk is.

Unfortunately, the list is missing the most dangerous risk in the home setting – YOU!

Before it abandoned the collection of information about home accidents in 2003, the Department of Trade and Industry figures provided evidence that the majority of people involved in accidents in the home were actually the cause of the accidents.

The conclusion must be that people underestimate the risks they take in their own home and sadly too many pay a high price for this.

Figure 5.10: *Stories such as the one reporting that children will be made to wear goggles when playing conkers are entirely untrue.*

The purpose of health and safety legislation

On its website (see 'Websites' on page ii), the Health and Safety Executive (HSE) – the body charged with enforcing health and safety legislation – clearly sets out its view of the purpose of the legislation.

> 'If you believe some of the stories you hear, health and safety is all about stopping any activity that might possibly lead to harm. This is not our vision of sensible health and safety – we want to save lives, not stop them. Our approach is to seek a balance between the unachievable aim of absolute safety and the kind of poor management of risk that damages lives and the economy.'

Such a statement may seem surprising, considering the horror stories that are constantly reported in the press about health and safety restricting traditional activities.

A view seems to have emerged that there is a '**nanny state**' approach to health and safety. HSE carried out research that identified three types of story.

- Myths with no basis in fact, for example that trapeze artists will be required to wear hard hats.
- Decisions by (usually very well-intentioned) individuals that go well beyond what the law and common sense require, for example requiring children to wear goggles when playing conkers.
- Health and safety used as a convenient excuse for a decision taken largely or wholly for other reasons, for example the closure of facilities for financial reasons mainly unrelated to health and safety.

(It may surprise you to know that on its website – see 'Websites' on page ii – the HSE has a 'myth of the month' page. Check it out! The HSE wants people to know it thinks that these myths are silly and distract attention from its real job.)

There is also a widely held belief, seemingly supported by extensive personal injury claim advertising, that the UK has become a 'compensation culture' similar to that of the USA.

The facts do not bear this out: there has been little change in the number of claims since 2000. However, the fear of this **compensation culture** can cause people to become more cautious and take action to avoid a perceived threat.

ACTIVITY

1. 'The HSE is a much misunderstood organisation.' Give some evidence to support or contradict this statement.

2. 'Every accident means someone gets compensation.' Is this the case?

VOLUNTARY CODES OR LEGISLATION

All of health and safety at work is covered by legislation. This means that certain things have to be done, and if they are not, there can be consequences enforceable at law.

In the field of health and safety in the home, RoSPA is concerned about a lack of legislative support. It believes changes are necessary to drastically reduce the deaths and injuries in the home. These will be very slow to come about if they are voluntary rather than compulsory, and more people will die and be injured in the meantime.

The experience of the HSE regarding the negative impact of 'nannying' health and safety on people's attitudes to its work may be a reason not to resort to law-making without careful thought.

It is one thing to be told you must wear a hard hat on a building site; it is something entirely different to be told what you must wear to mow the grass at home – and risk prosecution if you fail to comply.

STRETCH AND CHALLENGE

Is it possible for the government to pass laws to remove all risks from life? If it is, should they do it?

SUMMARY

This unit has explored the following points.

- What the Health and Safety Executive is and what it does.
- Issues of health and safety in the workplace and at home.
- The purpose of health and safety legislation and the debate around voluntary codes.

Unit 5.4 Health, healthcare and economic development

IN THIS UNIT YOU WILL LEARN ABOUT:

- different ways of measuring the health of a nation
- different risks to health in countries with contrasting economic development
- different patterns of healthcare in contrasting countries
- ways of improving health in LEDCs.

KEY CONCEPTS

Life expectancy
Infant mortality
Preventative medicine
Malnutrition
Diseases of poverty
Diseases of affluence

WHAT IS DEVELOPMENT?

Development can be defined as improvements in the ways of managing natural and human resources in order to create wealth and improve people's lives. It can relate to either **economic development** or **human development**, and can be measured by the use of **development indicators**.

There is no simple, single way to calculate the level of development of a country, region or people. As a result, there are a number of development indicators that can be applied to help determine a country's level of development.

Put simply, development is about how rich people are and therefore how good their quality of life is. This varies dramatically in different parts of the world. Countries are commonly divided into MEDCs (more economically developed countries, such as the UK, France and Japan) and LEDCs (less economically developed countries such as Egypt and Bangladesh). This categorisation does not fit all countries. Some, such as Brazil, are in the process of moving from the status of LEDC to MEDC. These are described as partially developed and generally have an improving standard of living.

CHARACTERISTICS OF MEDCs AND LEDCs

Table 5.5: Some of the characteristics of MEDCs and LEDCs.

	MEDC	LEDC
Birth rate	10–16 babies born per 1000 people.	20–45 babies born per 1000 people.
Death rate	Low, due to good healthcare.	High, due to poor healthcare and disease.
Infant mortality	Very few children die before the age of 5.	Around 35,000 babies die every day due to poor healthcare and malnutrition.
Housing	Adequate for the majority of people. Most have basic facilities of water power and sanitation.	Often inadequate with no access to any facilities.
Education	Usually compulsory and free, leading to high levels of literacy. University education is common.	Access to education varies and is poor in rural areas. Poor literacy levels, particularly amongst females.

(Source: www.Revisionworld.co.uk)

It is difficult to avoid stereotyping when making broad brushstroke definitions such as that of LEDC. Many people in LEDCs do live in poverty and have few opportunities, but there will be some people who have a good life with all the luxuries of an MEDC.

Around 1.3 billion people – that is 1 in 4 of the world's population – are believed to live in total poverty.

Table 5.6: Data that give a better picture of the health of a country.

Indicator	Description	UK	Brazil	Egypt	Bangladesh
Life expectancy	The average age an individual might expect to reach.	77	67	64	58
Infant mortality	The number of deaths per 1000 live births.	6.2	48	62	77
Access to healthcare	The ratio of patients to one doctor.	611	844	1316	12,884
Access to safe water	Essential to control water-born diseases such as cholera and dysentery.	96%	73%	68%	30%

(Source: WHO World Health Report press kit, 2002)

HEALTH DEVELOPMENT INDICATORS

Health development indicators can ask broad general questions such as:

- Do all the people in a country have access to medical care?
- What level of healthcare is available – basic or advanced?
- Is healthcare free or paid for?

They can also focus on very specific data to try give a more precise picture of the health of a country. These data might include those in Table 5.6.

Health risks in countries with different levels of economic development

Ten preventable risks are responsible for 22.4 million (40 per cent) of the 56 million deaths each year. These risks are:

- childhood and maternal malnourishment;
- unsafe sex;
- high blood pressure;
- tobacco;
- alcohol;
- unsafe water, sanitation and hygiene;
- high cholesterol;
- indoor smoke from solid fuels;
- iron deficiency;
- obesity.

Some of these risks are only found in the developing world. The remainder of the risks have spread throughout the developed, as well as the developing, world.

Around 170 million children in developing countries are underweight because they do not get enough to eat.

If no action is taken by 2020 the five million deaths per year caused by tobacco now will rise to an estimated nine million.

Action against all the preventable risks could increase life expectancy in parts of Africa by as much as 16 years.

HEALTH RISKS IN LEDCs

Table 5.7: The percentage of population in LEDCs affected by each of the health risk factors.

Risk factor	LEDCs % of population affected
Underweight	9.0%
Unsafe sex	6.2%
Blood pressure	2.8%
Tobacco	2.2%
Alcohol	2.6%
Unsafe water and sanitation and hygiene	3.7%
Cholesterol	2.6%
Indoor smoke from solid fuels	2.6%
Iron deficiency	2.3%
Overweight and obesity	1.2%

(Source: WHO World Health Report press kit, 2002)

The impact of specific risk factors and how to prevent them

Malnutrition: estimated to cause around 3.4 million deaths annually. Just under 2 million of these deaths are in Africa. Poor nutrition is a cause in more than half of all child deaths in developing countries.

Poor nutrition can be addressed in the short term by food aid but in the longer term this will require properly structured and funded development aid and debt reduction for LEDCs.

Unsafe sex: HIV/AIDS is estimated to cause around 2.9 million deaths annually. Life expectancy in sub-Saharan Africa is estimated at 47 years. Without the AIDS effect that estimate would rise to 62 years. It is believed that up to 95 per cent of HIV infections in Africa in 2001 were caused by unsafe sex.

This requires an education programme with ready access to family planning clinics. For those already infected, the drugs to slow the disease and prolong

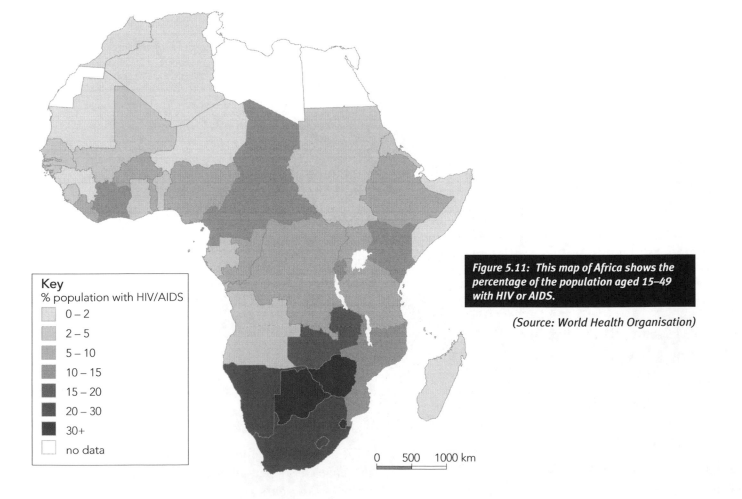

Key
% population with HIV/AIDS
- 0 – 2
- 2 – 5
- 5 – 10
- 10 – 15
- 15 – 20
- 20 – 30
- 30+
- no data

0   500   1000 km

Figure 5.11: This map of Africa shows the percentage of the population aged 15–49 with HIV or AIDS.

(Source: World Health Organisation)

life need to be provided by international drug companies at realistic prices.

Tobacco use: estimated to cause around 4.9 million deaths annually. As has already been indicated the use of tobacco is rising rapidly. Much of this increase is in developing countries.

The rise in the use of tobacco in developing countries is a direct result of the restrictions on smoking in developed countries. Cigarette manufacturers target these new markets which have less regulation.

Unsafe water, sanitation and hygiene: estimated to cause around 1.7 million deaths annually. A third of these deaths are in Africa and another third in south-east Asia. Almost all these deaths are in developing countries. Diarrhoea is the major cause of death.

Access to clean water needs to be a priority in development aid.

Iron deficiency: estimated to cause around 800,000 deaths annually. Around 2 billion people suffer from iron deficiency.

This is easily treatable either by an improved diet or food supplements.

HEALTH RISKS IN MEDCs

Table 5.8: The percentage of population in MEDCs affected by each of the health risk factors.

Risk factor	% of population affected
Underweight	0.1
Unsafe sex	0.2
Blood pressure	1.5
Tobacco	1.8
Alcohol	1.4
Unsafe water and sanitation and hygiene	0.1
Cholesterol	0.1
Indoor smoke from solid fuels	0.1
Iron deficiency	0.1
Overweight and obesity	1.0

(Source: WHO World Health Report press kit, 2002)

In excess of a billion people in developing and developed countries are deemed obese by the World Health Organisation (WHO). Of these, 500,000 die each year from weight related diseases in North America and Western Europe.

Deaths from obesity are currently running at 3 million per year and are expected to rise to 5 million. Action against preventable risks in Europe, the USA and the richer parts of the world could increase life expectancy by up to 5 years.

The impact of specific risk factors and how to prevent them

Unsafe sex: HIV/AIDS is a preventable risk in MEDCs. It is much more controlled than in LEDCs due to pro-active educational programmes and high quality medical care for those infected.

High blood pressure: is estimated to cause around 7.1 million deaths annually. Around 62 per cent of strokes and 49 per cent of heart attacks annually are caused by high blood pressure.

High cholesterol: is estimated to cause around 4.4 million deaths. Its effects often overlap with high blood pressure. Around 18 per cent of strokes and 56 per cent of heart disease are caused by cholesterol.

Prevention of both of these risk factors is a major strategy in MEDCs, based around medication and lifestyle change.

Tobacco use: numbers of people smoking in MEDCs is in decline due to rising prices of tobacco through government taxation and restrictions on smoking in public places. These actions are supported by advertising campaigns and medical help to quit smoking.

ACTIVITY

1. Explain what is meant by a preventable health risk.

2. What are the main differences between preventable health risks in LEDCs and MEDCs?

3. What action can be taken to prevent these health risks in LEDCs and MEDCs?

THE DEMOGRAPHIC TRANSITION MODEL

The demographic transition model tries to show how population changes as countries develop economically. It was developed by analysing events in Europe and the USA as they industrialised.

Four stages were identified and are shown in Figure 5.12.

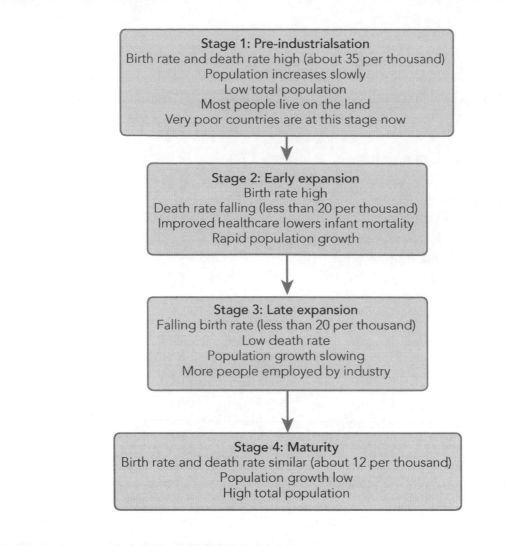

Figure 5.12: *The four stages of economic development and the impact on population.*

THE FUTURE OF HEALTHCARE

Many LEDCs appear to be following the transition pattern. Once they reach Stage 3, the impact on healthcare is significant. As more developing countries progress, it is anticipated that healthcare will improve in low and middle income countries over the next 25 years. The number of deaths due to infectious diseases such as diarrhoea, tuberculosis and malaria and poor nutrition will fall.

Unfortunately, as the way that people live changes, so will the way that they die. The old killers will decline only to be replaced by the diseases found in MEDCs.

Some of the new killers, for instance chronic obstructive pulmonary disease (a lung disease that makes it difficult to breathe), arise from lifestyle choices, such as tobacco use. Others, like road traffic accidents, grow as people become more prosperous and can afford to buy cars.

Examples of some of the expected changes in LEDCs are:

- HIV/AIDS. Deaths will rise from 2.2m in 2008 to a maximum of 2.4m in 2012 before falling back to 1.2m by 2030.
- Cardiovascular diseases. Deaths will rise from 17.1m in 2008 to 23.4m by 2030.
- Road deaths. Deaths will rise from 1.3m in 2004 to 2.4m by 2030.
- Cancer. Deaths will rise from 7.4m in 2004 to 11.8m by 2030.

ACTIVITY

'Development does not remove preventable health risks it just exchanges one set of potential killers for another.' How far do you agree?

Patterns of healthcare in contrasting countries

The World Health Report 2006 revealed an estimated shortage of almost 4.3 million doctors, midwives, nurses and medical support workers worldwide. Ironically, this shortage is worst in the areas in which it is most needed, especially sub-Saharan Africa.

In global terms, new medicines and technologies are making significant improvements in healthcare. These improvements are not universal. In many of the world's poorest countries, HIV and AIDS and the collapse of governments have, in some 'failed' states, led to life expectancy being drastically cut.

THE ROLE OF THE WORKFORCE

Crucial to improving health is the quality and size of the medical workforce. The outcome of health is dependent on the quality and quantity of doctors available. Improvement in the quality of healthcare is down to the workers on the ground, who can identify where there is a need and an opportunity to change for the better. Workers are integral to making sure resources are used properly.

The WHO estimates there are 59.2 million full-time paid health workers worldwide. Two thirds of these are practitioners while the other third are administrators.

These health workers are not evenly distributed across the globe. There are four nurses per doctor in Canada and the USA, while Chile, Peru, El Salvador and Mexico have less than one nurse per doctor. More than 70 per cent of doctors are men and more than 70 per cent of nurses are women – a marked gender imbalance.

WHO has calculated a workforce size needed to be able deal with essential healthcare and necessary to meet the health-related Millennium Development Goals.

Based on this, 57 countries can be identified with critical shortages in their health workforce. The shortages are greatest in sub-Saharan Africa, and are very large in south-east Asia because of the sheer size of that population.

Sometimes, shortages occur in countries that have large numbers of unemployed health workers, and this is often because of a lack of public funds, or government inefficiency, or sometimes both.

Table 5.9: The relative distribution of disease, health workers and health spending in two contrasting WHO regions.

WHO Region	Burden of disease	World health workers	World health spending
The Americas	10%	37%	50%
Africa	37%	3%	1%

(Source: WHO World Health Report, 2006)

These figures place Africa at the very centre of the global health workforce crisis.

The likelihood is that the crisis in Africa will deepen in the future. Demand for healthcare and therefore demand for health workers will rise in all countries – rich and poor.

In poorer countries still dealing with infectious diseases, chronic illness and the HIV/AIDS epidemic, the availability of effective vaccines and drugs to cope with these health threats poses practical problems, as they demand effective responses.

The gap between what can be done and what is being done is getting wider. Success in bridging the gap will only be achieved if the workforce develops enough to provide effective health systems.

Problems in MEDCs

Rich countries with a low birth rate and with a growing elderly population will need more care for those with **chronic** and **degenerative diseases**.

The low birth rate will leave a population with more old people than young people. Even if in relatively good health these older people will need more resources. There will be a labour shortage even with massively increased training for workers in wealthy countries, these changes will put more pressure on health workers from poorer regions to migrate to the richer countries.

STRETCH AND CHALLENGE

An estimated worldwide workforce of 59.2 million health workers should be enough to provide basic healthcare for everyone. Explain why this does not happen in practice. What measures could be taken to ensure a fairer sharing of healthcare? Is this likely to happen?

Ways of improving health in LEDCs

THE MILLENNIUM DEVELOPMENT GOALS

During the UN Millennium Summit in 2000, 189 nations adopted the Millennium Declaration. Taken from this declaration are the Millennium Development Goals (MDGs). These are meant to be achieved by 2015. There are 8 goals, which are listed below.

Goal 1: Wipe out extreme poverty and hunger.

Goal 2: Primary education for all children.

Goal 3: Equality for women.

Goal 4: Reduce child mortality.

Goal 5: Improve the health of mothers.

Goal 6: Combat HIV, AIDS, malaria and other diseases.

Goal 7: Ensure environmental sustainability.

Goal 8: Develop a global partnership for development.

Many of the MDGs would make a significant contribution to improving health in LEDCs.

In 2005, world leaders meeting at the World Summit agreed to take action on a range of global challenges. They restated their commitment to achieve the all of the MDGs by 2015. They agreed to provide an extra US $50 billion a year to fight poverty. Immediate support was agreed for initiatives against malaria and to support education and healthcare.

It was also agreed that they would help to finance development projects in the health sector. Debt relief, and even cancellation of debt, was raised along with measures to make world trade fairer for developing nations.

EXISTING WAYS TO REDUCE THE DEVELOPMENT GAP

To reduce the development gap, LEDCs need finance to develop their economic and social infrastructure. There are a number of methods being tried to achieve this.

Figure 5.13: NGOs such as the Red Cross can help provide relief from immediate crises, but cannot solve the healthcare shortfalls.

Investment: LEDCs can borrow money to finance development projects or encourage transnational companies to locate to their country. The latter will create jobs and help to generate wealth.

Government aid: LEDCs can use international aid offered by MEDCs. This can provide both financial and technical expertise but often it comes with strings attached, such as MEDCs linking the aid to trade deals. There is also the danger that LEDCs can become dependent on aid rather than developing.

Aid from non-governmental organisations (NGOs): This is aid from charities using voluntary contributions. It is often provided for emergency relief or small-scale projects. Its impact on overall development is therefore small.

Change the terms of trade: Trade often favours MEDCs at the expense of LEDCs. If this was changed to allow LEDCs to make more money from trade, they might be more able to self-finance development projects and avoid debt. Unfortunately, world trade is still dominated by the three big players: USA, Japan and the EU.

ACTIVITY

1. How should the MDGs improve healthcare in LEDCs?

2. What support was agreed for the MDGs by world leaders?

3. There is already an extensive network of development aid in place. Explain why this has failed to effectively reduce the development gap.

SUMMARY

This unit has explored the following points.

- How the health of a nation is measured.
- The health risks and problems in LEDCs compared to MEDCs.
- How patterns of healthcare differ between LEDCs and MEDCs.
- What can be done to improve healthcare in LEDCs.

Unit 5.5 The development of welfare provision in the UK

IN THIS UNIT YOU WILL LEARN ABOUT:

- the insurance principle and the foundation of the Welfare State
- the reconstruction of post-war Britain in 1945
- poverty today and criticisms of state welfare
- the advantages and disadvantages of state intervention in welfare provision.

KEY CONCEPTS

Welfare State
Means test
Private provision
National Insurance
Universal benefit

WHAT IS MEANT BY WELFARE?

Welfare is the name given to a system of benefits that the state provides in areas of need such as unemployment, medicine, education and housing. Its aim is to help everyone maintain a minimum standard of living.

This system in the UK is known as the Welfare State, especially since the changes after the Second World War ended in 1945.

The first attempts to create a Welfare State date back to the reign of Queen Elizabeth I (1558–1603). The Poor Law of 1601 was the first attempt to use the law to give the poor help to live.

By the end of the nineteenth century, it was clear that the Poor Law – even though it had been reformed in 1834 – was failing to meet the needs of the poor. This was highlighted by surveys carried out by two wealthy businessmen who believed it was their duty to help the poor and disadvantaged.

Figure 5.14: A contemporary poster, ridiculing the new Poor Law. This is taken from the National Archives and was produced in 1837. The new laws changed the way in which the poor of the parish were to be dealt with and not everyone thought it was a good idea.

These surveys were 'Life and Labour of the People in London' (1889) by Charles Booth and 'Poverty, A Study of Town Life' (1901) by Seebohm Rowntree, and both painted graphic pictures of life for the urban poor.

In addition to this, the government was shocked to find that when recruiting for the South African War (Boer War 1899–1902) a high proportion of army volunteers had to be refused on the grounds of their poor physical condition.

THE LIBERAL GOVERNMENT REFORMS 1906–1914

Rowntree's survey showed that there were three times in the lives of the poor when they were particularly at risk: as young children, when they were sick or unemployed, and in old age.

The Liberal government that was elected in 1906 brought in measures to help people when they fell into these at-risk groups.

There were two measures for young people. In 1906, local authorities were allowed to provide free school meals to children. However, this was not compulsory and some chose not to do this. In 1908, The Children and Young Persons Act made it illegal to neglect children or treat them cruelly. To keep them out of prisons, it established juvenile courts which sent children convicted of crimes to 'borstals' – now known as Young Offenders Institutions.

For the unemployed, **labour exchanges** were established in 1909 to help them find work.

Health insurance and unemployment insurance were introduced by the 1911 National Insurance Act. An entitlement to free medical treatment and sick pay of 50 pence a week for 26 weeks was available at an insurance premium of 1.5p per week. For another 1p per week, workers could claim unemployment pay of 37.5p per week for 15 weeks.

National Insurance was used to pay for these benefits because the Liberal government did not want to raise income tax to fund it.

In 1908, pensions were introduced. These were means-tested and provided 25p a week to a single person, or 37.5p to a married couple. They were available to people 70 years and over at a time when the average age of death for men was 48.

ACTIVITY

1. Why did the Liberal government of 1906 feel changes were needed in the Poor Law?

2. What changes did the Liberal government of 1906 make to welfare provision?

3. What were the main ideas that the Liberal government was trying to achieve by these changes? How successful do you think they were? Give reasons for your answer.

THE RECONSTRUCTION OF POST-WAR BRITAIN IN 1945

A major problem with the new system of welfare benefits up to the outbreak of the Second World War was that they only applied to some groups of people, and many of those most in need were excluded.

The move to extend welfare benefits to everyone gathered support, but the **Great Depression** of the 1930s made this difficult to finance.

The war itself produced the political will to provide an all-encompassing welfare system.

An enquiry was set in 1941 to produce a strategy to bring this about. This enquiry was led by Sir William Beveridge, an economist and expert on unemployment problems.

Beveridge's report aimed to provide a comprehensive system of social insurance 'from cradle to grave'. He proposed that all working people should pay an affordable weekly flat rate contribution to the government. In return, they would receive benefits for unemployment, sickness and maternity and old age as well as widows' pensions and funeral benefit.

The aim of this was to set a minimum standard of living with a safety net to stop anyone falling below it.

A series of laws was passed between 1945 and 1948 which established the Welfare State.

Free education, council housing and a commitment to support full employment completed the package.

Table 5.10: The most important laws that created the Welfare State.

Act of parliament	Benefits granted
Family Allowances Act 1945	25p a week for each child after the first.
National Insurance Act 1945	Unemployment pay for six months. Sick pay for as long as the sickness lasts.
National Insurance Industrial Injuries Act 1946	Extra benefits for people injured at work.
National Assistance Act 1948	Benefits for anybody in need.
National Health Service Act 1948	Doctors, hospital, dentists, opticians, ambulances, midwives and health visitors were available and free to everybody.

Criticisms of the Welfare State

For a period in the 1950s and 1960s, the Welfare State appeared to work well. There was general agreement that this was the way forward by all the political parties.

Events conspired against this agreement. The cost of the NHS was a constant concern. Demand for its services was driven upwards by a number of factors, including rising expectations, developments in medical treatments and a rapid increase in life expectancy.

It also became clear that benefits were not paid at a high enough level to prevent many pensioners, in particular, becoming poor.

ACTIVITY

1. What did the Labour government of 1945 hope to achieve when it created the Welfare State?

2. How successful was the Welfare State? What problems did it have?

THATCHERISM

In the more challenging economic climate from 1975 onwards, arguments began to be heard against the affordability of universal welfare benefits. Many believed that targeting resources on those who really needed it would be more economic, as most people were able to provide for themselves.

Another argument that began to be heard against the high welfare benefits was that it caused economic problems. It made for a lack of competitiveness and encouraged people not to work.

Here's to the brave new world!

Figure 5.15: This contemporary cartoon shows the high hopes people had of the Welfare State.

The real challenge to the Welfare State arrived when Margaret Thatcher became Conservative Party leader in 1975. As prime minister in 1979, her policies promised low taxes, less state intervention, and lower levels of public spending. This implied cuts in welfare spending.

Welfare spending cuts were implemented in two ways. Reduced benefits placed more claimants on means-tested payments. In 1979, one in six claimants was means-tested, and by 1997, this figure had become one in three.

In 1980, state retirement pension increases stopped being linked to rises in average earnings and instead increased in line with prices. This saved a great deal of tax payers' money but meant harder times for many pensioners. Pensioner groups are still campaigning to have this reversed today.

ACTIVITY

1. What did 'Thatcherism' promise for public spending?
2. How did this affect welfare provision?

NEW LABOUR AND 'WELFARE TO WORK'

The phrase 'welfare to work' is not new: it has been used by the government since the 1980s. It expresses the ambition to stop paying people for being unemployed by providing help and incentives to return to paid work.

New Labour adopted this approach in 1997 when it was elected into government. It then proceeded to expand its meaning.

In the past, the 'welfare to work' approach has been used for those actively seeking work and registered as unemployed. Since 1997, it has been extended to groups previously excluded, such as lone parents and disabled people. All working-age people living on benefits are now expected to at least consider entering the workforce.

Tax credits have been a major tool in this process. Originally, they were only available to families with children but they have since been made available to all full-time workers over the age of 25. Alongside the introduction of the minimum wage, it is hoped that this will provide an incentive to work by the establishment, guaranteeing a minimum income for those on low earnings.

ACTIVITY

1. What was the New Labour policy of 'welfare to work'?
2. What did it mean for welfare provision?

The advantages and disadvantages of state intervention in the welfare provision

There is a long history, since 1601, of government in the UK attempting to provide welfare for its citizens. Even before the passing of the Poor Laws, it was generally regarded as a Christian duty to carry out the instructions laid down in the Bible in Matthew's Gospel, chapter 25 – that all Christians should:

- feed the hungry and give drink to the thirsty;
- welcome the stranger;
- clothe the naked;
- visit the sick and the prisoner;
- bury the dead.

It is clear from the information given in this unit that there are different views about whether and how the governments should intervene with those in need. These views have changed over time and continue to change.

The major areas of argument might centre around questions such as the following.

- Is the wellbeing of the individual a personal or collective responsibility?
- Does welfare encourage people to be idle or help the unfortunate?
- Should benefits be universal or targeted at those in need?
- Should the state interfere with citizens' lives or should they make private provision?
- Does society have a responsibility to its less fortunate members?

At the time of the Poor Law, the state made a distinction between the deserving poor, who were poor through no fault of their own, and the undeserving poor, who were considered capable of working but chose not to do so. The deserving poor were either people who wanted to work but were unable to find employment or people in Rowntree's vulnerable categories who were too young, too old or too sick to work. These were supported.

The undeserving poor – also called idle beggars or sturdy beggars – were to be whipped through the town until they learnt their lesson!

The major advantage of state intervention is that it provides a safety net for all members of a society, whether deserving or undeserving. The major disadvantage is that this is at a financial cost to those members of society who might themselves never receive any benefits. They might willingly support the deserving but are also obliged to support the undeserving.

Hopefully, few people would wish to return to treatment meted out by the Poor Law. Is the modern equivalent to withdraw someone's benefit for refusing to actively seek work just as bad?

STRETCH AND CHALLENGE

The Welfare State established after the Second World War was meant to look after people 'from the cradle to the grave'. The fact that it has failed to achieve this ambition is more to do with cost than any change in the principle that the 'the overall responsibility for the welfare of the citizens must remain with the state'. This has been true of governments of all political parties. How far do you agree with this assessment?

SUMMARY

This unit has explored the following points.

- The origins of the Welfare State in the UK.
- Problems with the Welfare State and how different governments have tried to overcome these.
- The arguments for and against state intervention in welfare.

Figure 5.16: *A 16th century woodcut of a beggar being whipped through the streets, to the obvious enjoyment of the spectators.*

ExamCafé

Welcome!

The following sections will help you to prepare for your examination. It is important to remember that the exam is designed to test you not to trick you.

- The questions on the exam papers will be from the information that you have studied.
- The mark schemes will show you ways to build an answer that can reach the highest marks.
- The revision tips will give you ideas that have worked for some people and you may find helpful.

However, none of the revision tips and exam preparation activities can make a difference without your commitment to revise thoroughly to achieve the best result you can.

If you are properly prepared you should do well.

Individual revision

Revision tips

Revision is very personal. What works for you may not work for anyone else. That does not mean that you are wrong, just that you are you! It is essential that you find out what works for you.

There are some things that you cannot avoid. Most exams will expect you to have gained knowledge from the course you have been taking. Factual knowledge and appropriate skills are essential.

The need for factual knowledge makes it a sound idea to use the information gathered over the course as the starting point for your revision. **BUT** this is **only** the starting point.

Simply re-reading your exercise books or file will rapidly bore you to distraction and probably mean that you learn very little! There are many more effective methods of revising; but remember the ones you personally find useful, or enjoy using, are the ones that are likely to be most effective for you.

Use a variety of techniques to keep you interested. People learn in different ways. Four major methods have been identified:

- sight
- hearing
- reading/writing
- kinaesthetic – practical hands-on activities.

Most people learn by using a mixture of all the identified methods but if you have a particular learning preference, concentrating on that for revision could help.

- Copy out key points, words and phrases from your notes onto small revision cards.
- Make multiple copies and stick them up in places where you will see them regularly.
- Use diagrams. Design your own – you will remember them better!

- Mnemonics – use the first letter of important facts to create a word that will help you to remember the facts.

- Accept that revision needs to be planned as part of your course – not a bolt-on at the end.

- Set a timetable – try to keep to it – be realistic! Last-minute revision is useless.

- A short session once a day is better than one long session once a week.

- One subject per session – avoid confusion.

It may seem strange, but long sessions of revision are usually ineffective. They may make you feel virtuous, but the acid test is how much more do you know at the end of them than you knew before you started?

Ten minutes is plenty of time to revise a revision list you have created, and most people can manage not to get bored in ten minutes.

If you become tired or cannot remember what you have just read – stop. Do something completely different – give yourself a treat for being good – then start again feeling relaxed.

When to do revision is also a matter of personal choice. What is the best time for you? Work out the routine that you prefer and stick to it. (Late at night is not usually good.)

Common mistakes

Each section of the specification for B031 contains lists of key concepts and major topic areas. These are listed in the next section, the Revision Checklist.

Students often know too little about these. Exam questions will test your knowledge and understanding of key concepts, based around one or more of the major topics. When students don't know precisely what they mean, they can lose marks.

Revision Checklist
Unit B031 Cross-Curricular Themes

Chapter 1: Issues of Citizenship

Rights and responsibilities.	• What human rights are and how they developed.
	• UK and international law on human rights.
	• How individuals, organisations and governments have responsibilities as well as rights.
	• How individuals, organisations and governments are responsible for upholding human rights in the UK and the world.

Democratic process in the UK.	• How parliamentary democracy in the UK works. • Alternative systems of democracy. • The rights available in a democracy. • Dictatorship. • The importance of active citizenship in elections.
Judicial process in the UK.	• The role of the law in protecting rights and resolving conflicts. • The difference between criminal and civil law. • The operation of the different judicial systems. • The due process of criminal law.

Chapter 2 Issues of Economic Wellbeing and Financial Capability

The classification of economic activity and the nature of the modern economy.	• The classification of economic activity. • The reason for the relative decline of primary and secondary industry. • Changing global industrial patterns.
Different types of work and methods of reward.	• Changing patterns of employment within the UK. • Changes in technology, the organisation of work and the feminisation of the work force. • The link between reward and motivation.
Financial capability.	• Money management. • Financial decision making. • A range of financial products. • The financial implications of post-16 options.
Rights and Responsibilities at work.	• The rights and responsibilities of employers and employees. • The importance of the contract of employment. • The functions of trade unions. • The ways trade unions seek to influence employers and government.

Chapter 3: Environmental Issues

Climate change and its consequences.	• The causes and impacts of climate change. • The historical development of climate change as an issue. • The difficulty of identifying future trends and the problems for planners. • Controversies over climate change.
Resource management and the need for increased sustainability.	• The impacts of sustainable lifestyles on developed and developing countries. • The economic and environmental implications of sustainable development. • The range of methods of managing waste. • The purpose and implications of Agenda 21.

Chapter 4: Religious and Moral Issues

The nature of God.	• What religious people mean when they use the word God. • The different beliefs religions have about God • Where is God? • Why do many people believe in God?
The nature of belief.	• The ways in which worship takes place in religious buildings and privately at home. • The meaning of important religious festivals. • Ceremonies and beliefs associated with 'rites of passage'. • Beliefs about Holy Scripture.
Religious and personal relationships.	• The ways religious beliefs can influence relationships within the family. • Religious attitudes towards marriage and divorce. • Religious attitudes towards sexual relationships. • Religious attitudes towards race, other religions and gender.
Religious beliefs about good and evil.	• Religious beliefs about why there is suffering in the world. • The difference between natural and moral evil. • The religious attitude towards overcoming or coping with suffering. • How people cope with suffering through a belief in a better afterlife.
Religious beliefs about modern dilemmas.	• Religious and non-religious viewpoints about the origin of the universe and human beings. • Differences both within religions and outside religion towards issues such as abortion and euthanasia. • Religious and non-religious attitudes to war, violence and pacifism. • Religious and non-religious attitudes towards the poor and needy.

Chapter 5: Issues of Health and Welfare

Maintaining a healthy lifestyle.	• The benefits and risks of health and lifestyle choices. • The consequences for physical and mental development of these choices. • The effect of toxic substances on human development. • The characteristics of emotional and mental health.
The importance of sex education for social, moral and cultural development.	• The purpose and focus of sex education in the UK. • The sources of sex education and its effectiveness. • The joint responsibilities of parents, medical authorities and voluntary agencies for sex education. • The debate about where primary responsibility lies. • The importance of sex education for women and men.
Health and safety at work and in the environment.	• The potential risks to health and safety in the workplace. • The ways or reducing health and safety risks in the home. • The purpose, focus and effectiveness of health and safety law. • The case for and against law to reinforce voluntary codes.

Health, healthcare and economic development.	• Different ways of measuring the health of a nation. • Different risks to health in countries with contrasting economic development. • Different patterns of healthcare in contrasting countries. • Ways of improving health in LEDCs.
The development of welfare provision in the UK.	• The insurance principle and the foundation of the Welfare State. • The reconstruction of post-war Britain in 1945. • Poverty today and criticisms of state welfare. • The advantages and disadvantages of state intervention in welfare provision.

Understanding exam language

Different command words and what they mean

Questions in Unit B031 will use one of three command words. These words try to show how you should answer the question.

State – The answer should be factual, short and knowledge based. It could be a single word, a phrase or a short sentence. Writing more than a short sentence is not necessary and could cost you time.

Describe – The answer should be in some detail telling what something is like or how something might be done. A short paragraph would usually be enough.

Explain – The answer should be detailed. Good factual support is needed for the explanation. These questions have bullet points for guidance. These are not the points which must be included but guidance to what might be included. You are encouraged to provide your own response. An essay type answer is needed.

Different types of question and how they should be approached

In Unit B031:

Sections A to D have three different types of question: (a), (b) and (c).

Question (a) is knowledge based:

- The question has two parts.
- Each part asks you to **state** three facts about one key concept used in that unit.
- Each correct fact is awarded 1 mark.
- Single word or short sentence answers are all that are required.

Question (a) in each section is worth a maximum of 6 marks.

Question (b) is skills based: extracting information from a documentary source.

- The question has two parts.
- Each part asks you to **state** two pieces of information identified in the source.
- Each piece of information correctly identified is awarded 1 mark.
- Single word or short sentence answers are all that are required.

Question (b) in each section is worth a maximum of 6 marks.

Question (c) is knowledge based: constructing a short essay to answer a question.

- The question has 4 bullet points for guidance – these are not the only way to write an answer.
- The question asks you to **explain** your answer.
- Detailed factual support is expected for the explanation. An essay type answer is needed.

Question (c) in each section is worth a maximum of 10 marks.

Section E has two different types of question: (a) and (b).

Question (a) is skills based – extracting information from documentary sources.

- The question has four parts.
- Each part asks you to **state** some information identified from the sources.
- Each piece of information correctly identified is awarded 1 mark.
- Single word or short sentence answers are all that are required.

Question (a) is worth a maximum of 6 marks.

Question (b) is knowledge based and skills based.

Knowledge based.

- The question has 4 bullet points for guidance – these are not the only way to write an answer.
- The question asks you to explain your answer.
- Detailed factual support is expected for the explanation. An essay type answer is needed.

This part of the question is worth a maximum of 8 marks

Skills based – using documentary sources to support an essay type answer.

- The two sources should be used to support your explanation.
- Marks are awarded for the quality of support provided form the sources.

This part of the question is worth a maximum of 6 marks

Examiner tips

There is a lot to read in a question paper and it is important that you read the instructions and questions carefully. Misreading of questions or individual words can have a big effect on the marks you are awarded, for example employee and employer have only one letter different in spelling but that one letter makes a massive difference in meaning.

Time is vital in an examination. How much time should you spend on a particular question? There are a number of indicators on the examination paper. Each question has the number of marks it is worth shown in brackets. The space provided for your answer on the paper should also help you to write appropriately for each question.

One calculation that might help you plan your time is to divide the total time available by the total number of marks awarded on the paper. For Unit B031 the calculation is:

120 minutes/100 marks

therefore you have 1.2 minutes, or 1 minute 12 seconds to gain each mark.

This may seem a silly calculation, but if you multiply the number of marks by 1.2 minutes you will get an indication of how much time to spend on each question to maximise your opportunity to get as many marks as possible.

Each module is worth 20 marks therefore you should spend no more than 24 minutes on any one module.

Modules A – D have three types of question:

- (a) 6 marks: 7 minutes 12 seconds
- (b) 4 marks: 4 minutes 48 seconds
- (c) 10 marks: 12 minutes

You cannot be as precise as this, but if you do spend 40 minutes on one module you will seriously affect the time available for one or more other modules. Within a module, if you spend 12 minutes on question (a) you will squeeze the time available for the other questions and this may cost you marks.

The way you write is also important. There are two parts to this. Firstly, in your own interests, try to make your handwriting as readable as possible. Examiners will always try to mark positively – to reward what you have shown you know – but they can only do this if your writing is readable.

Secondly, write using the sort of language you are comfortable with. Do not try to use phrases or terminology that you are not entirely sure of. Examiners know that you are 16-year-old students and they generally have a wide experience of the way people in that age group write. As long as your writing clearly gets across your ideas you will be rewarded appropriately.

Structuring an answer

When planning an essay type answer it is important to understand how the examiner will assess what you have written.

Below is the outline mark scheme used by examiners to assess answers for Question (c) in all the modules of unit B031 Cross Curricular Themes.

[0 marks]	**No evidence** submitted or response **does not address** the question.
Level 1: [1–2 marks]	Candidate offers a **general statement** about the question with **limited information**.
	Text is difficult to read, poor spelling and grammar; little punctuation makes comprehension difficult.
Level 2: [3–5 marks]	Candidate writes about **one side of the argument** or the other identified in the question **with examples**.
	To reach top of the level candidates will clearly comment on **at least two examples**.
	Text is readable, there are mistakes in spelling, grammar and punctuation; comprehension of meaning largely clear.

Level 3: [6–8 marks]	Candidate writes about **both** sides identified in the question. Examples and discussion will be **more developed** than the Level 2. To reach top of the level candidates will comment on **both sides in depth**. Text is clearly readable spelling, grammar and punctuation are largely accurate; meaning is clear.
Level 4: [9–10 marks]	Candidate writes a **detailed and accurate account of both sides** identified in the question. To reach top of the level candidates will reach **a personal conclusion** based on the arguments made in their answer. Text is clearly readable spelling, grammar and punctuation are accurate; meaning is very clear.

Humanities mark schemes are Level of Response mark schemes. This means they contain descriptions of what a candidate answer should include to achieve a certain level.

The highlighted text in the table above shows the minimum information an examiner will expect to find to decide a candidate answer has achieved a particular level. Each level has more than one mark and the descriptions also assist the examiner to award a particular mark.

If you understand how this mark scheme works it can help you to plan an essay structure that will enable you to achieve a higher mark. For a candidate, the highlighted text provides the 'gateways' they need to go through to get from one level to the next.

Gateways

Level 1 to Level 2:

- Clearly write about **one** of the alternatives in the question.
- Give **some** factual support/examples.
- Possible maximum mark – **more than** one example.

Level 2 to Level 3:

- Clearly write about **both** alternatives in the question.
- Give **more developed** factual support/examples.
- Possible maximum mark – **discuss both sides in depth**.

Level 3 to Level 4:

- Write in **detail and accurately** about **both** alternatives in the question.
- Possible maximum mark – a **personal conclusion** based on evidence.

Unit B031 Cross-Curricular Themes

Although the example questions are drawn from Chapter 1 of the specification, the mark schemes, level descriptors and examiner's comments would also apply to the other chapters.

Chapter 1: Issues of Citizenship

Question and Mark Scheme
Section A Question 1 (a)

In Sections A to D (a) questions are knowledge based:

- They are two part questions.
- Each part asks you to state three facts about one key concept used in that unit.
- Each correct fact is awarded 1 mark.

Single word or short sentence answers are all that are required.

1(a)(i)	**State three facts about:** **The government** 1 mark for each correct fact relating to the term government e.g.: • Winners of (general) election/biggest party • Leader is prime minister/ministers make up cabinet • Runs the country • Suggest laws/taxes etc. If correct example(s) are given maximum of 1 mark	[3]
1(a)(ii)	**State three facts about:** **The opposition** 1 mark for each correct fact relating to the term opposition e.g.: • Other political parties who did not win election • Can be more than one party • Shadows the government • Challenges/alternative ideas/policies If correct example(s) are given maximum of 1 mark	[3]

Student answer:

The term government refers to the winner of an election. When all the votes are counted they are the ones who have won. The leader of the winners is made the prime minister. The government is in charge of the country. It decides what laws should be and what people have to do.

Examiner says:

This candidate has identified three facts:

- winner of an election
- leader is made prime minister
- in charge of the country.

The general tone of this answer is somewhat vague, possibly suggesting that the candidate is not totally sure of her/his facts. However three correct facts are identified therefore this is a good answer.

Advice:

The candidate should write more briefly, as in the bullet points above, to save time.

Question and Mark Scheme
Section A Question 1 (c)

Question (c) is knowledge based – constructing an essay to answer a question.

- The question has 4 bullet points for guidance – these are not the only way to write an answer.
- The question asks you to explain your answer.
- Detailed factual support is expected for the explanation. An essay type answer is needed.

1(c)	**Political systems are not all the same. One important difference is the protection given to individual freedom. Explain how this protection may differ in a dictatorship and a democracy.** **In your answer you could refer to:** • **the importance of the media** • **the role of the police and courts** • **freedom of speech** • **the right to protest and oppose** **[0 marks]** No evidence submitted or response does not address the question.
	Level 1: **[1–2 marks]** Candidate offers general assertion about individual freedom in a dictatorship e.g. it is a police state with no rights/ democracy e.g. individuals have rights which are protected etc. For top of level candidate attempts to develop example given. Text is difficult to read, poor spelling and grammar; little punctuation makes comprehension difficult.
	Level 2: **[3–5 marks]** Candidate writes about dictatorship **or** democracy. Dictatorship. Gives examples of infringements of individual freedom through censorship, lack of equality before the law, limits on personal freedom and the right to protest. Democracy. Giving examples of the protection of individual freedom through the power of a free press, equality before the law, freedom of speech, religion and association. To reach top of the level candidates will clearly comment on at least two examples. Text is readable, there are mistakes in spelling, grammar and punctuation; comprehension of meaning largely clear.

Level 3:

[5–8 marks] Candidate writes about dictatorship **and** democracy.

Will build on the type of information in Level 2 but will develop the answer by identifying that institutions can be used in the different systems to protect or limit individual freedom.

Dictatorship

The legal system is a tool of government used to repress individual freedom, the press is not free and is used for propaganda, the forces of law and order are deployed to restrict freedom of association and expression and especially the right to protest.

Democracy

The legal system is independent of the government and a bastion to protect the individual, police facilitate the right to protest, a free media provides a platform for freedom of speech, there is an acceptance of the right to protest.

To reach top of the level candidates will comment on both systems in depth.

Text is clearly readable spelling, grammar and punctuation are largely accurate; meaning is clear.

Level 4:

[9–10 marks] Candidate writes a comprehensive evaluation of dictatorship **and** democracy.

To reach top of the level candidates will reach a personal conclusion e.g. the restraints of dictatorship on the freedom of the individual can sometimes counterbalance the excess/ libertarianism of societies which emphasise freedom/ democracy demands a high level of active citizenship.

Text is clearly readable spelling, grammar and punctuation are accurate; meaning is very clear.

[10]

Student answer 1 :

Dictatorship is not as good as democracy because it stops people from doing what they want. The telly and papers is not allowed to tell you the truth. The police are allowed to pick on people for no reason and if you get taken to court you don't get treated fair.

If you say things about the way things are you will be in trouble with the dictator and if you were to try to do something about it like putting up a poster or signing a petition you might get arrested.

Democracy is much better than this because it does not have the same sort of control.

Examiner says:

This candidate goes beyond general assertions but the answer is lacking in detailed support for the statements made. At this point the marker is looking at a response above a Level 1. The answer has two other weaknesses. It concentrates almost entirely on the problems of dictatorship and it is too dependent on limited responses to the bullet points.

The examiner will consider whether the candidate has reached anything higher than Level 2. This will depend on whether the candidate meets the descriptor for Level 2 'candidate writes about dictatorship **or** democracy' or Level 3 'candidate writes about dictatorship **and** democracy'.

The candidate develops limited responses to the problems of dictatorship but only refers to democracy in passing. This candidate is working at Level 2. Given the range of marks, 3 to 5, what does the candidate deserve? The mark scheme indicates that the top of the level, 5 marks, should be awarded for 'clear comment on at least two examples'. This candidate has commented on all four of the suggested reference points and the answer is therefore worth more than the bottom of the level. However it is difficult to say that any of the four points is made clearly. The answer is a satisfactory Level 2 response.

Advice:

To improve this level the candidate would need to do two things. Firstly to answer all the question. The question asks about dictatorship and democracy but the candidate almost ignores democracy except for a passing reference at the end. This is not sufficient to move the answer into the next level. To do this some comparisons would need to be made about the differences between the two types of government. Secondly the candidate needs to write more clearly and in greater detail to explain fully what is meant in the supporting comments.

Student answer 2:

Democratic governments are elected on a regular basis by the people. Dictators are not. This means that democratic governments can be removed by the people voting against them. Dictators cannot.

As a result people living in democracies have rights which dictators do not allow their people because they might use them to get rid of the dictator. In a dictatorship the media is controlled by the government and does not allow information against them to be published. The media in a democracy spends a lot of its time digging out and publishing things the government might prefer that people did not know. This is perfectly legal and would be protected by the law.

In a dictatorship the police and courts would be used against any organisation or person who tried to speak freely or protest. They would be arrested and quite probably be gaoled. In a democracy, as long as the protest followed certain rules, the police and courts would be expected to protect the rights of people to do this.

Democracy assumes that people can use freedom in a mature way, dictatorship does not.

Examiner says:

This candidate makes clear reference to both dictatorship and democracy. The bullet points have been incorporated in the answer and been developed beyond the obvious. At this point the marker will be considering a response above Level 2.

The candidate identifies that state institutions can be used to protect or limit freedom. This is developed in some detail. The marker will conclude that this candidate is working at Level 3 and possibly at the top of Level 3. Does this answer reach a Level 4 response? A top Level 3 'comments on both systems in depth' Level 4 requires 'a comprehensive evaluation of both systems' with a personal conclusion.

There is evidence that the depth of the answer is limited. It also lacks a personal conclusion. The conclusion is that the candidate is working towards the top of Level 3.

Advice:

To reach a Level 4 the candidate would need to use more factual evidence to improve the depth of the answer, and more examples of what these two types of government mean to the individual. The candidate also needs to reach a personal conclusion based on the information that has been used.

Application of Knowledge
BO32

2

Unit 6.1 Different types and forms of evidence

IN THIS UNIT YOU WILL LEARN ABOUT:

- official statistics
- primary research
- secondary research
- quantitative methods of enquiry
- qualitative methods of enquiry.

PRIMARY RESEARCH

Research that is designed to produce new information is called primary research. Because this type of research is original, the data generated should have direct relevance to the research project. Primary research is also known as field research.

Primary research is subdivided into two basic types: qualitative and quantitative research.

PRIMARY SOURCES

Primary sources are original materials which contain original ideas, a discovery, or new information. They can include:

- things from the time, which are called artefacts;
- diaries;
- letters;
- original documents;
- government records;
- paintings, photos, cartoons.

QUALITATIVE RESEARCH

Qualitative research is designed to find out how people feel about issues and the reasons for these feelings. It is a research method that uses interviews, observations, small numbers of questionnaires, focus groups, subjective reports and case studies.

The results of this type of research cannot be analysed statistically or be used to make generalisations because qualitative research does not use a randomly selected representative sample. Instead the number of people taking part is small and they are not all asked exactly the same questions.

Qualitative research is largely exploratory. It produces ideas which might explain certain facts or observations and can then be tested through research. Its advantage is that it can look at topics in more depth than quantitative research. Its drawback is that it cannot generalise findings to a broader audience or the public in general.

QUANTITATIVE RESEARCH

Quantitative research is designed to find out how many people feel about an issue. It is a research method which uses large samples of people who fill in structured questionnaires with, mainly, closed questions. Closed questions are questions which offer a limited number of alternatives. The most common ways of collecting information are on-street, postal or telephone interviews. Once the information has been collected it can be analysed to produce numerical data and statistics.

The advantage of quantitative research is that when the survey involves a statistically valid random sample the findings can be generalised beyond the group which took part in the survey. The information produced can be anonymous which helps reliability in areas that people might consider sensitive. Its weakness is that the data generated tells us what people think but ignores the reasons why.

OFFICIAL STATISTICS AND RECORDS

What are they?

The Government Statistical Service is a government-wide body that is coordinated by the Office for National Statistics (ONS).

The government website (see 'Websites' on page ii) states that it provides:

> 'A comprehensive directory of all statistical censuses, surveys, administrative systems, publications and other services produced by government and a range of other organisations in the United Kingdom.'

Official statistics play an important role in informing government, business and the public about the economy, population, society and the environment. To do this official statistics should be useful and accessible to meet the public's right to freedom of information.

What does the public think?

The results of a 2008 poll conducted by the ONS show that:

- only 36 per cent of people thought official statistics were accurate;
- a large majority (84 per cent) thought that government manipulates statistics for its own purposes.

To try to resolve these public concerns, a new body, the UK Statistics Authority, has been set up and parliament, not the government, will control it.

SECONDARY RESEARCH

Secondary research is using information gathered by other people through primary research. The results of secondary research are fairly easy to find, but there are drawbacks to this kind of data. For instance, where have the data come from? They can be general, vague and difficult to use. Is the information current or is it out of date? Secondary data may cause problems if these concerns are ignored.

Secondary research is also called desk research because much of it is done sitting at a desk reading through material. There are a large number of sources for this type of secondary data. Researchers may use previous studies on similar topics such as reports, press articles and previous market research projects in order to come to a conclusion.

Other sources include periodical publications issued at regular intervals, usually more than once a year, for example newspapers, magazines and professional journals. These may be issued by particular bodies such as trade associations or professional bodies. Government statistics are readily available nationally and the Chambers of Commerce provide information on a local basis. The Internet is increasingly used.

SECONDARY SOURCES

This is material written about primary sources giving other people's views of the information in the primary source. They are not original evidence but discussions about evidence. They can include:

- biographies;
- encyclopaedias;
- histories;
- magazine and newspaper articles;
- textbooks;
- websites.

ACTIVITY

Explain in you own words what you understand from the terms:

- primary source;
- secondary source;
- quantitative research;
- qualitative research.

Unit 6.2 Using and evaluating evidence

IN THIS UNIT YOU WILL LEARN ABOUT:

- bias
- utility
- reliability
- validity
- significance
- triangulation
- sampling
- trend.

Evidence is selective, very often biased, and never complete. Much evidence is only available by accident, whilst some evidence is deliberately created to support a point of view. Primary sources are not all equally useful. Those that are closer to an investigation in time and location are usually regarded as more useful.

BIAS, VALIDITY, RELIABILITY AND UTILITY

Every source is by definition biased because it will reflect the views of the person or organisation which produced it. Each source needs to be analysed to identify its strengths – what makes it valid, reliable or useful – and weaknesses – what takes away from making it valid, reliable or useful. Every piece of evidence and every source must be read or viewed sceptically and critically.

No piece of evidence should be taken at face value. The author's point of view must be considered. This will involve cross-checking with other evidence and identifying the author of the source and the reason it was produced. This is relatively easy to do for some sources, such as individual attempts to persuade audiences or justify actions. It needs to be applied equally to all types of evidence.

It is vital to explain how a source is biased. Is it because it twists the facts, gives only one side of an argument or tries to give a false version of events?

Each piece of evidence and source must be cross-checked and compared with related sources and pieces of evidence.

The reason that bias is important in a document is that it throws doubt on how valid and reliable the source is. It can also affect how useful the document is but if the bias is identified it can still be useful to show what one group wanted people to believe.

SAMPLING

Social science research is often carried out by the use of sampling. This is the process of using a small number of people in a piece of research, but accurately reflecting the views of a much larger population. One result of sampling is that some errors will creep in. Sampling methods have been worked out to try to limit this error.

SAMPLING FRAMES

All sampling methods use sampling frames. This is a list of members of the total population the researcher is interested in. A population does not necessarily mean people, it is a term used to describe all the items about which the researcher wants to discover some facts, for example people who play a particular sport, accidents in the home or railway stations. A sample for a study can be produced from the list.

Simple random sampling

With simple random sampling any item on the list in the sampling frame has the same chance of being selected in the sample. The selection can be made by giving each item a number and then randomly selecting numbers to identify the sample. This can be done by relatively scientific methods or simply picking numbers out of a hat.

This method is simple to use as long as the population concerned is relatively small. It becomes less simple the larger the number of items in the population.

Stratified sample

One problem of random sampling is that it assumes that the whole population identified in a sampling frame is the same. This is based on the assumption that there are no distinct sub groups in the population which, in a large population, is unlikely. Such groups are ignored by the random sampling method which increases the likelihood of error.

To avoid this, sub groups – described as strata – can be identified. Making sure samples from all these strata are included should make the sample more representative.

Stratified sampling uses this method and the results are more accurate than random samples.

Quota sample

This is a sampling method often used by market research and opinion pollsters. It shares some of the characteristics of stratified sampling. The sample is chosen by setting quotas from each strata in an attempt to represent the whole population of the sampling frame.

Once quotas have been set the random nature of the sample is lost because it is then the responsibility of an individual researcher to choose the final sample.

Panel sample

This sampling method is used to identify trends. The direction of the trend can be defined by time, as long, medium or short-term and by direction, as up or down. A group is selected by random sampling and is questioned at regular intervals to identify the way views change over time.

TRIANGULATION

This is the use of more than one method in a study to check the reliability of the results. If different methods produce similar answers a researcher can be more confident that the results are significant and reliable.

Triangulation suggests the use of three methods because if two, or more, of the methods support each other this adds significance to the results. If the three methods produce conflicting results it is a clear indication that either the study, or the methods being used, need to be reconsidered.

ACTIVITY

1. What do the terms bias, reliability and utility mean when used about evidence?

2. Consider the different sorts of samples that can be carried out. List the advantages and disadvantages of each and indicate when each might be chosen to carry out research.

3. How is triangulation used to check the reliability of the results of a study?

Unit 6.3 Managing an enquiry

IN THIS UNIT YOU WILL LEARN ABOUT:

- hypothesis
- pilot study
- controlling variables.

ACTIVITY

What are the factors to take into account when choosing the methods to use in an enquiry?

The requirement to undertake an enquiry leading to the production of a written report, with a word limit of about 2000 words, is a requirement of the scheme of assessment for OCR GCSE Humanities. There will be list of tasks published each year by OCR.

GETTING STARTED

A hypothesis is a statement which can be investigated. For the independent enquiry hypotheses will be provided and one will need to be selected. Testing a hypothesis requires the collection of data about the statement being examined.

The hypothesis is a specific question or statement. The enquiry will attempt to gather evidence that will either support or disprove it. The introduction to the enquiry should start with what the investigation hopes to achieve. It then needs to indicate the research methods to be used. To achieve a balanced approach at least two methods should be used and possibly more.

COLLECTING THE DATA

The actual research should try to include both primary and secondary sources of information, and a mixture of qualitative and quantitative data. The research methods that are chosen should be capable of producing data that are directly relevant to the

hypothesis. It is important that results included in the report are relevant to the enquiry and should include any difficulties and problems that are encountered.

The easiest way to collect quantitative data is to produce a questionnaire. This sounds deceptively simple but is actually quite difficult. Questions that the researcher expects to be understood in a certain way may be misinterpreted. To avoid this it is good practice to do a pilot study with the questionnaire to be sure it actually works in the way it is intended.

Questionnaires can be administered as structured interviews, filled in while the researcher is present asking the questions, or as postal questionnaires to be filled in and returned to the researcher. The questions should be 'closed' questions to collect quantitative data.

CONTROLLING VARIABLES

Although questionnaires are a relatively straightforward research method they do have weaknesses as well as strengths. Questionnaire design makes it difficult for the researcher to examine complex issues and opinions. Even 'open' questions, designed to produce qualitative data and opinions, are less likely to produce the depth and detail than almost any other research method.

Structured interviews raise issues of respondents being intimidated or influenced by the presence of an interviewer. Postal questionnaires enable respondents to be anonymous and therefore perhaps more honest, but there can be no certainty that questionnaire has been completed by the person to whom it was sent.

Unstructured interviews which question each respondent in an individual manner can generate detailed responses, but these can be difficult to put together in a way which allows conclusions to be drawn. This could, however, be the first stage in developing a structured interview procedure to test the general truth, or otherwise, of the opinions identified.

Observation, either as a participant, or simply an observer, might be useful in this type of research.

Unit 6.4 Communicating the results of an enquiry

IN THIS UNIT YOU WILL LEARN ABOUT:

- introduction
- evaluation
- evidence
- referencing
- conclusion
- narrative
- annotation
- bibliography.

INTRODUCTION

The purpose of the introduction is to inform the potential audience of the nature and scope of the research topic being undertaken. A reader should have an understanding of the way in which the study will develop from this section.

It should include a description of the general topic being researched, including the hypothesis, as this is what the enquiry will focus on and attempt to either prove or disprove.

Describe the purpose of the research and how the topic was selected. Include the main aims and objectives of the research. List the research methods used and the reasons why these methods in particular were appropriate for this piece of research.

EVIDENCE AND NARRATIVE

When you have completed your research you will have primary and secondary evidence linked to your hypothesis. This needs to be included in your enquiry. At this stage you are not evaluating it you are simply presenting it as a narrative (events described in order, as in a story). In other words, you describe your evidence collection process and present the evidence.

EVALUATION

Evaluate the research methodology and the evidence it produced in a 'critical commentary'.

This is a judgement about the way the research was carried out. If there were any problems in using the research methods selected, describe what they were and suggest how they might have been avoided.

Describe the improvements that could be made to the methods chosen. Try to assess the reliability and validity of the research methods chosen. As well as critically analysing any difficulties, highlight the parts of the research that were successful. Explain why the research methods were chosen and justify why these methods were used.

CONCLUSION

The conclusion does not introduce anything new but sums up and draws together information presented throughout the research. Conclusions are what can be said about the results you have managed to gather. They are a description of the main findings of the research.

Conclusions could assess whether the study has met its aims and objectives – has it proved or disproved the hypothesis? Are there conclusions about the research process itself? Have areas for future research been identified?

Conclusions are unlikely to be definite. They are tentative and might change if further research was done. They are the author's opinion of what has been discovered by the research.

BIBLIOGRAPHY

This is a list of all the sources of information referred to in a study or used as reference material. It is a list of the secondary sources used, and possibly quoted from, by a researcher that is included at the at the end of a study. As well as the title and author of the source, the publisher and date of publication should be included.

REFERENCING

When a study is being written it is quite common for the researcher to use work originally produced by someone else. Often this will be a direct quotation of what the other researcher has written. Because this is not the work of the current researcher it is necessary for this copying to be acknowledged. There is more than one way of doing this.

Short quotations can be highlighted by being put in speech marks. Longer extracts can be indented in the text to show that they are quotations. Whichever method is used each quotation should be given a reference number. This will enable a reader to look to the end of the study where the information about the source of the quotation will be listed in a similar way to the bibliography.

ANNOTATION

Many of the results from quantitative research will benefit from being included in a study in the form of charts and tables. If these are simply inserted into a narrative it can be difficult to understand what there contribution is. A solution for this problem is to annotate visual images.

Annotations are comments, notes or explanations that can be attached to charts, maps, diagrams and photographs. With appropriate annotation the contribution of the visual image can be clearly explained to a reader.

It is therefore important that visual images should be annotated. The annotation should include a description of the image and what it shows and an explanation of its contribution to the argument being pursued in the study.

ACTIVITY

Describe all the stages needed to communicate the results of an enquiry.

ExamCafé

Unit B032 Application of Knowledge

The following sections will help you to prepare for the exam.

Common mistakes

Each section of the specification for B032 contains lists of key skills. These are listed in the next section, the Revision Checklist.

Students often know too little about these. Exam questions will test your knowledge and understanding of these key, based around sources on one of the chapters in this book. When students don't know precisely what they mean, they can lose marks.

Revision Checklist
Unit B032 Application of knowledge

Different types and forms of evidence	• Primary sources • Secondary sources • Quantitative methods of enquiry • Qualitative methods of enquiry
Using and evaluating evidence	• Reliability • Validity • Significance • Triangulation • Sampling • Trend
Managing an enquiry	• Hypothesis • Pilot study • Controlling variables
Communicating the results of an enquiry	• Introduction • Evaluation • Evidence • Referencing • Conclusion • Narrative • Annotation • Bibliography

Understanding exam language

Different command words and what they mean

Questions in Unit B032 will use one of three command words. These words try to show how you should answer the question.

State – The answer should be factual, short and knowledge based. It could be a single word, a phrase or a short sentence. Writing more than a short sentence is not necessary and could cost you time.

Describe – The answer should be in some detail telling what something is like or how something might be done. A short paragraph would usually be enough.

Explain – The answer should be detailed. Good factual support is needed for the explanation. These questions have bullet points for guidance. These are not the points which must be included but guidance to what might be included. You are encouraged to provide you own response. An essay type answer is needed.

Different types of question and how they should be approached

In Unit B032:

Section A has 2 different types of question.

Questions 1 and 2 are knowledge based:

- Each question asks you to **state** a piece of information identified in a source.
- Each piece of information correctly identified is awarded 1 mark.
- Single word or short sentence answers are all that are required.

Question 3 is knowledge based:

- The question asks you to **explain** an answer with reference to a source.

Question 3 is worth a maximum of 3 marks.

Questions 4 and 5 are skills based – using information from a documentary source/s.

- Each question asks you to **explain** an answer.
- Detailed factual support from the source/s is required.
- A short essay type answer is required.

Question 4 is worth a maximum of 5 marks.

Question 5 is worth a maximum of 6 marks.

Section B has one type of question.

Question 6 is knowledge and skills based:

- The question has two parts.
- Each part asks you to **describe** the advantages and disadvantages of a research method.
- A short essay type answer is required.

Question 6 is worth a maximum of 10 marks

Section C has 3 different types of question.

Questions 7 and 8 are knowledge based:

- Each question asks you to **state** a piece of information identified in a source.
- Each piece of information correctly identified is awarded 1 mark.
- Single word or short sentence answers are all that are required.

Question 9 is knowledge based:

- The question asks you to **state** two piece of information identified in a source.
- Each piece of information correctly identified is awarded 1 mark.
- Single word or short sentence answers are all that are required.

Question 9 is worth a maximum of 2 marks.

Question 10 is knowledge and skills based:

- The question asks you to **describe** an issue from information identified in a source.
- A short essay type answer is required.

Question 10 is worth a maximum of 4 marks.

Question 11 is skills based – evaluating information from a documentary source:

- The question asks you to **explain** an answer.
- Detailed factual support from the source/s is required.
- A short essay type answer is required.

Question 11 is worth a maximum of 6 marks.

Question 12 is skills based – reaching reasoned conclusion from documentary sources:

- The question asks you to **explain** arguments for and against a statement.
- Detailed factual support from all the sources is required.
- An essay type answer is required.

Question 12 is worth a maximum of 10 marks.

Examiner tips

There is a lot to read in the question paper and it is important that you read the instructions and questions carefully. Misreading of questions or individual words can have a big effect on the marks you are awarded for example quantitative and qualitative research sound very similar but not knowing for sure which is which can make a massive difference in marks awarded.

Time is vital in an examination. How much time should you spend on a particular question? There are a number of indicators on the examination paper. Each question has the number of marks it is worth shown in brackets. The space provided for your answer on the paper should also help you to write appropriately for each question.

One calculation that might help you plan your time is to divide the total time available by the total number of marks awarded on the paper. For Unit B032 the calculation is:

   75 minutes/50 marks

therefore you have 1.5 minutes, or 1 minute 30 seconds to gain each mark.

This may seem a silly calculation, but if you multiply the number of marks by 45 seconds you will get an indication of how much time to spend on each question to maximise your opportunity to get as many marks as possible.

Each section is worth a different number of marks therefore you should spend a different amount of time on the different sections.

Section A: five questions worth 16 marks. Total time available 24 minutes.

Section B: two questions worth 10 marks. Total time available 15 minutes.

Section C: six questions worth 24 marks. Total time available 36 minutes.

You can not be as precise as this, but if you do spend more time on one section you will seriously affect the time available for the other sections.

Structuring an answer

When planning an essay type answer it is important to understand how the examiner will assess what you have written.

Below is the outline mark scheme used by examiners to assess answers for Section A Question 4 of Unit B032 Application of Knowledge.

A comparison of two documents giving different opinions on the same topic.

[0 marks]
No evidence submitted or response does not address the question.

Level 1
[1 mark] Candidate makes a **general but unexplained link** between the two documents.

Level 2
[2–3 marks] Candidate makes a **developed statement** about the relationship between the two documents. Identifies **specific supporting information** from one document.

Level 3
[4–5 marks] As Level 2 but candidate additionally identifies alternative supporting information from **both documents**.

Humanities mark schemes are Level of Response mark schemes. This means they contain descriptions of what a candidate answer should include to achieve a certain level.

The highlighted text in the table above shows the minimum information an examiner will expect to find to decide a candidate answer has achieved a particular level. Each level has more than one mark and the descriptions also assist the examiner to award a particular mark.

If you understand how this mark scheme works it can help you to plan an essay structure that will enable you to achieve a higher mark. For a candidate the highlighted text provides the 'gateways' they need to go through to get from one level to the next.

Gateways

Level 1 to Level 2:

- Write a **developed** statement referring only to **one** document.
- Give **some** factual support from document.

Level 2 to Level 3:

- Write a **developed** statement referring to **both** documents.
- Give **some** factual support from both documents.

GradeStudio

Unit B032 Application of Knowledge

Section A: Analyse and interpret different types of evidence

Question 4

Document B

Results of Opinion Poll

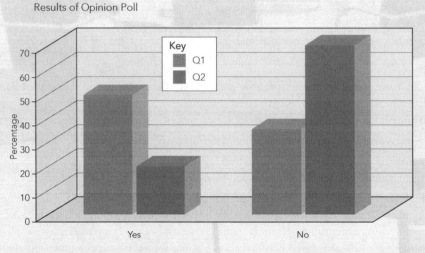

Questions asked:

Q1. Do you personally support the ban on fox hunting?

Q2. Should the police enforce the ban when it becomes law?

> The poll also found that 23% of Labour supporters were against the ban. Opposition to the ban was strongest amongst low earners bearing out claims that hunting is not simply for the better off.

Adapted from ICM opinion poll based on a random sample of 1000 adults aged over 18.

Document C

Police to enforce hunting ban

> The Home Secretary has told police chiefs they should use common sense and sensitivity when enforcing the ban on hunting. He stressed that any attempts to continue foxhunting would be clearly seen as a breach of the law.
>
> The Home Secretary announced that there would be no extra money for the police to do this. The money they had previously used to protect hunts from the disruption caused by hunt saboteurs could be used.
>
> The Association of Chief Police Officers stated that this was an extra job that will be difficult to do, but that as the job of the police is to enforce the law that was what they would do.

> In Document B 70% of the public believe that the police should not enforce a hunting ban.
>
> Use Document C to explain how far the Home Secretary and the police spokesman agree with them.
>
> **[0 marks]**
>
> No evidence submitted or response does not address the question.
>
> **Level 1**
>
> **[1 mark]** Candidate makes a general but unexplained link about the relationship between the ban and the need for policing hunts.
>
> **Level 2**
>
> **[2–3 marks]** Candidate makes a developed statement about the relationship between the ban and the need for policing. Identifies the switch of resources from protecting to policing hunts.
>
> **Level 3**
>
> **[4–5 marks]** As Level 2 but candidate additionally identifies the police attitude to the issue and the need for sensitivity.

Student answer:

The ban on fox hunting will need to be enforced. The Home Secretary says in Document C that there will be no extra money for this. It will be paid for by using the money that was used to protect hunts from protesters.

The Home Secretary says that enforcing the law needs to show sensitivity which perhaps shows he understands the public attitude.

The police spokesman comments that this will be an extra job that will be difficult. That they will enforce it because it is the law and enforcing the law is their job, suggests they would rather not. This would suggest the police might agree with the public attitude.

Examiner says:

This candidate has clearly used Document C to address the question. S/he has clearly identified the attitudes of the Home Secretary and the police. The evaluation of these attitudes has indicated that they are not necessarily the same.

Both recognise there is public opposition to the ban. The Home Secretary responds with a sensitive enforcement. The police it is suggested are not really in support but will do their job. This is a good Level 3 answer.

GradeStudio

Section C – Assess the reliability and utility of evidence and reach reasoned conclusions

Question 11

Document F

> Unexplained events are happening in the North Sea. Cod stocks are falling faster than over-fishing can explain. Mediterranean fish like red mullet are migrating north.
>
> Several species of sea birds are also in trouble. Kittiwake numbers are falling fast and guillemots are struggling to breed.
>
> Scientists suspect these events are linked. They are trying to work out how. Some believe a dramatic change in North Sea plankton is responsible. And, what is more, they blame global warming.
>
> Plankton are microscopic marine organisms that are eaten by fish. As global temperatures rise cold water species of plankton are moving out and warm water species are moving in. This is causing changes further up the food chain.

NERC Centre for Ecology and Hydrology

Explain the uses and limitations of Document F to a researcher studying the decline of fish stocks in the seas around the UK. Use your knowledge of research techniques to answer the question.
[0 marks]

No evidence submitted or response does not address the question.

Level 1

[1–2 marks] Candidate accepts the information in Document F at face value. Makes no attempt to explain the utility or reliability of the document.

e.g. Unexplained events are happening in the North Sea/not totally attributable to over fishing/scientists blame global warming/plankton moving north as seas' warm.

Candidate response simply assumes the information is valid and therefore useful and reliable.

Text is difficult to read, poor spelling and grammar; little punctuation makes comprehension difficult.

Level 2

[3–4 marks] Candidate considers the provenance of the source. The NERC Centre for Ecology and Hydrology. Supports the utility of the data because of the source.

e.g. they are involved in the process/scientists studying the process/therefore will be able to give information that will be useful.

Candidate response has simplistic response to utility but does not challenge reliability.

Text is readable, there may be mistakes in spelling grammar and punctuation; comprehension of meaning largely clear.

Level 3

[5–6 marks] As Level 2 but candidate is also able to identify the limitations of relying on one account.

e.g. questions reliability NERC Centre for Ecology and Hydrology/ has a view point and the information may be biased/ also they admit they do not know precisely what is happening.

A more developed response to utility and candidate may develop a challenge to reliability by identifying the need to contrast one source with other possibly alternative views.

Text is clearly readable, spelling, grammar and punctuation are largely accurate; meaning is clear.

Student answer 1:

The document says that things are happening. More cod have gone than caused by fishing. Other fish coming in. Seabirds are in trouble. Plankton what fish eat have changed. Water is getting hotter and fish move. This is useful to a researcher.

Examiner says:

This candidate has made the classic mistake on this question. The document has been taken at face value and information has been presented as though it is the truth. There is no attempt to question the utility or reliability. This is a Level 1 answer.

Advice:

To get to a Level 2 response the candidate would need to go beyond taking information at face value and start to ask questions about who wrote the document and why they wrote the document? Alternatively the candidate could challenge the usefulness and reliability of one document suggesting that it really needs the support of other documents to be believed.

Student answer 2:

Document F appears to come from a scientific source, the NERC centre for Ecology and Hydrology.

The scientists are involved in monitoring and researching what is happening in the North Sea. Their findings suggest that the fall in Cod stocks is bigger than can be explained by over fishing. They have also identified that the plankton that fish feed on has changed.

Their explanation is that the sea is warming causing cold water fish to move out and warm water fish like the red mullet from the Mediterranean to move in. These changes are also causing problems for other creatures like sea birds.

However this is only one source and to be sure that what it says is useful and reliable it would need to be checked against what other scientists are saying. The NERC centre might be reliable or it might have a particular viewpoint on this issue which would bias its opinion.

The document is useful for the information it provides but would be more reliable if there were other sources which supported it. No researcher should base any research on only one source.

Examiner says:

This candidate has grasped the essence of this question. No one source is reliable without external verification, and no researcher would base conclusions on such limited evidence. The document has been used to illustrate this point. This is a good Level 3 answer.

Question 12

Assess the Reliability and Utility of Evidence and Reach Reasoned Conclusions

Document D

Lobsters recover in no take zone

In 2002, an area of 3.3 km east of Lundy Island in the Bristol Channel became the first legally protected fishing 'no-take zone'. This designation means that no live sea creatures can be caught in this area.

English Nature reported that after 2 years there were three times more lobsters in this area than in areas where fishing had been allowed to continue. This increase also applied to crabs and other sea creatures. As this confirmed the results of the previous year it was concluded that this showed the 'no-take zone' was definitely working.

The government is seriously considering setting up more no-take zones in its new Marine Law as it believes that Lundy Island has been a major success.

Document E

Drastic and urgent action needed to save seas from fishing fleets!

30% of UK waters should be fish reserves!

Changes will be painful but essential if the fishing industry is to have a future!

| Control the amount of fishing not the amount of fish caught! | Continuing to fish is no longer acceptable! | Major shift in thinking is needed! |

Headlines extracted from the Royal Commission on Environmental Pollution

Document F

Unexplained events are happening in the North Sea. Cod stocks are falling faster than over-fishing can explain. Mediterranean fish like red mullet are migrating north.

Several species of sea birds are also in trouble. Kittiwake numbers are falling fast and guillemots are struggling to breed.

Scientists suspect these events are linked. They are trying to work out how. Some believe a dramatic change in North Sea plankton is responsible. And, what is more, they blame global warming.

Plankton are microscopic marine organisms that are eaten by fish. As global temperatures rise cold water species of plankton are moving out and warm water species are moving in. This is causing changes further up the food chain.

NERC Centre for Ecology and Hydrology

'The evidence that too much fishing is the cause of declining fish stocks is not proved! To what extent do you agree and disagree with this statement?

[0 marks]

No evidence submitted or response does not address the question.

Level 1

[1–2 marks] Candidate offers a rudimentary answer that either agrees or disagrees with the statement.

e.g. agree where fishing is controlled marine life recovers, Document D (not essential for mark). Disagree NERC say it is climate change, Document F.

Candidate response simply assumes the information is valid and therefore does not question utility or reliability.

Text is difficult to read, poor spelling and grammar; little punctuation makes comprehension difficult.

Level 2

[3–4 marks] Candidate agrees **or** disagrees with the statement and offers some evidence from the sources to support the stance taken.

e.g. disagrees Document D states that where fishing grounds are protected stocks recover more quickly than anticipated/ Document E shows from the headlines that this is a widespread problem.

Agree Document F newspaper headlines do not really give any evidence therefore not really useful/ Document F scientists clearly indicate that there is something else going on in the North Sea/ it could be linked to climate change.

Candidate has simplistic response to utility but does not challenge reliability.

Text is readable, there are mistakes in spelling, grammar and punctuation; comprehension of meaning variable.

Level 3

[5–6 marks] Candidate agrees **and** disagrees with the statement and offers some evidence from the sources to develop a comparative narrative.

e.g. makes use of the arguments made in Level 2 and explores both sides of the argument.

Candidate implicitly accepts the utility of the sources but does not challenge reliability.

Text is readable, there may be mistakes in spelling grammar and punctuation; comprehension of meaning largely clear.

Level 4

[7–8 marks] Candidate agrees **and** disagrees with the statement **and** offers detailed evidence from the sources to support the narrative.

e.g. uses the documents to develop a balanced narrative exploring the arguments for and against the proposition/examines not only what the sources say but their provenance.

Document D:

challenges the proposition because it is a report on English Nature/integrally involved in this process/easily challengeable statement made in the public arena.

Document E:

challenges the proposition/extracted from the Royal Commission on Environmental Pollution/ easily challengeable statement made in the public arena

Document F:

supports the proposition because sees other causes/NERC scientific research organisation/does not rule out over fishing/lacks certainty.

Candidate examines the utility of the sources and therefore implicitly challenges reliability.

Text is clearly readable, spelling, grammar and punctuation are largely accurate; meaning is clear.

Level 5

[9–10 marks] As Level 4 but in addition candidate is also able to identify the limitations of relying on limited accounts Candidate offers a comprehensive evaluation of the content of the sources to support a personal conclusion.

A more developed response to utility and candidate will develop the challenge to reliability by identifying the need to contrast sources with each other to identify and challenge conflicting views.

Text is clearly readable, spelling, grammar and punctuation are accurate; meaning is very clear.

Student answer 1:

I disagree because Document D proves that where fishing is cut down fish stocks recover and quicker then people thought. This is backed up by Document E which is newspaper headlines showing that lots of people believe this.

I agree because Document F says that other things are happening like some fish moving out and others moving in which might be because of global warming making seas hotter. It is written by scientists. Document E is not evidence only paper headlines which cant be trusted.

Examiner says:

This candidate very clearly says that s/he both agrees and disagrees with the statement. This suggests to the marker the possibility of a Level 3 answer. To confirm this evidence from the documents for both arguments is needed. This is present in the answer though it cannot be described as detailed. The candidate has also dealt with the arguments against with little attempt to compare the evidence. The answer implicitly assumes that the documents are useful but makes no attempt to challenge their reliability. A fair Level 3 answer.

Advice:

To achieve a Level 4 response the candidate would need to write about the evidence in more detail and draw comparisons. Some consideration of who has produced the documents, and why, to consider their usefulness and therefore challenge their reliability is also required.

Student answer 2:

The evidence from these three documents does not all point in the same direction. Document D says that banning fishing in a particular area of the North Sea has had a surprising effect after a fairly short space of time.

The report from English Nature says that there are three times as many lobsters in this area than in areas that still allow fishing. It is reasonable to assume that the cause of this increase is because of the fishing ban. This suggests that Document D does not agree with the statement. The fact that this statement is made by English Nature might be important because it is a well known body which does not make statements that cannot be supported.

Document E certainly disagrees with the statement. This collection of headlines all demanding that fishing should be cut back, presumably because of the fall in fish stocks, were collected by a Royal Commission.

The number of headlines could make you think that this is a commonly held view and the body which collected published them is not likely to be telling lies.

Document F is the only document that questions the impact of fishing and so could be said to agree with the statement. It identifies other causes that may be causing fish to move because of changes in the sea. It does not completely rule out over fishing as a cause of falling fish stocks. The general impression it gives is that it is not really sure what is causing the situation.

I would disagree that this statement is not proved but I would have some questions about whether there are other reasons, as well as over fishing causing falling fish stocks.

Examiner says:

As this candidate clearly identifies agreement and disagreement with the statement the marker would begin to look at the response in the area of Level 3/4. The crucial issue is the level of support the candidate gives to the narrative argument from the sources.

This candidate clearly uses each source, and implicitly refers to the content of each source. The utility of the sources are challenged as is there reliability. Both these actions place the candidate in Level 4 not Level 3.

Consideration of Level 5 depends on the quality of evaluation of the sources and the quality of any personal conclusion, if any. The evaluation could reasonable be described as detailed but not comprehensive. The personal conclusion is limited.

This candidate therefore scores Level 4.

Advice:

To achieve a Level 5 answer the candidate would need to provide a more detailed evaluation of all the sources and use this to produce a personal conclusion which is based on the arguments made.

Glossary

A

Abstinence – A personal decision not to engage in certain activities. Often used in relation to sexual intercourse

Acquired immunodeficiency syndrome (AIDS) – A potentially fatal disease of the immune system passed on through blood products, sexual contact or contaminated needles

Act of parliament – A law passed by both houses of parliament and signed by the Queen

Alcohol dependence – The need for alcohol to feel good or to avoid feeling bad

Arbitration – A way in which two parties in a dispute agree to allow a third party to decide their dispute

Atheist – Someone who believes that gods do not exist

B

Barrister – A lawyer who specialises in speaking on behalf of clients in court

Bill – A proposed new law which needs to be agreed by parliament to become law

Binge drinking – Drinking large quantities of alcohol in a short period of time with the intention of becoming drunk

Biodiversity – The number and variety of species of plant and animal life within an area

Body Mass Index (BMI) – Measures individuals' weight in relation to their height. Commonly used to identify obesity

Bond – A certificate of debt issued by a government or business to raise money

Budget – A plan of income and expenditure over a period of time

By-election – An election held when a seat in parliament becomes vacant between general elections caused by a death, resignation or for other reasons

C

Carbon footprint – The amount of carbon dioxide produced by an individual, organisation or country over a period of time

Census – The process of recording data about every member of the population of a country. Usually taken once every 10 years

Chief whips – Members of political parties who are MPs and who organise their party colleagues in the House of Commons

Chlamydia – A sexually transmitted infection which is difficult to detect as many sufferers have no symptoms

Chronic – A disease that can be treated but not cured. Any condition that lasts longer than 6 months is classed as chronic

Circuit judges – Senior judges in England and Wales who preside in the Crown Court

Class A drugs – The drugs that the UK government says are most dangerous. Supplying or possession of them carries the most severe penalties

Climate – The average weather conditions of a place over many years

Climate change – Changes in the earth's climate, especially those produced by global warming

Common law – Law based on custom, common practice and court decisions

Compensation culture – Anyone who has suffered a personal injury claims compensation by taking legal action against anyone connected with the injury

Constituency – A geographical district from which an MP is elected

Contraception – The use of a device or procedure to prevent conception as a result of sexual activity

Council of Europe – Founded in 1949 it is the oldest international organisation working towards European integration

Council tax – A household tax paid to local authorities based on the estimated value of the property

Credit – In personal banking terms, this is a sum of money put into an account

Credit score – A numerical score, based on an individual's credit history, that measures an individual's credit worthiness

Crown Court – This court hears mainly criminal cases

Crown Prosecution Service (CPS) – An independent agency responsible for public prosecutions in the UK

D

Debit – In personal banking terms, this is a sum of money taken out of an account

Deforestation – The process of destroying a forest and replacing it with an agricultural system

Degenerative disease – A disease marked by the progressive failure of an organ or body

Deity – A supernatural being worshipped as a god or goddess

Democracy – A political system in which supreme power belongs to citizens who elect people to represent them

Denomination – A religious group with its own organisation and distinctive beliefs

Development – Ways of managing natural and human resources in order to create wealth indicators and improve people's lives

Devolution – The delegation of particular powers by a higher level of government to a lower level of government.

Dhamma – The law discovered and proclaimed by the Buddha that is summed up in the Four Noble Truths

Dictatorship – A political system in which supreme power is held by one person who is not limited by a written constitution, laws or any opposition

Direct debit – A payment system allowing organisations to collect variable payments directly from customers' accounts

Disciplinary action – A formal action taken by an employer in response to unacceptable performance or misconduct by an employee

Duty of care – A legal duty imposed on all employers to provide a safe place of work

E

e-Commerce – Buying and selling goods using the Internet

Economic development – The stages a country will pass through from a simple low-income economy to a modern, high-income economy to create wealth and improve the standard of living for its people

Electoral register – A register of parliamentary or local government electors maintained under Section 9 of the Representation of the People Act 1983

Ethnic group – People of the same race or nationality who share a distinctive culture

European Union (EU) – A political and economic union of 27 member states. It was set up by the Maastricht Treaty in 1993 as successor to the European Economic Community (EEC)

F

First past the post – A voting system where the candidate with the most votes wins

Flexi-time – A variable working day instead of the standard 9am to 5pm working day. There is a core time when employees are expected to be at work; the rest of the working day is worked to suit the employee

Fossil fuels – The decayed remains of plants and animals, such as coal, oil and natural gas, which are used to provide energy

Free will – The ability to make personal life choices without outside interference

G

Generation Y – People in the workforce who were born in 1981 or later

Government – The system by which a country is run

Great Depression – The economic crisis which began when the American stockmarket crashed in 1929 and which lasted throughout the 1930s

Greenhouse effect – Warming that results when solar radiation is trapped by the atmosphere

Greenhouse gases – Gases that increase the temperature of the earth's surface. They include water vapour, ozone, chlorofluorocarbons, carbon dioxide, carbon monoxide, methane and nitrous oxide

Green paper – A government document containing policies for discussion with no promise of putting the policies into effect

Grievance – A wrong or hardship suffered (real or imaginary) which leads to a formal complaint.

Gross misconduct – Behaviour at work which could lead to an employee being disciplined by an employer, potentially ending in dismissal

Guru Granth Sahib – The Sikh sacred scripture

Gurus – Each of the first ten leaders of the Sikh religion

H

Hereditary peers – Unelected members of the House of Lords whose right to be there is inherited from their parents

Hire purchase – A way of buying an item where the buyer pays regular instalments to use the item but does not own it until the final payment

Holy Scripture – The texts which various religious traditions consider to be sacred. Many believe they are the actual words of their god.

Home Office – UK government department responsible for security and order

House of Commons – The lower, but most important, house of the UK parliament

House of Lords – The upper house of the UK parliament

Human development – The process of growing to maturity

Human immunodeficiency virus (HIV) – The virus that causes AIDS

Humanitarian – A person involved in improving people's lives and reducing suffering

I

Individual savings account (ISA) – Tax-free savings accounts launched in April 1999 allowing investment in stocks and shares

Infrastructure – The basic services needed for a community to function, for example transport, communications, water, power and public institutions such as schools, post offices and prisons

Interest-only mortgage – A mortgage where a borrower pays only the interest on the loan. The loan is paid off by a savings plan that matures at the end of the mortgage term

Intoxication – A temporary state resulting from excessive consumption of alcohol

J

Job sharing – An employer allowing two employees to share one job

Just war – The idea that going to war can be just (right) under certain conditions

Justices of the Peace (JPs) – Citizens appointed as magistrates; they do not need to be legally trained

L

Labour Exchanges – These were set up by an Act of Parliament in 1909. Their purpose was to help the unemployed find jobs

Legal precedent – A legal case which makes a rule that all courts will follow

Less Economically Developed Country (LEDC) – Developing country which has not reached Western-style standards of living

Life peers – Members of the House of Lords who are appointed for their lifetime. Their children have no right to follow their parents as members of the House of Lords.

Liturgy – A set of rituals that is performed as part of a religion

M

Magistrate – A judge who administers the law in a court dealing with minor offences

Mantra – A phrase repeated to assist concentration during meditation

Miscarriage of justice – The conviction and punishment of a person for a crime that they did not commit

Moral evil – Evil that results from the misuse of free will

More Economically Developed Country (MEDC) – Country with a developed economy

Multiculturalism – The idea that different cultures can coexist peacefully in a single country

Multinational corporation (MNC) – A company which operates in more than one country

Mutation – A change in an organism resulting from alteration to chromosomes

N

Nanny state – Government institutions interfering in and controlling people's lives

Natural evil – Evil that results from natural processes; no human being is responsible

Non-Governmental Organisation (NGO) – An international organisation that is not part of any government

O

Obesity – A condition in which excess body fat has accumulated to such an extent that health may be affected

Omnipotent – Unlimited power; usually relating to a god or gods

Omnipresent – The ability to be in all places at the same time; usually relating to a god or gods

Omniscient – All-knowing; usually relating to a god or gods

Overdraft – A short-term bank loan which allows a customer to spend more money than is in their account

P

Pacifism – The opposition to war or violence as a way of settling disputes

Parliamentary democracy – A system of government where the people use their political power by electing representatives to parliament

Primary pollutants – Pollutants that are put directly into the air by human or natural activity

Primary sector – The agricultural and mining sectors of the economy

Private member's bill – A proposed law introduced by a backbench MP

Prophet – Someone who speaks on behalf of god and explains what god wants

Proportional representation – An electoral system where the number of seats won is directly linked to the number of votes cast for each party.

Prosecution – Legal proceedings taken against a defendant for criminal behaviour

Public bill – A bill which proposes a law of which applies throughout the country

Q

Quaternary sector – Information services, such as computing and ICT, consultancy and research and development

Qur'an – The Islamic holy book considered to be Allah's message for mankind as revealed to the prophet Muhammad

R

Racism – The belief that one race is superior to others

Radiation – Energy that is radiated or transmitted in the form of rays or waves or particles

Radiation sickness – Sickness that results from high exposure to radiation received in a short time

Referendum – The electorate voting directly on an issue of public importance

Refugees – Someone who flees their own country for safety

Repayment mortgage – A mortgage which repays the capital and interest on a loan in monthly instalments over an agreed number of years

Representative democracy – A form of democracy in which the citizens elect others to act on their behalf

Revelation – Knowledge given to man by a god

Right of appeal – The right to ask a higher court to consider the verdict of a lower court

Risk assessment – The process of identifying the risks from an activity and the potential impact of each risk

Rite of passage – A ritual that marks a change in a person's social or sexual status

Royal assent – The official signature by the Queen to an act of parliament which makes it law

S

Secondary pollutants – Pollutants that are formed in the atmosphere as a result of chemical reactions

Secondary sector – The part of the economy concerned with the manufacture of goods

Secured loan – A loan where the borrower pledges their house as security for a loan; if the money is not repaid the property can be taken instead

Sexually transmitted infection (STI) – A disease transmitted through sexual contact

Shares – A financial interest in a company

Single transferable vote (STV) – A voting system designed to minimise wasted votes and provide proportional representation

Solicitor – A lawyer who gives legal advice and prepares legal documents

Standing order – An instruction a bank account holder gives to their bank to pay a set amount at regular intervals to another account

Statute law – The laws passed by parliament

Stewardship – A religious belief that people are responsible for the world, and should take care of it

Subsistence – The food necessary to sustain life

Sustainable development – The use of resources to meet human needs while preserving the environment now and in the future

T

Tertiary sector – Industries providing services, both private and public

Thatcherism – Conservative policies under Margaret Thatcher, prime minister between 1979 and 1990

The Five Pillars of Islam – The term given to the five duties every Muslim should perform

The Trinity – A Christian belief that God exists as three persons but is one being

The Vedas – The most ancient sacred writings of Hinduism written in early Sanskrit

Theist – Someone who believes in the existence of a god or gods

Torah – This refers either to the five books of Moses or to all of Judaism's religious texts

Trial by jury – A trial in which a jury makes findings of fact guided by a judge

Tribunal – A term for any body acting like a court

U

Unauthorised overdraft – An overdraft that has not been agreed with the bank

Unsecured loan – A loan which is not secured on property

V

Voluntary code – Rules which people agree to follow

W

Welfare state – The government looks after the welfare of its citizens through public health and public housing and pensions

White paper – A government document containing government policy on a law that is to be brought before parliament

Index